THE ROOTS OF A

THE ROOTS OF ARTIFICE
On the Origin and Development of Literary Creativity

Jay Harris, M.D.
Cornell University Medical College

Jean Harris
Rutgers University

HUMAN SCIENCES PRESS
72 Fifth Avenue   3 Henrietta Street
NEW YORK, NY 10011 ● LONDON, WC2E 8LU

Printed in the United States of America
123456789   987654321

Library of Congress Cataloging in Publication Data

Harris, Jay, 1936–

   The roots of artifice.

   Bibliography: p. 311
   Includes index.
   1. Creation (Literary, artistic, etc.)
2. Literature—Psychology.   I. Harris, Jean A.,
joint author.   II. Title.
BF408.H315   153.3'5   LC 80-23061
ISBN 0-89885-004-5

CONTENTS

INTRODUCTION

The study of literature and writers' lives indicates that writers share a distinct, syndromatic pattern of development. This pattern animates written works of art. Though a similar pattern may lie at the heart of unwritten art, the unwritten lies outside the reach of this study.

Literary works testify to their writers' identities as artists. Every creator experiences a split between the ordinary identity that structures his experience of his life and the creative identity that structures his experience of his work. He also feels an intimate relationship between these two aspects of identity. This book explores the nature of the relationship between ordinary and creative identity. Its theme is that creative identity screens the creator from the traumas of ordinary life.

In each stage of his life cycle, as it is neuropsychologically conceived, man experiences necessary and particular stimuli as trauma. The creator makes a special imaginative structure of identity in response to traumas. In the creator's lifetime these alternative structures of identity constitute a syndrome which we call the "creator's syndrome."

We must include a social and a neuropsychological perspective in our examination of the development of the creator's syndrome. Keats referred to the artist's adaptive ability to accept unpleasant experience—and to transform it by creating a broader and imaginative context—as "negative capability." The artist fulfills an adaptive function in society by extending his social perspective to encompass disturbing forms of information. He does this by adapting language to deal with trauma. Literary devices are neuropsychologically innate species of thought adapted to accepting the essence of an experience, while neutralizing overwhelming emotional impact.

Our approach relates the creator's syndrome to consecutive stages of the life cycle. This approach allows us to describe an ontology of literary devices and to project a composite creator. The caricature is a purposeful one, for creators arrive at universal imaginative solutions developed in response to particular stages in their life cycle which are signs of creative fixation. Assuming we have read our authors right, the range of fixations illustrates creative identity formation in each stage of the life cycle.

The creative process and identity formation are two sides of the same coin. When the creator engages his work he enters a process which impels him to search for the roots of his present-day conflict. He disassembles his identity, the format of his present-day consciousness, in search of the roots of his trauma. His creative process is structured by an innate and ordered sequence of mental acts. The sequence recapitulates the essential neuropsychological steps that occur in the process of identity formation, realigning consciousness in each stage of the life cycle. If we are to understand the nature of the creator's work, and if we are to perceive the residue of this work in the product, then we must understand the origin and development of identity in its neuropsychological context.

Chapter 1

THE ROOTS OF ARTIFICE

The concept of identity will act as a fulcrum for our consideration of the creator's development. Therefore we would like to explain the various levels in which we find it a necessary concept. At the neurological level, the function of identity joins the two spheres of cortical consciousness into a common process, for each cortical hemisphere promotes a separate integrated form of consciousness which must be integrated into cortical consciousness.

Freud referred to this context of identity in *The Project for a Scientific Psychology*. He contended that an identity in perception occurs when the motor image of an act coincides with the visually imaged appearance of an object. It was Freud's idea that the resulting identity in perception is the prelude to the release of discharge processes.

We take it that the motor and the sensory image of the object are integrated separately in each cortex and made to coincide in a process we call "neuropsychological identity." *Identity* is also a term used in ego psychology to refer to the intrapsychic process wherein an organized ensemble of motor images constituting a "subjective self" *(I)* is unified with an organized ensemble of visual and tactile images constituting an "objective self" *(me)* forming a whole self image. This in turn can form the basis for a relatively enduring structure which we call "intrapsychic identity."

Identity is a term which also refers to an intermediate stage in the development of object relations. In this sense it connects the intrapsychic world with the extrapsychic world of real people and objects. Used in this way *identity* comprises an experience of communality with the extrapsychic object. We call this "experiential identity." As Freud pointed out in his paper "On Narcissim," identity is an experience of fusion during the process of falling in love.

Identity has one more common meaning, perhaps the commonest. As Erikson uses the term it refers to an inherent unity in the reflective awareness of one's enduring psychological sameness. Operationally defined, identity regulates the flow of consciousness through the coordination of subsidiary systems.

In our discussion of identity we have raised some assumptions about consciousness to the status of terms in an implicit paradigm. The terms we have used to describe the components of consciousness are "subjective," "objective," "experiential," and "reflective." These are terms, like identity, which have a neuropsychological as well as a common referent. These four major components of consciousness, four directions on the mental compass, are involved in the organization of every mental act.

A consideration of the effect and aftermath of trauma indicates the importance of developing a generalized context for understanding the relation of these components of consciousness. A prototype for understanding how trauma stimulates the process of new mental structure formation is provided in Freud's paper on "Screen Memories." In that paper Freud contends that the hallmark of a screen memory is the appearance of the self objectified in the recollection. The presence of the objectified self in the memory is an indication that an intense, overwhelming experience has triggered a shift in the focus of consciousness to pure, reflective self-observation. The sense of imminent danger is such that the subjectively initiating active self is removed from the scene of action, replaced by the objectified image of the self suddenly locked into the reflective position. In other words, trauma sets off a neuropsychological mechanism for taking refuge from experience through becoming a spectator. This mechanism also induces the immediate formation of long-term memory pictures as intensified impressions, proximal to the traumatic ones. This screens out the traumatic experience, and the sense of identity as observer is preserved forever after.

This is a familiar mechanism. We all recall the responses to the question, "How did you feel during the period that you were kidnapped?" "Very neutral and detached, like an observer, like it was happening to someone else." And when this mechanism of detachment fails to protect from the life-threatening imminence of danger, "My life passed before my eyes." We can see in these statements that when trauma reaches extremity the reflective cohesion of identity is suddenly released and all manner of experience floods the mind.

Thus, to understand the development of new identity in response to the naturally occurring traumas of life cycle, we must understand the working relation among reflection and experience, subject and object. In the new identity formation that occurs naturally during the life cycle rather than artificially, neurological propensities for change in mental structure are triggered, and the creative process is set into motion. We shall contend that the creator does not resolve life-crisis traumas completely, and that in the fixation on responding to trauma with new identity formation, the creator is impelled to bear witness to, and to document the formation of new identity.

THE NEUROPSYCHOLOGICAL PARADIGM OF CONSCIOUSNESS

The creative process of identity formation is simultaneously a neurological and a psychological process. To support this contention we offer the evidence that the different components of consciousness are grounded in functionally distinct anatomies of the cerebral cortex. After decades of work in identifying functional and mental damage due to brain pathology, followed by anatomical dissection of the autopsied brain, Luria, the great Russian neuropsychologist, concluded that the prefrontal neocortex supports the general function of *evaluating* sensory experience, while the posterior areas of the neocortex are involved in producing new sensory experience. His findings relate reflection and experience as one polarity of consciousness —a north and south on the neuropsychological compass.

The other evidence we cite for a neurological-psychological congruence of consciousness is the effect of splitting the two cortical hemispheres of the brain by severing their connection. Neuropsychologists found that when the corpus callosum is cut so that the two hemispheres are separated, except for their subcortical connections, the two separate spheres of integrated consciousness are released from a previously unapparent bondage to one another.

The sphere of consciousness, integrated in the nondominant hemisphere, processes sensory emanations of the external world and images of the body as an entity existing in space. This organization of consciousness, in what we may term loosely the "object sphere," provides information and experience about the object of the real world.

The sphere of consciousness integrated in the dominant hemisphere, however, processes the subjective initiation of movement, gesture, and verbal meaning. This organization of consciousness, in what we may loosely call the "subject sphere," provides information on the genesis of intent.

This neuropsychological East and West of our consciousness combines the initiatory I of the subject sphere with the person-in-the-world *me* of the object sphere in the process we have termed "neuropsychological identity."

THE DRIVES

Freud defined instinct, or drive, as the demand that the mind produce work. It is consistent both with psychoanalytic theory and with recent work on neurotransmitter systems to consider three separate drives. We must therefore include in the neuropsychological paradigm we have introduced (1) a libidinal need-engendering drive that fuels the subjective side of consciousness via a dopamine neurotransmission system; (2) an aggressive frustration-engendering drive that fuels the objective reality-seeking side of consciousness via a norepinephrine neurotransmission system; and (3) a neutral drive that fuels reflection via a seratonin neurotransmission system.

The nature of the neurotransmitter systems is of no moment in our discussion in this book. What is important is the notion that twin, sexual and aggressive drives exact a neuropsychological engagement in experience, while a separate neutral drive requires the mind to work at assessing that experience.

THE DEVELOPMENT OF CONSCIOUSNESS IN INFANCY

The basic components of consciousness we have been discussing are assembled from infantile prototypes. The creator resorts to the raw materials of consciousness in his reconstruction of identity.

We must follow Freud in assuming not only that the infant discharge process structures nascent consciousness, but also that the development of conditions prerequisite to infant satisfaction is the prototype for all identity processes. It follows that the earliest sense of psychological experience inheres in the identity of sensations. The registration of libidinal and aggressive drives attaches to this identity a sense of pure, unstructured existence, a barely qualified blank of unreflective awareness.

The rudiments of primary neuropsychological identity are structured when a libidinally (or subjectively) generated wish produces in the mind a kind of kinesthetic, effortful image of satisfaction. This same wish is visually or tactiley imaged in the object hemisphere. When a precursor of the reflective sense affirms the presence of real, tangible, milk-producing humanity, there is an identity formed, a congruence perceived, between the subjectively and objectively imaged wish and the object of wishing.

An infant comes into the world with both an inborn readiness—a neurological predisposition to associate or make mental content out of an indwelling sense of balance experienced when held in its mother's arms—and an inborn capacity to bind this sense with indwelling drive. Inevitably, the warmth and feel of the mother's body are associatively bound to movements of infantile libido.

Genetically, this nascent kinesthetic-libidinal sense of subjective existence is balanced against a nascent sense of the object, a sense which develops a more or less cutaneous image. The infant feels coldness, a lack of accommodative support when the mother/object puts it down. In this feeling is a precursor of primary subject/object identification.

There is another matrix of kinesthesia/vision around the reflexive smiling response that develops at two or three months. So, from the beginning of postnatal life, vision and cutaneous sensation must be instrumental in the process of differentiating images of extrapsychic origin. In the smiling response, the libidinal pressure is channeled instinctually into the oral masculature, and the activity of sucking is libidinized as the satisfaction of hunger comes to be accompanied by new libidinized cathexis. Sucking is associated with an image of the mother's face and this association becomes the primary, organizing basis for the identification of the image of the mother's face with satisfaction.

Beyond this, the infant must come to distinguish the intra- from the extrapsychic image of the object through the instinctu- ally triggered agency of judgment. Reflective consciousness must, in the first months of life, work in a highly undifferen- tiated fashion. In infancy, when an identity of perceptions oc- curs and that identity is followed by discharge, then reflection must also release its working energy and so add to the pleasure gain. But when needful states arise and no perceptual identity can be established, the reflective sense must take the infant away from the state of frustration into evanescent states of prototypical reflective awareness. In this way reflection, or in- wardly directed consciousness, must discriminate between in- trapsychic and extrapsychic images.

Now the image of the mother's face has been associated with the extrapsychic appearance of the mother, and so with libidinal satisfaction and reduction of the process that led to need. However, when the maternal image occurs intrapsych- ically, but not extrapsychically—that is to say, when the infant hallucinates the means of satisfaction—then there must be an intensification of aggressive pressures, need tension, frustration. This is the core of the instinctual collocation of frustration/cry- ing. Crying is the affective prototypical response that comes to be identified with the appearance of mother, an appearance associated with a diminution of conscious and needful pain. Need and frustration, pleasure and pain, are the rudiments of experience. Judgment discriminating between the intrapsychic and extrapsychic is the prototype of reflection. When crying is ineffective and judgment lapses, trauma occurs.

During the first year and one-half of life, the components of consciousness are somewhat loosely tied together as intrapsy- chic indentity in what may be termed the transitional mode. Winnicott's notion of the transitional object is that subjective effort in bringing about the arrival of the desired object of gratification is not clearly demarcated from the object itself. Thus, although judgment can discriminate between the intra- psychic and the extrapsychic object, it cannot yet firmly dis- criminate between the effort induced by need and the appearance of the object. Primary intrapsychic identity of this kind escapes the province of judgment until the first well-structured synthesis of identity occurs in the aftermath of the primal scene.

PRIMAL SCENE

We may define the primal scene as a mutually exclusive engagement of the parents with each other, carried out despite overwhelming pressures for satisfaction occuring in the infant. It is only in the resolution of this neuropsychologically determined frustration, triggered by reality, that the first thoroughly functional structured reflective identity occurs. The future creator remains fixated to the transitionally optimistic premise that his efforts must result in the appearance of the need-satisfying object in reality. The effect of this fixation is to provide the future creator with an illusion of alternative means to resolve trauma, as he continues to half-believe in the efficacy of intense wishful effort.

If we conceive of the effect of the primal scene on the infant, it must be such that an overwhelming pressure of drive triggers an escape to reflection at the same time that the reflective mechanism breaks down and the drive floods the neuropsychological apparatus, opening up new and biologically readied cortical areas for drive reception. Soon the infant comes into possibilities of new experience, and a new, traumatically objectified, real identity, which is to center on auditory and anal perceptions. This, after trauma has induced a loss of consciousness when reflection fails to hold the drive in check.

It is our thesis that the future creator manages to resist the full loss of consciousness attendant to this trauma. The future creator maintains his transitional optimism that even this situation can be subjectified through extreme effort. Thus he continues to reflect on the nature of the identity change being induced under the impact of circumstances and his drives.

The identity change that occurs, and to which the future creator is fixated, goes through a sequence of phases. These fixated nuclear phases become the unalterable prototypes for the creative process. During his creative process the adult creator maintains an intensely effortful awareness of his work in process, in the face of potential identity-quenching trauma. The creator cannot relax until he has constructed an alternative identity sufficent to dispel the trauma. This process determines the states in creativity, just as it determined the future creator's response to primal scene trauma.

THE CREATIVE PROCESS

The identity making phases appear to be inevitable and ubiquitous in identity-formulating works of literature. Because dreams are innate neuropsychological prototypes for identity making, we assume that the process of dream formation is the prototype for identity-formulating creative works. In this context we take Freud's description of the dream formation sequence as a guide to the creative sequence: in the dreaming it is only a conflictual idea or fragment of identity that undergoes degradation; in the work-in-process the creator's identity is degraded and reconstructed.

Phase 1—Frustration

The first phase in the creative process consists of frustration in reality. The creative person is faced with some dilemma in his life that cannot be resolved through ordinary problem-solving techniques. Problem solving is the method for evaluating proposed courses of action according to the success of previous courses of action. Possibilities are limited by the prevailing identity structure operating within a framework of logic maintained by the inherent nature of reflection. The identity worked out in response to the stage-appropriate trauma that precipitated the individual's entrance into a particular stage of life is ordinarily sufficient to structure an approach to overcoming frustration.

Failure in the ordinary modes of problem solving requires either a particular creative effort, or a more general, thoroughgoing creative effort whose end result is a basic change in the structure of personal identity. Putting this in terms of dream formation, some critically important fragment of intent is broken off from the possibilities of action because of its dynamic incompatibility with the ordinary methods of solving problems and of finding satisfaction.

Phase 2—Regression

The second phase in the creative process occurs when the conflictual intention begins to undergo degradation as an idea. Its verbal content becomes reduced to more primitive verbal form, while the effort that filled the intention is diffused and degraded to the status of primitive impulse. In the language of dream interpretation, we may say the latent thought loses its logical coherence and enters into associative confluences of various kinds. Its libidinal energy is spread throughout any number of derivatives. It is a kind of searching for earlier verbal formulas of success.

Phase 3—Primary Process

The now transformed latent intention enter the realm of primary process of dynamic unconscious. Here in this neuropsychological bedrock the transformed latent idea undergoes a more radical transformation according to the laws of the primary process: condensation and displacement. The transformed latent thought comes into contact, and is reinforced by the raw stuff of long-term memory. This part of the process is one in which the radical transformation consists in change from verbal content to visual imagery. We may view this as the phase in the creative cycle in which the actual new product is formed. The form of the original idea takes on its affective significance, is enhanced by contact with primary wishes, and appears to conscious reflection as newly experienced imagery. It is the new idea melded in the furnace of the drives.

Phase 4—Revision

If the movement in stage 2 deserves to be called regressive, then the movement in stage 4 is progressive. The raw, imaged form of the now transformed latent idea is reshaped as it takes on verbal equivalence in preparation for its full re-emergence into the world of mental reflection. In finding a new verbal form, the now transformed latent idea has undergone a revision similar to the genetic revision that occurs in development when the verbal mode begins to take precedence over the visual mode in the formulation of new experience. It remains for the new verbal product to pass that last barrier to full reflective consciousness by passing through another—secondary—revision which insures that only logical thoughts shall enter into full reflective consciousness.

Phase 5—Resolution

In this last phase of the creative process the revised product is considered from the standpoint of its utility. Judgment determines the goodness and trueness of the product before any attempt is made to use it for social communiction. The product is judged according to the standards which determined its entrance into the creative process in the first place.

THE CREATOR'S SYNDROME: THE PLEASURABLE RESOLUTION
OF TRAUMA

We come to the heart of our argument! Every professional creator is afflicted with a clinically identifiable syndrome which should properly be called the creator's syndrome. The creative person maintains and has maintained an alternative to his normal identity structure at each level of his psychogenic development. The creative person feels that his works exist as the fruits of a provisional identity. His activities as a creator can only be legitimized through the active mediation of an audience. We shall argue (1) that the transitionally fixated identity of the person with the creator's syndrome determines much of what is common to all creative works, (2) that it determines the nature of the relationship to the audience, and (3) that it leaves its signature on every work in clearly perceivable ways.

In essence the creator's syndrome is a way of communicating designed to overcome traumatic frustration by producing "works" which will command attention felt to be otherwise unobtainable. Now, in normal development at every stage in the life cycle there is some product which naturally issues from that period and which becomes the medium of communication to the central persons in reality. For the creative person each and every period produces a provisional product which, if accepted, ensures the continued gratification of the one engendering the product through what is felt to be a special and effortful act of creation. The creative person uses the creative cycle, repeatedly, to avert present frustrations. In that sense the past is repeatedly made present, past pleasures are constantly used to screen present conflicts, and the sense of personal identity as creative person is constantly undergoing revision.

A syndrome of aversion, the creator's syndrome has much in common with psychosis. But here the psychosis is averted through the auspices of the work, whose provisional reality can become verified as real through the consensus of an important, parentally conceived audience. Thus the work serves the function of externalizing a kind of psychic repair.

THE LIFE CYCLE

We assert that the major stages of life are ushered in by insoluble dynamic conflicts whose solution requires new identity formation. In the sitution of the primal scene, for instance, the heightened libidinal wishes for satisfaction and the overwhelming aggressive response to the situation of exclusion from the possibility of satisfaction sets up a regressive process that brings reflection into renewed contact with the experiential sources of drives. The quantitatively excessive amount of drive stimulation opens up new neurological ground in the experiential neocortex. Unbound drive stimulates new autonomous nuclei for the binding of the drives, while subsequently, by means of what may be called a progressive current in the neuropsychological creative process, reflection makes a new identification which comes to serve as the identity prototype for the anal/auditory stage of life.

With the formation of a new, enduring, neuropsychological pattern of identity, the person is in the position of having one developmentally appropriate pattern of identification and another hierarchically circumvented pattern of identification. The circumvented pattern is available to organize what may now be called the primary process, containing an imagistic, oral and unconscious world.

Erik H. Erikson is the psychoanalytic theorist who must be given most credit for tying together the notions of identity formation and biologically unfolding stages in the human life cycle. We will follow Erikson's schematization of the human life cycle (1959, p. 170). (See Table 1-1.)

Table 1-1. Erikson's Stages of Identity Formation

Erikson's stages	Identity stages (our designation)	Approximate ages
1. Trust vs. mistrust	Primary identification	Infancy 0 to 1½
2. Autonomy vs. shame, doubt	Identification with aggressor	Early childhood 1½ to 3
3. Initiative vs. guilt	Secondary identification	Play age 3 to 4½
4. Industry vs. inferiority	Superego identification	Latency 4½ to 11
5. Identity vs. identity diffusion	Adolescent identification	Adolescence 11 to 21
6. Intimacy vs. isolation	Adult identification	Young adult 21 to 40
7. Generativity vs. self-absorption	Mature (societal) identification	Adult (maturity) 40 to 65
8. Integrity vs. disgust, despair	Aged identification	Old age 65 and over

LIFE CYCLE IN THE CREATOR'S SYNDROME

A person like Freud who develops the creator's syndrome, undergoes a normal resolution, and a simultaneous specifically pathological irresolution in each stage of the life cycle. In our view the creative person undergoes a normal and a wishful enduring response to each of life's neuropsychologically inevitable crises.

The alternative solutions prevent a firm closure to the neuropsychologically determined pattern of enduring drive distribution which accompanies each genetic stage of development. Consequently, regressive channels and progressive channels are more facilitated in the creative person. Moreover the more or less normal resolution achieved in each stage of life insures against a psychotic outcome. Thus, the primary fantasies or constructs act as guardians of the sanctity of neuropsychological channels. In this sense the actual event, say the primal scene as witnessed parental intercourse, is not normally available to adult consciousness. When it is, as it was with the Wolf Man, it may well imply psychosis, as it did in his case.

Let us now briefly project the elements of the creator's syndrome as they contribute to the outcome of each stage in life. Each stage we will mention forms the topic of a single chapter of this book. We begin in infancy. The transitional era belief that one creates the world as an extension of one's own effort, should, we think, normally be relinquished with the advent of the primal scene. However, the future creative person attempts to preserve the primary sense of making the world through the insistence that the primal scene is also his own making. The resulting fixation on the primal scene gives rise to the persistent formation of images, the real creative product of the infant. The signature of this fixation will be seen in such creative works as Keats' "Ode To A Grecian Urn" and Arnold's "Dover Beach."

Resolved or not, mental life shifts to an anal and auditory focus between the ages of 18 months to about three years. The world is given, not created. It is the possession of the aggressor, and it may be possessed through the magic of words. The introjections of this era, described so well by Isakower (1939), are taken in their neuropsychologically determined cadenced rhythms. The foundations of syntax and what Chomsky calls a "universal grammar" are necessary outcomes of the distribution of a heavy charge of a new drive into the neuropsychological territory which is opened up in the aftermath of the primal scene.

Poets like Dylan Thomas, who retain their magical belief in the efficacy of words to possess reality, also present in their heavily cadenced language creative changes in syntax, rearrangements of the basal grammar. This approach evokes a new interpretation of "Do not go gentle into that good night,/Rage, rage against the dying of the light," which echoes the anal child's tantrum, his refusal to give up consciousness to the overwhelming significance of the primal scene; instead words are used to maintain full consciousness and the illusion of control.

During the oedipal period a system of fluctuating, alternative identities is developed by future creators as a means of refusing to give up childhood masturbation. We believe that in this period a bisexual identification structures the realm of the imagination. The creative child resolves the oedipal dilemma on one hand, but on the other, he imaginatively identifies himself with what may well be called the phallic woman, the composite parent who is held as a fantasy object capable of purveying all gratification.

Now this composite, phallic woman representation reorganizes the earlier, alternate creative solutions under a single aegis. In this way the bisexual, composite identification comes to have a special effect on the formation of the reality testing which distinguishes between reality and fantasy during the oedipal era and thereafter. The creative person maintains an illusory belief in the possible efficacy of his fantasy productions.

The effect of this development on latency is that the creative person comes to believe—see—that he is capable of intuiting a world as replete as the real one, with a plethora of content and potential experience. As Sartre's autobiography *Words* shows, while the normal latency child ascribes the rules and regulations of society to a world outside of his own imagination which is to be explored and discovered, the creative child maintains the alternative belief that the real world is capable of basic mutative possibilities. Utopian books like Bacon's *Atlantis* will be seen to owe their fixation of origin to the alternative for the normal resolution of this period.

Adolescence is a period of new identity formation. The surge of genital drive demands a new experience in loving, and it intensifies the subjective experience of self. During this era the creative person begins to realize that a creative and a normal self represent alternative possibilities for identity. The creative adolescent tends to be suffused with love for the phallic woman, the long-limbed ideal woman who can, if found, inspire the most profound feelings.

For the creative adolescent such adolescent epiphanies are full of the possibilities for creative production. Whitman's recollection of adolescent epiphany, "Out of the Cradle Endlessly Rocking" ("Out of the mocking-bird's throat, the musical shuttle,") gives voice to the adolescent's yearning for an adult life full of inspired significance. This is the era when the realm of the imagination develops conscious significance; personal symbols, often representing the muse, take on significance in the creative life. It is also the era when the creative process, full of regressive longing and progressive inspiration becomes the prototype of both personal identity accretion and of the production of works of art. Insofar as these are synonymous, the adolescent creator begins to accept his identity as a creator. Stephen's epiphany and personal identification with his bird-woman in *Portrait of the Artist* is a case in point.

The problem for the creative individual's adult life is the acceptance of the creative mode as a focus of identity for professional life. A paradox is presented, because all along the creativity has been experienced as an alternative mode of life. To take on this mode as a basis for one's social identity before one has produced works that justify such an identity is taking a terrible risk, either of being perceived as odd or grandiose, or somehow pathological in the world of normal people.

This dilemma is well expressed by Eliot in a poem of entry into adult life. The "Love Song of J. Alfred Prufrock" is not a poem of old age, but a declaration of the terrible risk involved in accepting the life of poetry. The woman of the poem is the muse. Will she accept the poet's advances? Eliot asks if the poem itself, and the impostor poet (Prufrock), can succeed in producing an authentic work. The poet asks, just as the irony-laden adolescent asks whether he can hope to have his fantasy of satisfaction ever realized in the world of real satisfaction.

The problem for the adult creator is to produce real galvanizing objects, works which bring confirmation from a critical audience that his efforts at reconciling the creative and the normal selves can succeed. The works of the adult creator reduce the disparity between the creative and the normal self by addressing the indwelling muse of the poem or the work itself as if it were the real object. Thus in Shakespeare's "Shall I Compare Thee to a Sumers' Day?" "Thee" stands for the poem itself and for the indwelling muse of the poem.

The mature creator finds it not enough to produce the galvanizing object of adulthood. He feels that his ideas must receive sufficient recognition to enter into the mainstream, life of the mind of the social group with which he identifies himself. Then the aged creator must resolve the dying and disappearance of his muse, as well as the loss of personal identity. Thus, Shakespeare's Lear must deal with the loss of his fool, as well as with personal mortality, conceived of as the loss of his love, Cordelia. Yeats also faces the loss of his immortality musings in "The Tower," as he longs for his literary self, Hanrahan, to re-establish the poet's past greatness.

Chapter 2

THE CREATOR'S SYNDROME
Early Infancy

Comparing the creator's syndrome with schizophrenia will help define and shed light on the syndromatic aspects of the creator's experience, for creative people alter reality in ways that resemble the flight from reality into psychosis. The will to alter reality which expresses itself in a creative product has the legitimate function of making the unacceptable acceptable. Transforming unacceptable experience, each poem is a form of denial. But the poem is also elucidation of reality.

While using the poem to alter his reality, the poet must be in contact with and acknowledge distasteful experience. So must the audience contact and recognize the material to be transformed. To alter reality creatively, you must be fairly conscious of what really exists. Psychotic delusion works differently. It is designed to obscure reality. Psychotic delusion is not transferable into generally accessible creative objects; it is an obfuscation made in terms of entirely personal symbols.

What is the origin of these different truths? In infancy, during what has come to be known as the oral period of development (we are calling it the transitional stage), the future psychotic person is sometimes exposed to a mothering person genuinely opposed to her child's expressions of need. Such a mother is "schizophrenegenic," and unable to summon the appropriate kinesthetic and emotional responses of mothering. Schizophrenegenic mothering forces a disjunction to appear between the infant's instinctual behavior—rooting for the breast or nipple—and the mothering person's arbitrary handling of the infant. A schizophrenegenic mother is unable to respond to the infant's subjective need. Ordinarily, mothers, in loving their children, help them develop a sense of satisfying subjective being.

An infantile syndrome sets the stages for habitual ways of relating. The future schizophrenic is likely to vest as much of his life's energy in the hope for maternal care as is humanly possible. As a result, his future relationships remain heavily rooted in a sense of the pervading presence of his mother.

The future creative person is the child of another set of parents. These parents make inflated performance demands. In this case the mothering person is likely to resemble the schizophrenegenic mother in opposing the infant's libidinal (pleasurable) drive expression. Setting up a situation in which the infant's pleasure is deferred obliges the infant to see pleasure as depending on the completion of some "special" act. As for the parental behavior, it arises in that narcissistic extension which allows the parent, whose own creativity is somehow frustrated, to see the infant as potentially *special*. For narcissistic reasons, these parents are exceptionally liable to taking rooting (breast seeking) movement as gesture, grimaces as smiles, and babbling as speech. This contributes to an infantile fixation which amounts both to a premature transitional development and to a sort of precocious development of the prototype for synchronizing reality and experience.

Under a terrific weight of parental pressure, the "creative" infant manages to turn the tide of cathexes toward his own pleasure. This is an act of talent depending on the preverbal reflection that the pleasure process of the infant's internal world is best served by reproducing behaviors that elicit pleasurable and gratifying parental response. Such epoch-making reflective syntheses occasion the first memories of childhood. As we know, in rare individuals these memories extend back at least as early as six months.

Thus the mode of synthetic mental activity is aroused in the creative infant as the preferred method for averting frustration and gaining access to pleasure and consciousness. Quite simply, in infancy a vivid experience of reflective consciousness is attendant on these moments of mental synthesis. The talent that inheres in the creator's syndrome is the ability to synthesize reflective consciousness precociously.

This is part of a special pattern. The "talented" infant learns to avert frustration through acts liable to increase his nascent consciousness, and to preserve it from extinction. Phyllis Greenacre (1960, p. 712) reports that infants under pressures producing unusual tension are capable of using neurological channels inappropriate to their age. In the same way high tension may conceivably trigger activity in that segment of the frontal lobe in which resides the neurological basis for reflection.

The memory material organized in approximately the first year and a half of postnatal life is predominantly oral-visual in nature. In most children speech organization is in harmony with later anal/auditory developments. In potentially creative infants the habit of verbal response often develops at an early age (within the first year) with the result that the creative fixation is inalterably tied to an engagement in oral-visual thinking. Words evoke the primary oral-visual world in a facilitated way when they have been linked to this world by precocious development.

When people are said to exhibit the marks of a classifiable syndrome, they are so classified because all people with that syndrome have undergone similar patterns of fixation, and have formed similar strong, habitual responses. Fixation has two sources in experience: (1) instinctual overstimulation, or (2) reality-induced trauma. We have been examining the "stimulating" origins of the creative syndrome. We should also examine its traumatic origin.

Let us explain what we mean by the trauma-ontology of the creator's syndrome. Normally, the transitional illusion of having created the real world is shattered by the overwhelming impact of the primal scene. One literally relinquishes consciousness in the face of such overwhelming trauma. However, the future creative person remains fixated in his transitional beliefs. The fixation leaves its impact on the developing personality through the construction of the fixated illusion that under some special set of circumstances one can indeed excape the inevitable loss of consciousness involved in the primal scene. This means that the creative person believes that he can assert his transitional construction on the primal scene, making it his own. This optimistic illusion tends to keep open the gates of re-entry to the oral visual world of primary existence. Thus it is characteristic of the creative person that he can summon consciousness to avert trauma, since the primal scene is the prototype of trauma.

Of course, every primal scene image is covered over by an oedipal overlay. This is why Freud was so long in discovering it. We take Freud as a prime example of a literary creator. The wealth of available data about his life makes it possible to surmise the origins of his literary fixations with confidence.

TRANSITIONAL CREATION

There is a transitionally derived quality to Freud's writings common to that of many professional creators. Freud dramatizes and demonstrates his ideas in the formal stuctures of his essays. His imagery and other literary devices support the constructed form. We contend that embodying ideas in this way recapitulates the transitional mode of creativity. But Freud's most common formal device is an even more specific form of transitional creation. Freud often used the device of the "straw-man." He makes the straw-man responsible for the wrong idea, then he demolishes the straw-man, substituting the correctness of his own ideas about the truth. This corresponds to a transitional creation and destruction of an image of identity alternative to his own.

In Max Schur's biography of Freud, *Freud: Living and Dying,* S. observes that "Freud was the oldest child born to his father's third wife, Amalie. Next came Julius, who died at the age of 8 months, and then sister Anna, born on December 31, 1858 when Freud was nearly 2 years and 8 months old. . . . (Schur, pp. 340–341).

According to Schur, Freud was superstitiously obsessed with the possible death of those who were close to him. Freud's interest in and contribution to theories about death and the maintenance of consciousness probably originated in two events, both traumatic and both developmentally overlapping.

Freud himself analyzed these nuclear conflicts, relating them to an intense, envious hatred of his younger sibling, Julius, who actually died after 6 months, when Freud was 23 months old. Julius's birth and death coincided with the period of Freud's primal scene interest. The death and disappearance of Julius acted as a traumatic fixation point interfering with Freud's ability to resolve the primal scene.

Surely Freud's obsession grew out of transitional thinking. He must have felt power over the appearance and disappearance of Julius and the appearance of Anna, for transitional thinking has to do with feelings of creating objects by naming them, pointing them out, or taking them over. As parents know, creative children develop a pattern of making transitional objects. Whereas a normal child feels he has power to make and unmake one or two transitional objects—a blanket or a stuffed animal—a creative childs exercise control over an entire transitional world.

Julius's death or disappearance, coincided with an era of

envious hatred. Surely the omnipotent thinking common to the anal period was given a boost by the late transitional fixation, centered on Julius, which overlapped it. Taking Freud as one who manifests the creator's syndrome, we see the accessibility of his oral-visual world to the products of his later thought. We have surmised that he treated Julius as a transitional creation, and that his tendency to maintain reflective consciousness in himself and to elicit it in others grew out of a fixation to transitional thinking.

On "Screen Memories"

There are a number of striking instances of transitionally fixed creative thought in Freud's writings about trauma, especially in those that are autobiographically tinged. These exhibit an array of oral visual imagery. One thinks of Freud's 1899 essay on "Screen Memories." The essay is a demonstration of the proposition that analysis can recover conscious impressions laid down in the past. These impressions are hidden behind screen memories. The detective work involved in successful attempts to bring back the past recreate Freud's transitional mode. The kinds of recollections entangled in screen memories are dressed in heightened, visual, sensual, oral imagery.

The first thing to notice is Freud's statement that the earliest childhood memories are visual; the second is that in screen memories the subject (the maker and possessor of the memory) appears as an object in the recollection. The third notion to be grasped is that screen memories are erected to hide traumatic events. Fourth is in the construction of screens there is a displacement of emphasis: one attempts to deny an unforgetable and traumatic happening by remembering and substituting adjacent proximal impressions for the original. In this, screen formation resembles the building of dreams. Fifth, the screen memory has two potential values: it may organize later impressions or it may be a device for hiding earlier, traumatic impressions behind a later, more innocent memory.

The screen memory of this essay is claimed to be of the first sort: a group of early impressions hide a group of later ones. However, we think it must also be of the second sort. The memory is placed in time near the birth of the sister, Anna, which must screen the earlier disappearance of the brother, Julius. The presence of the self in the memory screens out the unwanted sibs. The memory is rather beautiful.

> The scene appears to me fairly indifferent and I can not understand why it should have become fixed in my memory. Let me describe it to you. I see a rectangular, rather steeply sloping piece of meadow-land, green and thickly grown; in the green there are a great number of yellow dandelions. At the top end of the meadow there is a cottage and in front of the cottage door two women are standing chatting busily, a peasant-woman with a handkerchief on her head and a children's nurse. Three children are playing in the grass. One of them is myself (between the age of two and three); the two others are my boy cousin, who is a year older than me, and his sister, who is almost exactly the same age as I am. We are picking the yellow flowers and each of us is holding a bunch of flowers we have already picked. The little girl has the best bunch; and, as though by mutal agreement, we —the two boys—fall on her and snatch away her flowers. She runs up the meadow in tears and as a consolation the peasant woman gives her a big piece of black bread. Hardly have we seen this than we throw the flowers away, hurry to the cottage and ask to be given some bread too. And we are in fact given some; the peasant woman cuts the loaf with a long knife. In my memory the bread tastes quite delicious—and at that point the scene breaks off. (*Standard Edition* vol. III, p. 311)

The memory, which happens to cover an array of oedipal strivings, is remarkable for its imagery: the yellow flowers, the emphasis on the taste of the bread. Parenthetically, the description of the knife happens to be the signature of an element of castration anxiety translated back into oral visual terms.

The essay's form is its remarkable feature. In it Freud disguises his subjective involvement with the unraveling of the screen's composition, so that one of his personae is externalized and, in a way, separated from identity. The patient is both the subject of the memory and the object of analysis. In the retrospective dialogue, Freud's identity resides in the person of the analyst, a reflective observer. The patient is an objective sort of being, reasonable, and capable of affirming or denying the pronouncements of the analyst who reflects upon the memory. In the course of the analysis, the analyst is moved to ask questions which revive related memories in the patient, who is good enough to confirm the analyst's hypotheses and interpretations in an exceedingly reasonable and automatic way. This dialogue recreates an imaginary Freud separated from his current identity, much like the child figure in the memory.

As we have been saying, this formal device approximates certain of the paper's conclusions, those that witness the defensive processes proper to screen memories. *The hallmark of screen memories is in the subject's entering the memory in objective form.* This is a form of transitional thinking, creating an image of personal identity.

An image of surpassing clarity precedes the imaginary retrospective dialogue between patient and analyst. It is itself an image describing the transformation of identity:

> The assertion that a physical intensity can be displaced from one presentation (which is abandoned) onto another which thenceforward plays the psychological part of the former one) is as bewildering to us as certain features of Greek mythology—as for instance, when the gods are said to clothe someone with beauty as though it were with a veil, whereas *we* think only of a face transfigured by a change of expression. (S.E. vol. III, p. 309)

The image has a transitional function in the paper, separating an abstract formulation about the nature of the displacement necessary to the formulation of screen memories from the concrete, empathically accessible dialogue. The image of veiling aptly precedes a discussion of screens.

The resort to imagery and rhetorical figure is characteristic of the creative person's tentative exploration of a difficult concept. It has to do with a way of making necessary connections, of reestablishing communication between the reflective concept and the sensual basis of perception. In the veiling image, "features" heralds a visual, facial impression embodied in an image. The image is one of disguised or transfigured identity, "whereas," Freud continues, "we think it is only a change of expression"—that is, only a change in the motoric self-expression.

The image is more than happy, indicating, as it does, Freud's change in identity in response to an oedipal turmoil. The turmoil is documented in the analysis of the screen memory. The change in identity structure is recapitulated—demonstrated really—in the form of the dialogue. In it Freud masters his creation, his method for assuring the interpenetration of experience and reflection.

Thus, we now see the transitional object is an integer of mental structure. D. W. Winnicott, (1953) who is responsible for the concept has demonstrated that transitional object formation is a sign of evolution beyond the era of hallucinations. For the potentially creative infant, the object gains utilitarian value in becoming a means to the end of satisfaction. The infant's activity in object formation has a peculiar subjective accompaniment. In adult terms, creating a transitional object is synonymous with endowing some article with a projection of subjective value. For the infant, however, this creation has another meaning. The infant perceives what we would call his endowment as an act of literal creation. He feels that he is creating the transitional object. The infant's satisfaction is meted out on the basis of adult recognition. Recognition reinforces the infant's belief in his having created the object out of thin air. In a subjective figure, the infant has created a satisfying object which mediates his needs Vis-à-vis reality.

In incorporating the transitional mode, creative people develop a primal optimism around their own ability to create the means of expression. Broadly conceived then, creativity is primal longing for expression. One of the great creative tasks is establishing means (and it is in the ability to establish such means that the optimism lies) through which the created object will implement the primal longing for expression. The optimism is based on some assurance that the search for an expressive object will be rewarded.

The means of representation are originally visual. The visual mode is more plastic than the auditory, more given to permutation and rearrangement. The first forms of thinking are visual. By the time the verbal mode is thoroughly organized, the creative person has an elaborated picture of the world, which is available for annotation in the auditory mode—in which it may also be completely re-created. Genetically normal infants experience a sense of the world's becoming objectified and newly created only after a resolution of the primal scene in a flowering of auditory-verbal-anal-autonomous locomotoric experience.

The creative infant, however, already has a sense of the past when his verbal system has come into being; he feels that words evoke the past and take the place of visual imagery. His ability to articulate the world in two modalities, visual and verbal, lends itself to the building of alternative systems of objective organization, one of which might be called "normal," while the other serves the later building of an alternative self-system, a more secret, more visual repository for fantasy. The interaction between these systems provides some of the tension and drama ordinarily provided by interaction with the object world.

In summary, the mental activity encompassed in transitional object formation is the prototype for an amalgam of reflection and experience. It is a comprehensive procedure arising from a need to find in reality the fulfillment of the libidinal drive for expression. The cohesion of reflection and experience is eased by the innate mechanism that links a frustration to a mental object and a mental object to a real object. The real object is then correlated with gratification and frustration's end. Moreover, during the early period which culminates in the formation of a transitional object, the potentially creative infant achieves his first synthetic image of identity. For what else is the transitional object but a synthesis of what is given by the environment and what is felt to be created from within?

How Objects Reveal Themselves

So far, we have defined neither creativity nor the "creative object." We feel that any definition, barring a definition on genetic principles, fails to be meaningful. Therefore the latter portions of this essay attempt a genetic examination of creativity. We will not try to define created products, or creative objects, for it seems that almost any object may be the result of the creative process.

More concretely, we will begin to offer, in what follows here, an hypothesis and its corollary. Our hypothesis is that the creator endows his object with a portion of his subjectivity and his characteristic manner of synthesis. The nature of synthesis has a great deal to do with a process Ernst Kris (1952) calls regression in service of the ego. The corollary is more explicable in context. It is that *the creative object recapitulates the process of its own development.* Without demonstration, the corollary appears inapplicable to a great many cases. Yet it describes one of the basic beliefs of psychoanalysis, that dreams, speech, and most other personal productions are available to analysis.

This recapitulatory tendency of creative objects is rooted in infantile necessity. In the transitional phase of development, young infants regularly begin a passioned search for some constellation which includes the mother's face and breast. This search has to do with an overpowering desire for nurture. At the beginning of this period, an infant's mother is not any particular purveyor of satisfactions; she *is* satisfaction. Her image, precisely her image felt in this particular constellation, wrests the infant—who is quite overwhelmed by it—from the clutches of his own pressing need (the instinctual drive) for gratification.

Later, somewhere around the age of six months, there is a rather complete development of a purely neurological activity that may as well be called "scanning." Scanning is a functional precursor of the more mature activity of self-reflection, or self-observation. At this point it is directed toward material reality, and especially toward judging the potential reality of external objects. This primitive, neurological activity provides, at least potentially, the germ for later creative integrations.

Remember, the image of the maternal constellation provides the early infant with the feeling of existence. When this constellation fails to materialize in hallucination or reality, a young infant experiences a sort of neurological shutdown, going off to sleep or falling into passivity. However, an older infant, caught in the turmoil of his instinctual drives, begins to scan an array of stored impressions relating to the missing object. He is beginning to learn a primitive, primary process: satisfaction.

Primary process has to do with the ability to familiarize oneself with the achievement of congruence between motor and perceptual imagery. More simply, it is a synchronizing of the elements which go into memories of movement (action sets, kinesthesia, muscular posturing) with a qualitatively real (sensory and usually visual) image. A completed primary process maneuver (unnoticed and habitual in adults) leaves the infant in a state of great satisfaction unless (and this happens first) the infant has produced a hallucination and deceived himself with it, in which case he is quite distressed. This activity, which in the infant's mind is wholly joined to the image of the gratifying constellation, verifies the primary sense of existence and imbues the primitive relfection with existential quality.

What happens is something like this: At first infants respond to instinctual pressure by producing hallucinations of the gratifying object. This is sort of "an easy way out" and obviously doomed to failure. Hallucinations do provide temporary relief from a load of painful craving. But pain, with the pressure of experience, is bound to force the infant into a new sort of consciousness. Inevitably, there comes a time when the infant arrives at the capacity to produce, in the wake of debilitating hallucination, a mental image qualitatively different from an hallucination. To the mother's probable joy, the learning infant becomes reflectively *aware* that there is a distinction between the mental object and the object in reality. That is, the infant comes to add a reflective belief in the reality of objects as opposed to hallucinations. This produces the capacity to form transitional objects, which the infant has the illusion of having created on his own, but which exist simultaneously in the world. Transitional object formation is reinforced by the appearance of the object in the world. The synthesis of motor and externally derived sensory elements is reflected on and fixes the synthesis as mental structure.

For, from the first, judgment, objectification of desire, and self-protection are intimately associated. The mental image (the objectified desire) or *object of desire, comes to stand for the solution to a problem.* In the most primitive language, the problem might be stated in the following way: "I feel pain. If I had the breast/mother's face [hallucination], I would feel no pain [mental representation of the object desired as the solution to the painful and genuine problem of object lack.]"

Remarkably, this neurological pattern which employs scanning has much to do with the adult notion of "embodying." Adults, creative adults, come to articulate need in general, and the need to create in particular, in a derivative way. By and large, the impulse to create forces itself on the potential creator before the precise object is determined, but in such a way that the object may be located.

Creative adults engage in the regression in service of the ego postulated by Ernst Kris (1953) as a basic mechanism in their ability to find solutions to reality problems by taking a point of view consonant with an infantile view in order to make new integrations, which are then reconceived in secondary process—thinking—terms. This controlled regression requires an ability to maintain reflective consciousness intact at its most mature levels of organization while matching this reflective consciousness with progressively more infantile forms of mental integration. Old, submerged combinations of infantile experience (with attendant reflection) are reinvoked as temporary organizers of the intrapsychic world.

The interesting thing about this descent into an underlayer of mental experience is that it is tied to a sense of frustration. Since the creative adult can find no program analogous to the potential solution of his problem—the problem of object formation or location—the creative adult chooses, or has a tendency to seek, solutions of potentially satisfying form in a previous era of his existence. The creative person feels that he will find a solution to a current problem by analyzing the successful solutions achieved in his past.

This is simply a more complicated version of the infant's scanning the stuff of raw memory. In the infant, the path is from need to scanning, which produces an hallucination, followed by an objectified image qualitatively different from an hallucination the search for the transitional object is the precursor of the creative person's creation of work as a solution to a problem.

Creative experiences are organized so that they become immediately accessible to memory. The infant, eventually, comes to remember what actions produce a warm maternal response and learns to repeat those actions or those kinds of actions. As Freud has taught us, that part of memory is accessible which has been tied to seeking satisfaction in the past. Other memories undergo repression.

To clarify, the regressive aspect of creative scanning is remarkably similar to adult dream formation. Dreams are formed from interrupted wishes. In fact, they are fulfillments of wishes that have been frustrated during the day. Their fulfill-ments require a certain amount of regression. Since they repre-sent wishes inadmissible to adult consciousness, they find their outlets at more primitive levels of consciousness. These levels are only available during sleep. There is something familiar in this. We feel as if dream images were found by rummaging through old mental closets. Creative scanning, regressive or otherwise, has something of this quality.

Chapter 3

PRIMAL SCENE

Late Infancy

A primal scene experience fixes the pattern of the intrapsychic images of the transitional era into a set design and locks the primary process into a permanently unconscious mental space which can be visited but not inhabited. We shall argue that the primal scene is, in essence, an inevitable, age-approriate, traumatically overwhelming concatenation of infantile experience. It triggers a reorganization of reflection and, at the same time, establishes an imperative shift of the grounds of experience to verbal encounter. A corollary to this is that the person with the creative syndrome makes only a provisional resolution of the primal scene trauma, so that the patterns of thought common to the transitional era remain accessible to the synthesis of identity established at this time.

The primal scene is an experience which brings infancy to an end. The foundation laid for stability in early childhood is a concrete reality, and the young child cannot alter it. The lesson learned in the primal scene is that the parents have their own mutual and exclusive world. This world cannot be created or destroyed by the young child's supercharged wishes. More neurologically, the primal scene locks the experience of reality into a smoothly synthesized system for composing visual/kinesthetic identities. Judgment is a major function operating within reflective consciousness to determine when the conditions exist in reality for satisfaction to proceed.

Insofar as the person with the creator's syndrome must think of reality as mutable, for him the structuring activity of the primal scene will be compromised. It will not absolutely put a lid on the world of infancy. For the adult creator, who enters into a process of regression in service of the ego, there will come a time in the creative cycle when some echo of the primal scene must be evoked. In other words, the primal scene becomes activated again when the artist's work requires that he question the fundamental nature of what he has taken to be real beforehand. We believe that derivatives of the primal scene are as evident in literary products as derivatives of oedipal conflicts. In the present chapter we will define the primal scene and look at the way in which primal scene derivatives enter into literary works.

THE WOLF MAN'S DREAM

Freud's famous Wolf Man study enters the primal scene through the window of the Wolf Man's dream. A window is a common image for the entry into the primal scene, just as it is almost a universal dream symbol for the actual entry into the visual world of imagery. In the Wolf Man's famous dream—which Freud used to demonstrate the existence of the primal scene—the window "opens of its own accord" as the dream scene begins. A window opens, curtains part, there is a revelation, reality is transformed—such is the imagery that re-searches the primal scene:

"I dreamt that it was night and that I was lying in my bed. (My bed stood with its foot towards the window; and in front of the window there was a row of old walnut trees. I know it was winter when I had the dream and night-time). Suddenly the window opened of its own accord, and I was terrified to see that some white wolves were sitting on the big walnut tree in front of the window. There were six or seven of them. The wolves were quite white, and looked like foxes or sheepdogs, for they had big tails like foxes and they had their ears pricked like dogs when they pay attention to something. In great terror evidently of being eaten up by the wolves, I screamed and woke up." (S.E. vol. XVII, p. 29)

THE PRIMAL SCENE

The primal scene is a universal construct. It maintains structural intactness for the primary identification that organizes awareness in the oral/visual world. Genetically, the scene binds and makes content out of the primary identification, inaugurates the anal auditory phase of development, and initiates a new pattern of identification shaped by aggression.

Psychologically, the primal scene or something like it shatters the transitional illusion. Infancy comes to a neurological end, and when it does the infant is bound to realize, through the agency of the primal scene or other deep engagement between his parents, that he, the infant, is no longer the maker and shaper of reality. After a certain moment, it cannot escape the infant's observation that his parents possess each other and are on certain occasions oblivious to their offspring—and this at times when the infant is wild with supercharged wishes to possess and receive gratification from each. Thwarted in reality, the infant is left to encompass quantities of libidinal and aggressive stimulation too great for discharge through ordinary channels.

This becomes plain in a consideration of Freud's Wolf Man case, itself an exploration of the universal movement from the transitional to the anal auditory phase of development. As is commonly agreed, during the anal auditory stage, the infant conceives of power as existing outside of himself. As a means of encompassing the now liberated quantities of drive, during the genetic interval following the primal scene, the infant necessarily identifies with his own aggression by means of the mechanism known as identification-with-the-aggressor.

In his "Notes From the History of Infantile Neurosis," Freud argues that the Wolf Man witnessed the primal scene. In Freud's reconstruction, the child's parents were copulating *a tergo*—in a position requiring penetration from behind. The woman was on her hands and knees in a position resembling the copulatory attitude of a female dog, wolf, or sheep. Following the reconstruction, in his excitement, SP (the Wolf Man) passed a stool. The scene's effect on the one-and-one-half-year-old child was immediate. It became a fixation point, shaping his destiny in each succeeding stage of life crisis.

After the primal scene experience, the child became aware of, and remained aware of, a veil or twilight over his sense of reality. The veil was penetrated and the Wolf Man achieved lucidity only after passing a stool. In the course of the psychologically regressive illness which began as SP entered adult life and which followed a gonorrheal infection, SP became perpetually constipated. Seeming to lose personal control over his bowels when he first came to Freud, the Wolf Man depended on a valet for the administration of enemas. The veil would lift only after an enema.

The veil imagery is provocative, suggestive, diagnostically useful. Suppose the primal scene to include the traumatic witnessing of a deep and exclusive engagement between the parents and a frustrated reemergence of the wishes appropriate to the time of primary identification; then the veil may be conceived of as a screen or amnesia hiding the scene from verbal and memorious consciousness. For it must be immediately obvious that when the primal scene experience is understood to include the wishes blossoming in the spectator, the infant must be thought of as, in the course of the scene, expressing his excitement, his wishes to participate, and his angry frustration through the mechanism of primary identification. Effectively, the primal scene liberates in the infant libidinal and aggressive derivatives. These are movements toward libidinally and aggressively cathected satisfactions achieved through expressive behaviors. They are to be distinguished from movements toward primary, immediate satisfactions. When the derivatives exceed the discharge capacities of the primary system, the infant must, to contain or channel his surfeit of psychic energy, appropriate another channel for expressively discharging derivative energies.

From this we deduce that witnessing the primal scene triggers an anal/auditory synthesis and brings on a new variety of neurological identification. In our understanding, the Wolf Man in particular and infants in general enter into childhood after some primal scene experience.

Since evidence from patients points to the universality of the primal scene construct, and since it appears that the primal scene mediates between the oral and anal phases of development, it seems likely that a deep, excluding parental encounter amounts (at the time of its occurrence) to a special kind of trauma, an inevitable and final blow to transitional thinking which falls only upon an organism ready to be traumatized, only upon an organism neurologically predisposed to begin the anal/auditory synthesis, only upon an organism capable of opening a new channel of neuropsychological identity.

Consider, for example, the fixation to primary identification in the background of the Wolf Man's primal scene experience. The Wolf Man (like Freud) was born in a caul. In the final stages of SP's analysis, Freud discovered that the Wolf Man associated the veil or *tenebre* perpetually surrounding him with his lucky caul. Freud traced the association to a rebirth fantasy and the fantasy to archaic wishes for *a tergo* penetration by his father and to opposing wishes to so penetrate his mother. But, granted that the rebirth fantasy carried with it a train of anal and oedipal meanings, it seems likely that the Wolf Man's feelings of rebirth, experienced in the aftermath of passing a stool, pointed also to a feeling of clear and comfortable re-entry into the oral visual world, the paradisal first estate, the mental territory predating the primal scene trauma.

Evidently the Wolf Man could not achieve the necessary identity formation to seal off the primal scene. It seems likely, too, that in the stool passing symptom, the Wolf Man achieved a condensed wish-fulfilling kind of satisfaction, a feeling of having been penetrated by his father, of having produced an excrement baby, and of having simultaneously and successfully identified with his mother's position in the primal scene.

Since SP was ill and therefore already somewhat traumatized at the time of the primal scene, and, as Freud tells us, subject to an innate predisposition to maintain any libidinal position ever entered into, the Wolf Man fell subject to an infantile fixation, an untenable wish to possess eternally the objects of primary identification.

POETRY AND THE PRIMAL SCENE

Screening and illuminating characterize the play of imagery in primal scene poetry. Poets who fixate the primal scene show those characteristics in their poetry which Freud attributed to screen memories: visual and oral imagery, displaced illuminating intensities, the subject objectified, and reference to veiled trauma. Some works contain more than these formal qualities, they contain trains of imagery suggesting the primal scene as a literal infantile experience of parents coupling. These works show consciousness fluctuating. They show identity seeking refuge in profound formulations. Works that explore the significance of the primal scene evoke a rudimentary sense of reality. They explore the movement from the visual paradise of the primary world to the sound figures beyond the early paradise. The poets of this transition might well be called "primal scene poets."

THE PRIMAL SCENE POETRY OF JOHN KEATS

Lionel Trilling (1956) and W. Jackson Bate (1963) both point to Keats's unusual openness to sensuous experience. Keats was devoted to intense pleasureful eating, drinking, sucking, and sensing, and to their reflective equivalents: making identity, coming into knowledge, synthesizing beauty and truth. These experiences and reflections particularly, taken in toto, comprise the elements of the primal scene era.

Trilling quotes a story, attributed to Keats's friend Haydon, that Keats put cayenne pepper on his tongue, the better to savor a draught of cold claret. He quotes Keats's letter to his friend Dilke, "Talking of pleasure, this moment I was writing with one hand, and with the other holding to my mouth a nectarine—good God how fine. It went down soft, slushy, oozy —all its delicious enbonpoint melted down my throat like a beatified strawberry." (Trilling, p. 12) Keats's felicity of pleasure, and the attendant identity formation reach inward to the breast of infancy in his famous quote to his brother George and sister-in-law, Georgiana: "the heart is the teat from which the mind or intelligence sucks identity."

Bate points out that "negative capability" is the ability to expand identity by entering into something larger or more meaningful. The capability refers to a simultaneous suspension and expansion of identity. The experience is consonant with infantile feelings of existence. Trilling stresses that Keats has the negative capability to appreciate the essence of what is beautiful and true and to engage in successful "soul-making" because he accepts what is evil into his perspective of what is knowable. The concept, then, is suitable to represent the kind of knowledge that the infant acquires during the primal scene. The creative infant, refusing to be completely overwhelmed by the primal scene, insists that he can turn the situation to his own satisfaction. For a nascent Keats beauty is the image of perfect satisfaction, and truth is the image of the satisfying object in reality, and negative capability is the ability to identify, and to identify with the object in reality despite its traumatic overtones of unavailability.

Keats's biography lends itself to this kind of formulation. Keats was the first-born, much desired child of a young, sensuous, and beautiful mother. Keats identified with her emotional, giving nature. He was to be very protective of his brother George, who was 16 months younger, of his brother Tom, four years younger, and of his sister Fanny, eight years younger. The birth of a sibling when an infant is at the primal scene age often acts as a fixation stimulus. The prime story of Keats's attachment to his mother has him at the age of five with his toy sword drawn, keeping everyone away from his ill and bed-ridden mother. The image of the ill mother is to recur with Keats. The sick or dying mother is a common fantasy screen for the mother of the primal scene.

When Keats was eight his maternal grandfather died. Then, in short order, his father died suddenly in an accidental fall from a horse. According to Bate the death of her husband left Keats's mother in an economically desperate situation. She remarried within two months to keep the livery business and the inn afloat. The marrige appears to have been a disaster.

By divorcing her new husband Mrs. Keats lost the livery stable. She was depressed, apparently she drank, and began a physical decline, probably due to tuberculosis, which ended with her death when Keats was 14. The children went to live with their maternal grandmother, who appointed Mr. Abbey to be their legal guardian. Keats nursed his mother in her dying days, as he was later to nurse Tom, who died of tuberculosis in his arms.

We do not know if Keats's dashing, handsome father, and his beautiful, sensuous mother ever provided the child with a primal scene. The inn with its itinerant revelers must have been a rich source of imagery at the least. Suggestively, a fantasy weaves through Keats's poems, through "Endymion," "Hyperion," "The Eve of St. Agnes," "Lamia." It is a fantasy of a young man who descends by extraordinary arrangement into the chamber of enchanted God and Goddess lovers. The young man enters a concourse of love with the Goddess as she lies dying, or almost dying, sleeping, or almost sleeping. In the end the Goddess loses the grace of real female loveliness. In "Lamia" she reveals she is the bisexual, serpent woman. The fantasy, equated with the realm of imagination, is penetrated by the hero who has the special vision to discern the felicity of pleasure available in the sleepy realm.

These poems span the five or six years in which Keats was a poet. For a period of a month, from mid-April through mid-May, 1819, Keats wrote his greatest poetry. The adult creator achieves his identity through his involvement with germinal works which achieve resolution of otherwise insoluble dilemmas of adult life.

The winter and spring of Keats's twenty-fourth year were especially intense. He had nursed his brother Tom through the final death throes of his tuberculosis. His brother George, with Georgiana, had gone to America. After their departure John Keats had gone on a long walking tour of Scotland, which instead of reviving him, left him with a residual sore throat. It showed little improvement through the fall and the following winter and spring. John Keats's tuberculosis had taken hold and was not to let go.

First he wrote his great poems, full of new identity as a professional poet. Then, in the aftermath, still in the thrall of the negative capability of knowing his own impending death, he fell full in love with 18-year-old Fanny Braune, the muse model of his short remaining life. Opiate illusion though she was, she still made love real to Keats. Keats bemused longings, condensing fantasy of love and death, attached to this half-accessible woman.

During the long winter and spring of 1919, Keats kept a

journal—a long letter to George and Georgiana—documenting both his physical decline and the attendant development of himself as a poet. The early poems of his month-long identity cycle are included in this journal. The whole set of odes, preceded by "La Belle Dame Sans Merci," encompass, express, and formulate an identity-transforming period in the life of the literary artist Keats.

As the realization of tuberculosis set in on the man Keats, he tried to transform the trauma through creative effort. The dawning realization of impending death was covered by the imagery of Keats's earliest primal scene trauma. In "La Belle Dame" the woman-death brings man into the dark gloom of her eternal sleep. Keats transforms the circumstances of dying into the overwhelming wish to be part of the primal scene. It is no longer mother and father sharing the marriage bed, rather the young creator and his poesy woman united in poetry. Throughout this whole period Keats drinks wine to ease the tubercular sore throat which reminds him continuously of his painful mortality. The wine weaves in and out of his identity, transforming poems and affecting the poetic voice as much as his sick throat affects his real voice.

On February 14 Keats says he thinks he must decline an invitation to dance five days hence because "a dance would injure my throat very much." (Trilling, p. 222) On February 18, Keats refers to the ability of wine to ease his pain and lead him into pleasure: "now I like claret whenever I can have claret I must drink it,-'tis the only palate affair that I am at all sensual in . . . it fills the mouth ones mouth with a gushing freshness—then goes down cool and feverless." (Trilling, p. 226)

In the late April portion of the letter, Keats expounds on his aesthetic theories of poetry. These statements, which are in effect formulations of identity attempting to reconcile his poetic with his ordinary identity, prepare the way for his active poetic descent into creative regression. He asserts that identity arises most strongly in response to the foreknowledge of death. "Call the world if you please vale of 'Soul-making.' . . . I say 'soul making' Soul as distinguished from an Intelligence—There may be intelligences or sparks of the divinity in millions but they are not Souls till they acquire identities . . . the Heart . . . is the mind's experience, it is the teat from which the Mind or intelligence sucks its identity." (Trilling, p. 257–258)

Keats goes on to assert his belief that individual experience accrues like sparks of divinity to enhance God. Thus Keats accounts for the sad experience of pain and premonition of death as part of the experience that promotes his identity as poet. Keats ends his long letter to George and Georgiana with this image: "This is the third of May, and everything is in delightful forwardness, the violets are not withered before the peeping of the first rose." (Trilling, p. 260)

KEATS'S IDENTITY FORMATION AS ADULT POET

Phase 1—Frustration

"La Belle Dame Sans Merci" begins with an invocation of death. The young man is dying and feverish. A woman comes to him, and they make love all day, but the young man is wooed into sleep, and he dreams of young men and old who tell him he is in the thrall of "La Belle Dame Sans Merci." Thus Keats's evocation of new identity begins "with a declaration" that he is dying. The woman, his mother, his poetic muse, has had many lovers; all have been brought through sleep into the realm of death. The primal scene is invaded.

Then in three short poetic pieces on "Sleep," on "Fame," and "On the 'Sonnet,' " Keats thinks sequentially about the decline into sleep, about the ambition that would still arouse him, and about the muse who must be satisfied if his ambition is to be fulfilled. In essence he personifies the woman (objectifies the subject) who lulls him into the dreamy state of poetry; the man who wants to overcome his fever and life's woes, to realize the identity-making experience; and the woman-man with whom he must share his identity as poet, the muse. These personifications, which are re-externalizations of the primal scene triad, comprise repeated elements in Keats's conscious symbolism. The deliberate use of symbols facilitates the intra-psychic entry into creative regression.

Phase 2—Regression

In "Ode to Psyche" Keats "represses" in order to revise his identity as poet. He seeks to find a mental position from which he can express the love he feels in the service of his identity as a poet. At the same time he must bind the pain still in his throat and mind. The poem begins with a tribute to Psyche, who is his muse of poetry, and at the same time his own audacious voice. He says he dreamed—or saw—the winged psyche as two eternal lovers in the grass.

> They lay calm-breathing on the bedded grass;
> Their arms embraced, and their pinions too;
> Their lips touched not, but had not bade adieu,
> As if disjoined by soft-handed slumber,
> And ready still past kisses to outnumber
> At tender eye-dawn of auroean love:
> The winged boy I knew;
> But who wast thou, O happy happy dove?
> His Psyche true.

We see in these lines that Keats has remade the primal couple of the primal scene into a unity of male and female, symbolized by the bird creature who is bisexual. Thus the poet usurps, unifies, and condenses the imagery of the primal scene to make an identity serviceable for the expression of love, for he goes on later in the poem:

> Yes, I will be thy priest, and build a fane
> In some untrodden region of my mind,
> Where branched thoughts, new grown with pleasant pain,
> Instead of pines shall murmer in the wind.

Thus Keats is using the imagery of his vocation to forge a new expressive voice strong enough to shut out—and include —the physical pain and foreknowledge of the real, physical death he feels.

Phase 3—Primary Process

In "Ode To A Nightingale," a beautiful and accomplished poem, Keats has assumed the voice of an adult poet. The identity condensation of the youth and his muse are so complete that the song of the nightingale issues out of reality straight into the poet's expression. Beauty and truth are utterly synthesized in the voice of the poet. Here, the poet, Keats, uses wine to flee into the realm of the imagination, leaving physical pain and the reality of imaged death far behind. Characteristically reporting the prelude to primal-scene imagery, the poem begins with an image of descending toward, but not totally into sleep

> My heart aches, and a drowsy numbness pains
> My sense, as though of hemlock I had drunk,
> Or emptied some dull opiate to the drains
> One minute past, and Lethe-wards had sunk:

The first stanza begins with an image of pain, altered by the wine of sleep or death, and ends with the nightingale: "Singest of summers in full-throated ease." Contrast this with Keats's sore-throated disease. The second stanza is an ode to the wine "With beaded bubbles winking at the brim." It takes Keats into the poetic reverie of the nightingale's song. In the third stanza the bird's song is made to image the movement away from his sickly state.

> The weariness, the fever, and the fret
> Here, where men sit and hear each other groan;
> Where palsy shakes a few, sad, last grey hairs,
> Where youth grows pale, and spectre-thin, and dies;

The next stanza turns away from physical pain to a place where "the Queen-moon is on her throne." Likely, the night mother, shining as the moon, is both the mother of the primal scene as well as the dead mother in the heavens. In the next stanza Keats returns to the present again, imaging the coming of death to youth rather than the coming of maturity in summer. The language Keats uses alters the end-image of the letter to George and Georgiana. The imagery turns to the dying perfume of the rose rather than the oncoming surge of summer.

> Fast fading violets cover'd up in leaves;
> And mid-May's eldest child,
> The coming musk-rose, full of dewy wine,
> The murmurous haunt of flies on summer eves.

The sixth stanza moves from this bemused winged image of death back to the song of the nightingale. That song is the voice which begins to transcend the death imagery of the midnight of the primal scene.

> Darkling I listen; and, for many a time
> I have been half in love with easeful death,
> Called him soft names in many a mused rhyme,
> To take into the air my quiet breath;
> Now more than ever seems to rich to die,
> To cease upon the midnight with no pain,
> While thou art pouring forth thy soul abroad
> In such an ecstasy.

In the seventh stanza Keats thinks of the illusion of immortality conveyed by the image of the bird—his poetic voice. His poetic voice reunites him with his mother, for the voice of the nightingale is

> Perhaps the self-same song that found a path
> Through the sad heart of Ruth, when, sick for home,
> She stood in tears amid the alien corn;

It is his mother after the death of her husband and father, exiled from family and children.

> The same that oft-times hath
> Charmed magic casements, opening in the foam
> Of perilous seas, in faery lands forlorn.

The casements, the window on the primal scene, is evoked, imaged, and bounded by the voice of the nightingale, the poet's voice full of the reality which issues from the closing of the infantile era. It is an image of separation.

In the last stanza the word *forlorn,* tolling like a bell for the departed, brings Keat back to the image of the fading reality of the nightingale's voice as it recedes into the next valley. The primal scene is gone, and the voice of the poet remains in its stead.

Thus in this poem Keats uses the voice of poetry, his poetic self, to explore the affectively reverberating past which ties death to the image of separation from the transitional mother of earliest infancy. Having found the roots of his poetic voice, Keats is free in his next poem to begin to move toward awakening. In fact "Ode to a Nightingale" ends, "Do I wake or sleep?"

Phase 4—Revision

Having fixed his identity as a poet, and identitifed his poetic voice with the realm of the imaginery, Keats now goes on to use the voice in a moment suspended between sleeping and awakening. "Ode on a Grecian Urn," which Keats wrote next in the sequence of his identity formation, suspends the primal scene as in a tableau.

We think the tableau is engraved on the urn from which Keats sucks the honey mead of life. The wine is the milk of satisfaction which makes the primal scene an illusion of ever-lasting life. For in the poem, springtime comes to a full stop,

the burning forehead and the parched tongue are left far behind, and thoughts of death are collapsed by an *antimetaboli*
which makes an identity of subject and object: "Beauty is truth,
truth beauty." It is perhaps, the last thought before the primal
sleep which wine brings on.

I

Thou still unravish'd bride of quietness
Thous foster-child of silence and slow time,
Sylvan historian, who canst thus express
A flowery tale more sweetly than our rhyme:
What leaf-frig'd legend haunts about thy shape
Of deities or mortals, or of both,
In Tempe or the dales of Arcady?
What men or gods are these? What maidens loth?
What mad pursuit? What struggles to escape?
What pipes and timbrels? What wild ecstasy?

II

Heard melodies are sweet, but those unheard
Are sweeter; therefore, ye soft pipes, play on,
Not to the sensual ear, but more endear'd
Pipe to the spirit ditties of no tone:
Fair youth, beneath the trees, thou canst not leave
Thy song, nor ever can those trees be bare;
Bold lover, never, never canst thou kiss,
Though winning near the goal—yet, do not grieve;
She cannot fade, though thou hast not thy bliss,
For ever wilt thou love, and she be fair!

III

Ah, happy, happy boughs! that cannot shed
Your leaves, nor ever bid the spring adieu;
And happy melodist, unwearied,
For ever piping songs for ever new;
More happy love! more happy, happy love!
For ever warm and still to be enjoy'd
For ever panting, and for ever young;
All breathing human passion far above,
That leaves a heart high-sorrowful and cloy'd
A burning forehead, and a parching tongue.

IV

Who are these coming to the sacrifice?
To what green altar, O mysterious priest,
Lead'st thou that heifer lowing at the skies,
And all her silken flanks with garlands drest?
What little town by river or sea shore,
Or mountain-built with peaceful citadel,
Is emptied of this folk, this pious morn?
And, little town, thy streets for evermore
Will silent be; and not a soul to tell
Why thou art desolate, can e'er return.

V

O Attic shape! Fair attitude! with brede
Of marble men and maidens overwrought,
With forest branches and the trodden weed;
Thou, silent form dost tease us out of thought
As doth eternity: Cold Pastoral!
When old age shall this generation waste,
Thou shalt remain, in midst of other woe
Than ours, a friend to man, to whom thou say'st,
"Beauty is truth, truth beauty,"—that is all
Ye know on earth, and all ye need to know.

In its opening the poem contemplates (1) the "unravished bride of quietness"—the untouched mother quiet before the primal scene—(2) the "foster-child of silence and slow time"—the eternal child—(3) thoughts of sexual ecstasy. Then it moves from the sight of imminent union to the sexual sound of soft pipes. The sound signals a retreat to reflection; the "unheard melodies" play the young child's retreat from the sounds of the primal scene.

The poem moves through a sense of timeless longing for a coupling at once permanent yet unfulfilled. It represents the sense of memory, the wish for the ecstasy of union, a longing never fulfilled. Here, the infant's wish to return to the sense of perfect fusion with the mother is a longing to be reunited through sexual engagement. In its ending one sees the resolution of the primal scene. It is the primal synthesis of reflection, the two hemispheres engaged, beauty and truth the perfect couple, the foundations of reflection, the dual requirements of judgment. For the primal scene is resolved by the formation of the most neutral of knowledge, fixing the reality of experience once and for all as subordinate to the primacy of reflection.

The perfection of the urn is a recollection of the sense of complete satisfaction attendant upon the experience of nursing the breast. The synthesis of beauty and truth is a metaphor for perfect satisfaction. In Freudian neuropsychological terms the synthesis of beauty and truth is tantamount to the formation of the judgment that the primary object of satisfaction, the breast, is ready.

The poem, then, is a vehicle of transitional thought restoring the conditions that prevailed before the primal scene when the infant could still completely enter into the illusion that he could create the conditions of his own satisfaction. The form that teases us out of thought, the breast-urn, is a longed-for object, one that can never be regained after the trauma of the primal scene. To be teased out of thought is not to lose all consciousness, but it is to lose access to consciousness. This is the trauma of the primal scene. One loses access to the primary sense of the timelessness of consciousness. Instead one is bound to the temporal sense of reflecting on one's own thoughts, maintaining consciousness only so long as the verbal means exist, only so long as the poem of awakened consciousness can go on.

Phase 5—Resolution

In the final phase of identity formation the wakening must be completed and set against the regressive tide which has turned the creator away from reality. The last two poems of this series of identity-making creativity are "Ode on Melancholy" and "Ode on Indolence." These poems have a recapitulatory, summary quality. Keats is returning to the reality of his life, and the experience of forging his identity anew begins to recede into the past. In the beginning of the "Ode to Melancholy" he says,

> . . . nor the death-moth be
> Your mournful Psyche

It is a warning against equating the poetic muse with the Maiden Melancholy, who will end all poetry and love, giving little but death in return.

The "Ode on Indolence" is a reconsideration of the image of the urn on which the primal scene triad are engaged. Banishing the primal triad, Keats finishes the poem as the mortal spectator at the deathless scene he has again evoked to escape his own mortality. The essence is in the fourth stanza:

> A third time pass'd they by, and passing, turn'd
> Each on the face a moment whiles to me;
> Then faded, and to follow them I burn'd
> And ached for wings because I knew the three;
> The first was a fair maid, and Love her name;
> The second was Ambition, pale of cheek,
> And ever watchful with fatigued eye,
> The last, whom I love more, the more of blame
> Is heaped upon her, maiden most unmeek—
> I knew to be my demon Poesy.

The end of the poem exiles Keats's images of the primal scene, and of his death, and even of his freshened identity as a poet. He wants to wake completely:

> So, ye three Ghosts, adieu! Ye cannot raise
> My head cool-bedded in the flowery grass;
> For I would not be dieted with praise,
> A pet-lamb in a sentimental farce!
> Fade softly from my eyes, and be once more
> In masque-like figures on the dreamy urn;
> Farewell. I yet have visions for the night,
> And for the day faint visions there is store;

Vanish, ye phantoms! from my idle sight,
Into the clouds, and never more return!

Keats puts Fanny Braune in place of the banished phantoms. He falls in love with her immediately upon completing
his identity transforming works. She becomes the image of his
muse, and her presence wrests him from the entangling embrace of the death Goddess. Though in his love for Fanny,
Keats stays in the present reality, Bate tells how Keats felt that
his room was like a sepulcher. His love letters begin on July 1.

> . . . in the Letter you must write immediately and do all you can
> to console me in it—make it rich as a draught of poppies to
> intoxicate me—write the softest words and kiss them that I may
> at least touch my lips where yours have been. For myself I know
> not how to express my devotion to so fair a form: I want a
> brighter word than bright, a fairer word than fair. I almost wish
> we were butterflies and liv'd but three summer days—three such
> days with you I could fill with more delight than fifty common
> years could ever contain. (Bate, p. 538)

Tragedy infiltrates Keats's declaration of love, making it
somewhat ironical as the fact of death still clings to his identity.
The bright butterfly of words he wants her to be makes her the
image of the inspiring muse-woman. All the imagery of his
great primal scene poems is condensed in his wish for her fair
form. Still, Keats manfully tries to take on the responsibility of
an ordinary adult in his love for Fanny:

> I look not forward with any pleasure to what is call'd being
> settled in the world; I tremble at domestic cares—yet for you I
> would meet them though if it would leave you the happier I
> would rather die than do so

The dark shadow death casts on his identity spares Keats
the necessity of living long in the dual identity of creator and
ordinary individual.

Matthew Arnold's "Dover Beach"

Arnold's "Dover Beach" is another example of the primal scene poem. As Norman N. Holland (1968) points out, it is one of the most widely quoted and popular of poems. Holland's subjective and objectively researched interpretation of the poem leaves little doubt of its primal scene nature. Holland holds that the presence of the poet's woman-companion provides the protagonist with a defense against the pertubation of the primal scene.

To us, his most telling observation is that the woman appears regularly at junctures where visual imagery gives way to auditory imagery. We surmise that the woman, as the ind-welling muse of the poem, defends the poet against the primal scene much as Fanny Braune signified as the muse who protected Keats from the primary terrors of the primal scene. It is precisely the introjection of the real person, as an auditory presence, that demarcates the illusiary primary world of infancy from the verbal world that follows. Arnold is most starkly presented as a primal scene poet in a quote Holland cites as an association of Louis Bonnerat's to "Dover Beach":

> Only when one is young and headstrong can one thus prefer bravado to experience, can one stand by the Sea of Time, and instead of listening to the solemn and rhythmical beat of its waves, choose to fill the air with one's own whoopings to start the echo. (Holland, p. 122)

This is as stark an image as there can be of the primal scene infant making the transition to the auditory world, by making his own voice sole evoker of the primal scene.

> The sea is calm tonight.
> The tide is full, the moon lies fair
> Upon the straits;—on the French coast the light

Gleams and is gone; the cliffs of England stand,
Glimmering and vast, out in the tranquil bay.
Come to the window, sweet is the night-air!
Only, from the long line of spray
Where the sea meets the moon blanch'd land,
Listen! You hear the grating roar
Of pebbles which the waves draw back and fling,
At their return, up the high strand,
Begin, and cease, and then again begin,
With tremulous cadence slow, and bring
The eternal note of sadness in.

Sophocles long ago
Heard it on the Aegean, and it brought
Into his mind the turbid ebb and flow
Of human misery; we
Find also in the sound a thought,
Hearing it by this distant northern sea.

The Sea of Faith
Was once, too, at the full, and round earth's shore
Lay like the folds of a bright girdle furl'd.
But now I only hear
Its melancholy, long, withdrawing roar,
Retreating, to the breath
Of the night-wind, down the vast edges drear
And naked shingles of the world.

Ah, love, let us be true
To one another! for the world, which seems
To lie before us like a land of dreams,
So various, so beautiful, so new,
Hath really neither joy, nor love, nor light,
Nor certitude, nor peace, nor help for pain;
And we are here as on a darkling plain
Swept with confused alarms of struggle and flight,
Where ignorant armies clash by night.

Arnold is one of the many poets who wrote criticism. The
intense identification with the formation ·of language is very

naturally paired with the detached and neutral judgment of the critic. We believe that this disposition arises in fixation to the primal scene.

A careful examination of the progress of imagery in "Dover Beach" shows the same sequence that characterizes "Ode on a Grecian Urn" as a primal scene poem. It begins with an image of the calm night, anticipating some rhythmic interruption. The waves come with a regular rhythmic force, a cadence which animates the beginnings of language. A note of high longing is introduced. The peaceful unity of the vision of the twin coasts of France and England is to give way to the emotional sea surging between the coasts. The image personifies nature and recalls the parental figures. As is often the case in primal scene poetry, a window opens to movement of the primal imagery. And the vision of peace is replaced with the sound of uproar. The immediate sequence of the primal scene is recalled in this way. Then, in the poem's progress, refuge is sought in detached contemplation of a sea of faith. But this gives way.

Arnold could not attain the synthesis of reflection Keats does with his beauty and truth. Arnold does not show a resolution of the primal scene. Rather it returns, like a symptom, with full fury. In the last stanza the imagery of the primal scene becomes alarming, building to a climax in the poem of "ignorant armies clashing by night."

The child in the primal scene is overwhelmed. He wants to possess the mother—and the father—but as his passions are stirred without satisfaction; with inordinately increasing frustration, he must take refuge in reflection. Arnold looks to his audience, whom he is addressing, to join with him in a restoration of faith. He wants to find an image of perfect quietness. His recourse is the poem, and whatever acceptance he can muster of the situation on the darkling plain, the bed where the child must endure his perturbation. Saying that the world is like a land of dreams is one attempt to deal with the confused alarm of the primal scene, for in the infantile period primary identity is relegated to the unconscious, to the land of dreams after the advent of the primal scene.

LITERARY LANGUAGE FORMATION

A great deal of language useful to the literary creator issues from the time of the primal scene, because, as we have said, it is a time when language takes on the function of forming a new basis for conscious experience. Many of the schemes and tropes that act as tools of expression are useful in locating kinds of experience that emanate from this period in the formation of mental life. When the creative person enters into his period of regression, schemes and tropes of language act as locators in the search for revised sources of new experience. What we use as imaged language in adult life was concrete and immediate in the past in which it was developed.

We would now like to enter into an exploration of a range of language figures, some of which recreate the transitional thinking and primary identification of the earliest era of life, some of which take root in the transforming period of the primal scene, and some of which develop in the aftermath of the primal scene. In this exploration we use "primal scene" in a neuropsychological sense: a stimulus to the transition to a new kind of expression of consciousness and identity. We use the term *primary revision* to refer to the change in the focus of conscious experience from pictures to words. This is a terminology which fits in with the language useful in describing the progressive portion of the creative process. Definitions are taken mainly from Edward P. J. Corbett's (1971) *Classical Rhetoric*.

Personification

Personification is a trope in which inanimate, abstract or nonhuman living things are invested with human abilities, attributes, or qualities.

EXAMPLES

Death Stands Above Me

Death stands above me, whispering low
I know not what into my ear;
Of his strange language all I know
Is, there is not a word of fear

—*Walter Savage Landor*

The Love Song of J. Alfred Prufrock

Let us go then, you and I,
When the evening is spread out against the sky
Like a patient etherized upon a table;
Let us go, through certain half-deserted streets,
The muttering retreats
Of restless nights in one-night cheap hotels
And sawdust restaurants with oyster shells:
Streets that follow like a tedious argument
Of insidious intent
To lead you to an overwhelming question . . .
Oh, do not ask, "What is it?"
Let us go and make our visit.

—*T. S. Eliot*

Trees

A tree whose hungry mouth is prest
Against the earth's sweet-flowering breast

—*Joyce Kilmer*

To personify is to vivify. The trope's name describes its action. The object personified is endowed with a kind of rudimentary subjectivity, and—as examination indicates—with a will to fuse, to encompass or be encompassed by something, or someone or anything else. The mechanism is infantile, uses primary identification, and is potentially nightmarish. In using personifications naively, like Landor or Kilmer, a writer tends to overdo or to use several personifications, or, reactively to sound unusually neutral or detached, to somehow decline the nightmare of primary fusion—anything to maintain a reflective distance, to know very well that one is personifying.

Onomatopoeia

To use onomatopoeia is to use words which sound like their meanings—bang, boom, splash, babble—or whose sounds imitate their sense, as in Coleridge's phrase, "slow spondee stalks."

EXAMPLE

Essay on Criticism

'Tis not enough no harshness gives offence,
The sound must seem an echoe to the sense:
Soft is the strain when Zephyre gently blows,
And the smooth stream in smoother numbers flows;
But when loud surges lash the sounding shore,
The hoarse, rough verse should like the torrent roar:
When Ajax strives some rock's vast weight to throw,
The line too labors, and the words move slow;
Not so, when swift Camilla scours the plain,
Flies o'er the unbending corn, and skims along the main.
—*Alexander Pope*

Onomatopoeia takes sounds as concrete, almost morphemic objects. The sound objects, prototypes of words, enter, for example, into lines of poetry denoting and imitating objects in nature. It seems likely that the figure springs from a total identification of sounds with objects, so that it describes a kind of neurologically primary, auditory process. The object is the sound it makes, revised from its primary existence as visual image. Onomatopoeia identifies meaning by lifting morphemes out of their matrix of auditory sensation. This trope is therefore derived from transitional thinking. The example from Pope is an essay in onomatopoeia: the primal scene shifts experience from the visual tableau to concrete sound-meaning. Such words can be more easily and selectively distanced than can the visual world.

Oxymoron

In oxymoron, contradictory terms yoke together.

EXAMPLES

The Faerie Queen

But full of fire and greedy hardiment,
The youthful knight could not for ought be staide,
But forth unto the darksome hole he went,
And looked in his glistering armor made
A little glooming light, much like a shade,
By which he saw the ugly monster displayede,
But th'other halfe did woman's shape retain,
Most lothsom, filthie, foule, and full of vile disdaine.
—*Edmund Spenser*
Book I, Canto 1, 14

Romeo and Juliet

Here's much to do with hate, but more with love,
Why then, O *brawling love,* O *loving hate!*
O *anything* of *nothing* first create
O *heavy lightness, serious vanity!*
Misshapen chaos of *well-seeming forms!*
Feather of lead, bright smoke, cold fire, sick health!
Still-waking sleep, that is not what it is!
This love I feel, and feel no love in this
—*William Shakespeare*
(Act I, Sc.i)

Oxymoron defines a condition that exists between poles. That condition is not the golden and rational mean, but the anti-mean, the irrational chaos of well-seeming forms. The trope undoes the reordering of primary revision, and it expresses a deliberate, or accidental, or unconscious falling back into primary process, into an unreflective, irrational chaos incapable of clarity or distinction. For oxymoron suggests the primary state in which psychic energies have not yet become bound to clearly distinguishable percepts when energy is still evoked in a more sensational and unstable fashion. Oxymoron destroys singleness and clarity of sense perception. A light cannot be like a shade. The trope describes denial of perception, the primary defense against trauma. The young knight obliterates the true state of the female anatomy.

Antithesis

An antithesis is a schematic juxtaposition of ideas which are at least contrasting and which are usually antithetical.

EXAMPLE

> Though studious he was popular; though
> argumentative, he was modest;
> though inflexible, he was candid;
> and though metaphysical, yet orthodox.
> —*Dr. Samuel Johnson*
> *London Chronicle,* May 2, 1769

Antithesis depends on the comparison of opposing attributes. The contents can often be reduced to primary concerns—separateness/no separateness, or primary consciousness/no consciousness. Divided syntactically, the two attributes are nevertheless provisionally united through juxtaposition.

The figure is primary revisory, for objects develop attributes in the course of primary revision. Light and dark are released from associatively blank visual sensation. As associations clothe sensation, percepts distinguish between qualities. That is to say, primary revision draws a primitive but decidedly experiential world out of sensation, instinct, and automatic behavior.

Now the achievement of unity in basal grammar and the coherence of subject and object as mediated by the verb seem to us to constitute the first step in primary revision. That is to say, in infancy, the self-verb-object relation exists at first as a sort of primary language descriptive of the oral/kinesthetic/visual world of infantile sensation. To develop that relation is to enter into primary revision.

Addressing the notions of oxymoron and antithesis genetically, we should say that oxymorom springs from the era when the subject did not have a clearly distinguishable different relation to the self and to the object. Therefore language could not yet be employed to make this distinction clear. Oxymoron can only approximate the synesthesias of this era. Antithesis seems to us rather more evolved. In it, primary boundaries are maintained with a degree of firmness. In fact antithesis describes the coalition of self object as intrapsychic, or self/not self boundaries.

Puns

A pun is a play on the meanings of words.

EXAMPLES

Julius Caesar

Flavius: What trade, thou knave? Thou naughty knave, what trade?

Cobbler: Nay, I beseech you, Sir, be not out with me. Yet if you be out, sir, I can mend you.

Marullus: What mean'st thou by that? Mend me, thou saucy fellow?

Cobbler: Why Sir, cobble you.

—*William Shakespeare*
(Act I, Sc. i)

Your argument is sound, nothing but sound.

—*Benjamin Franklin*

Puns recapitulate certain primary revisory acts. Primary language arises from morphemes—Ma, Pa, and so on. In the course of primary revision, phonemes take on significances. The acquisition of meaning establishes the morphemic nature of sound. Each morpheme is initially loaded with an array of significance. These are only gradually differentiated in language. Puns throw language back to the ambiguities of its morphemic origins. Plays on words re-enact the state of identifying phonemes with meanings. The identification is, as it was in infancy, facilitated by reflection. It is the business of puns, then, to force an act of primitive, distinguishing reflection on the hearer or the reader.

The verbal creator is sensitive to the roots of the language he uses. The evocation locates some general sense of the origin of the trauma he is now expressing, and expunging, in his work. We are trying to define something of the essence of language which remains fast—in devices—to each stage of the life cycle. For language is revised, as consciousness is revised, in each stage of the life cycle, though words learned may appear the same. The advent of the primal scene gives primary revision to language that had heretofore acted as transitional object. Granting language an existence of its own, much like granting the parents a life of their own, changes the whole experience of language. We shall proceed to look at the revision of language, and consciousness, which occurs during the next stage of life synthesis—the anal-auditory era.

Chapter 4

THE SPOKEN WORLD
18 to 30 Months—Anal/Auditory Period

The possessor of language locates the sources of experience more finely than the infant who must be satisfied with discriminating between visual data and visual imagery. In early childhood the sentence becomes the basic neuropsychological unit that accounts for the various levels of identity which organize the world all the way from the neuropsychological level to the level of a socially defined identity. The grammatical parts of speech may be viewed as the essential locators of the neuropsychological origins of experience.

The subject and the object of the sentence correspond to the subject sphere and the object sphere. Take a simple sentence such as "I want my bed," for instance. The subjective "I" generates the wished for action "want." In the object sphere the personal possessive pronoun "my" locates the objective self, and "bed" indicates the object in reality. Thus, in this simple sentence, subjective need is fused intrapsychically with an objective self bearing some relationship to an object in reality which can provide the desired gratification.

We have seen that the transitional era develops along the lines of a subjective generation of needs which come to be equated with simple objects in reality, whose intrapsychic or extrapsychic origins are themselves not yet clearly discriminated. Thus early speech consists of subjectively generated vocal gestures of need fused with prototypical words which stand for an array of objects whose extrapsychic origins are not yet distinguished.

In the anal/auditory period, however, language which relates extrapsychic objects to the self develops through the neuropsychological readiness to take in whole sequences of sound patterns (phrases) which contain the necessary distinctions between intrapsychic and extrapsychic reality. These introjected phrases contain the seeds of syntactical distinction.

A future creator develops an alternative and grandiose self which is devoted to the proposition that personally improvised verbal magic can circumvent the givens of reality and maintain reflective consciousness in the face of frustration engendering the rage which is the bane of this era. The normal resolution of frustration-engendering rage and tantrum behavior is the vesting of power over external reality in parental figures identified as carriers of aggression. The child believes in the supraordinate perfection of his syntax. But the future creator insists that he can find some verbal order, some formula of words which can exert a personally omnipotent control over the apparent givens of reality. The alternative self of reflection is inflated with the magical illusion that it can employ an ever new and conscious formation of language to insure its pre-eminence.

NEUROPSYCHOLOGICAL CONSIDERATIONS

The resolution of the primal scene brings neuropsychological life into a new era. The transitional era illusion of creating reality gives way to a vested interest in granting reality to external agency. The problem for the new stage of life, early childhood, is how to control and manipulate the givens of external reality. The neuropsychological basics of this era center on anal and auditory experiences. Subjective efforts and pleasures come to be experienced in the anal musculature in efforts of control and release. The object world comes to be embodied, first, in the products of the anal zone, and in other materials which come to be equated with and derived psychologically from these products; and, second, from auditory experiences of spoken language.

Whole phrases are experienced in the unity of their syntax in this stage, and these introjected phrases come to be figurative or concrete representations of the givens of external reality. The object world is divided into an external reality of phrases and concrete presences, *the object,* and an internal reality of bodily and emotional products, *the self.* The reflective perspective on reality in this era culminates in that recognition which is so fundamental to object constancy—that objects in the external world have their own internal reality.

The problem that poses itself in this era is how to achieve power over the external givens of reality through bodily, linguistic, and emotional products which are controlled by subjective initiatory function. This power, until it comes to be a product of an autonomous identity, is vested in the illusion of magic. It is in the pursuit of the magical manipulation of reality that the child gradually learns to formulate the rules of syntax and the manners which insure a response from the figures in reality who have the real power.

The powers in reality are formulated as the prerogatives of the aggressor, for the young child experiences the failure of reality to grant his wishes as a frustration engendering rage. But expressions of rage by the child only elicit a more formidable aggressive response from the powerful parental figure, who comes to be seen as the aggressor with all the power of aggression at his disposal. Magic involves the belief that one's own aggression can usurp the power vested in external reality. It is evident to the young child that this power is somehow vested in the right combination of verbal sequences. Further, the phrases which are taken in whole from the external figures at this time are experienced in their full neuropsychological cadence. They are punctuated like thunder with a primitive, ineluctable rhythm that becomes the natural origin of chants and curses. The young child wants to take in this magic of phrase making, and it becomes the denotation per se of the power of the aggressor. Thus identification with the aggressor is fueled by the rage to take on all the power of language for personal gratification.

Autonomy is the key word for the reflective organization of this era. Reflective identity comes to take on an autonomous character in this stage of development. Whereas in the primary period *judgment* is the reflective quality that determines whether discharge processes are to proceed, in the era of young childhood, *autonomy* is exercised to determine whether discharge is to proceed. The means of this autonomy is the reactive ability to say "no" to experiential wishes. The conscious use of the word "no" is at the root of the reflective speech development of this era.

Reflection is able to employ speech (as a medium of intrapsychic communication) in making decisions about going ahead with some planned discharge operation. For instance, the child must decide whether or not to let go and discharge the contents of the bowels. This is certainly a prototype for the decision-making function that operates autonomously through the jurisdiction of speech and the reflective ability to say no. The discrete form of negation is at the basis of the mental organization which reflection imposes on experience in this era.

In the visual world, trauma can be averted only by denial —negative hallucination, blotting out—or through total loss of consciousness. In the world of verbal presentation and reception, trauma can be averted through the mechanism often described as "reaction formation." What *is* may be negated and so verbally converted into what *is not.* "No" allows for discrete negation and for partial obliteration.

CLINICAL MATERIAL FROM THE ANALYSIS OF A MUSICIAN

To give the reader a retrospective view of this period we would like to explore some verbal testimony from an analytic session of a young musician. One would expect that a musician would retain a special sensitivity to the products of the anal/auditory era. In the following example one sees the return to a mode of mentation in which the "aggressor" is vested with the authority to determine the meaning engendered by words. In this particular session the patient shows evidence of real intrapsychic change. He seems to have returned to the site of his original formation of autonomous expression under the pressure of an impending final examination in his musical performance. He feels he must take on new mastery of the sounds he produces in order to complete the performance successfully. We present a part of the session verbatim:

> Some change took place yesterday as a result of the session. I started thinking in an analytical way again, and the immediate result was that I felt resentful again. Before the session I had the illusion of power. It was something that I felt. When I had thought about going to school to practice, it was very matter of fact, but after the session I felt tired, more than physical fatigue. When I deal with the situation myself I feel basically in control. After the session I became hypersensitive. I see and hear a lot more. I listened to an hour of music on the radio and I paid close attention to what was pleasing. Before, when Alan had said that he didn't understand Mahler's Ninth it didn't make sense to me, but now I know what he means. Before, when I had thoughts about it I compared the thoughts with what Alan might think. Whatever I felt I was receiving, such as a criticism of the rhythm, I was doubtful of. I would just catalogue the stimulus. Now it's just being imprinted. I just know that it's there. Before I would be doubtful of what I sensed, and it wouldn't stay with me.
>
>   I watched "Judgment of Nuremberg" last night, and I found myself paying attention to sentence structure, and sensitive to the director's touch. Small details in the trial, like earphones that the girl would hold up to her ear, only when they were needed—Was it her decision, or the director's decision? Or

small details of the action such as when the man who was on trial
had been a judge himself, before, fingered his lapel to show that.

I commented that he was becoming his own authority, and
that this increased his openness to what he was experiencing.

A question about what you just said is why would I want to be
this sensitive or receptive. It's like an infant flexing his muscles,
for the first time grasping something, feeling the ability and
testing it out. This book I'm reading by Arthur Clark about this
new breed of earthlings with a greater destiny, flexing their
muscles to change the solar system. I have the feeling: Am I
doing it right? There is also an element that I don't have faith
in my own senses. What I'm doing now is saying, "This is what
I sense, and I trust it." If I feel that way about it I can let it
imprint, instead of feeling, "Is this really what's happening? I'd
better check."

THE ANAL/AUDITORY ERA IN THE CREATORS SYNDROME

For the creative person, the primary effect of the anal
period is one of confirmation. We hypothesize that the increased bowel control and the experience of control over physical production is taken by the infant as confirmation of what
the transitional mother had led the infant to believe—that he
is a creator. Now that the infant is sure he is creating something, he feels sure he has always been creating something. The
experience of creation is intensified. Creation becomes synonymous with power.

Power is closely linked with the ability to create words.
First the infant notices a greater ability to use words in relation
to the transitional object world. Objects are given names. At the
beginning of the anal period, words assume two related functions. First, having progressed beyond the transitional level, the
infant is able to use words to ward off the transitional primary
world.

The primary world has special meanings and terrors for the child who has recently passed out of it. Since the anal child's great achievements are bowel control and linguistic ability, the increase in these functions teaches the anal child something about organization. For the first time, he is aware of what is within and what is without. Regression in the anal child is a blotting out of the newly acquired distinctions. The terrors of the primary world are very like an adult's nightmare in which the distinctions collapse between what is acted upon and what is acting.

Lewis Carroll's Alice in Wonderland

Alice in Wonderland has many links to the anal world. In particular, the tumble down the rabbit hole is a falling back through it into the primary world. *Alice* was written by an adult and is filled with bits of information exceeding the information available to an anal child. Still, Alice's drive toward linguistic mess demonstrates a sort of failure. The first lots of organization to go are bits of introjected information acquired with some difficulty, in school or in imitation of older people. So Alice falls down through her long tubular schoolroom-cum-nursery as though she were falling out of the reflective state of knowledge:

> Either the well was very deep, or she fell very slowly, for she had plenty of time as she went down to look about her, and to wonder what was going to happen next. First, she tried to look down and make out what she was coming to, but it was too dark to see anything: then she looked at the sides of the well, and noticed that they were filled with cupboards and book-shelves: here and there she saw maps and pictures hung upon pegs. She took down a jar from one of the shelves as she passed: it was labeled "ORANGE MARMALADE," but to her great disappointment it was empty: she did not like to drop the jar, for fear of killing somebody underneath, so managed to put it into one of the cupboards as she fell past it. (Carroll, p. 18–19)

In her fall from neatness and organization, the careful child scrupulously observes the injunction not to make a mess.

Unfortunately, things get messier. In a vain effort to amuse herself in the almost tedious fall, Alice starts a conversation with her cat, Dinah. Dinah is, of course, not with Alice, so the conversation has a rather "wish you were here" quality.

> "I wish you were down here with me! There are no mice in the air, I'm afraid, but you might catch a bat, and that's very like a mouse, you know. But do cats eat bats, I wonder?" And here Alice began to get rather sleepy, and went on saying to herself, in a dreamy sort of way, "Do cats eat bats? Do cats eat bats?" and sometimes "Do bats eat cats?" for, you see, as she couldn't answer either question, it didn't much matter which way she put it. (Carroll, p. 20)

The linguistic order is going fast, and with it notions of logical performance. These notions appear during the anal phase of development. We have a sense that all is lost when Alice begins to sing

> How doth the little crocodile
> Improve his shining tail,
> And pour the waters of the Nile
> On every golden scale!
> How cheerfully he seems to grin,
> How neatly spreads his Claws,
> And welcomes little fishes in
> with gently smiling jaws!
> > (*Carroll* p. 29)

The normal version of this ditty begins, "How doth the little busy bee improve each shining hour?" Alice has transformed an improving and puritanical little song on the order of "busy hands are happy hands" into a prototype for the opening lines of "Mack the Knife." If "how doth the little busy bee" has any message at all, it is intended as an allegory on something tidy and difficult, like self-reliance. The idea is that a child singing this song should pick up, by a kind of osmosis, the idea that his purpose as a self is to act neatly, industriously. It is a song about the work ethic.

In Alice's translation, it is none of these. Alice has so altered the song that the bee acting on the flower has become a crocodile inviting fishes. The result is that the concept of selfhood, which has been firmly invested in the little busy bee song is now equally distributed between the crocodile and the fish. Alice's recitation of the bee song is supposed to demonstrate that she is she. It is intended as an expression of her separate reality and ends up mediating between Alice and reality in just the style of a transitional object. In the same way re-forming a transitional object of the external world demarcates that loss of consciousness leading to sleep. Precisely, the bungled demonstration does not prove to Alice that she is she; it proves she is an unfortunate little girl named Mable.

In the anal period, play develops a functional utility. It provides an assemblage of whole figures which begin to constitute the basis for an aggregate of identities or roles. One may have one body (one's own) or another—the experience of the body becomes objectified only as an enduring framework of constant proportions through the realization that one's own child body is the only aggressive instrument of consequence to one's intentions. Alice's regressive experiences and the stability of her neat resolutions undo development of the corporal basis for the autonomous ego. For Lewis Caroll, Alice is a vehicle for the lovely slips and puns and messy business which his mathematics must oppose. If mathematics is his orderly reaction formation, Alice is the substance of his defiance. In *Alice,* the maintenance of intentional consciousness is the story of a developing sense of control.

An Anal Creator in Analysis

The analytic productions of creative people free associating in analysis reveal something about the complexity of the creator's syndrome. We take an example from the recent case of a young man, a 22-year-old writer, who is trying to reconcile creative necessity with the pressures of daily life. The following session focuses on material which shows the interaction between the anal trends in the patient's personality structure and his creativity.

The session begins with a description of a large roll of toilet paper the patient had seen unrolled at a distance on the lawn. The paper presented itself to him as the figure of a dead man. Then he tells two dream fragments from the preceding night:

> I went into my younger sister's room and lay face down on the bed. I was naked and I had to get up without exposing my genitals to her.

> A lecturer took out a giant bottle of red brown viscous wine to illustrate a point. My girl friend was with me and as we left we came to a manhole. She was hanging from it over a rushing stream of sewage. She said she would end it all since she would be no good to a writer. I tried to talk to her into not dropping into the river of sewage.

His immediate associations to the first fragment concerned a wish to exhibit himself to his sister. "As I sat in my sister's room teaching her division I noticed a large doll she had which seemed to be possessed, as though the devil were sitting there glaring at me." He connects this with the movie "The Exorcist," and hence to his fear of conscience and of the analyst.

He complains about his writing. "I began the thing again. The old stuff was terrible. It's telegraphic. I finish everything instantaneously. I did the whole story in one written page. Last night I did an exercise of writing a Virginia Woolf story." That is, he wrote as if he were Virginia Woolf. The story was, essentially, a transformation of an unpleasant wedding he had attended with his girl friend. In the story men and women become mixed up in their sexual identity. "I find Virginia Woolf saying that the feeling of wanting to be the other sex is not horrible."

The patient describes an episode which had occurred while he was paying a visit to another young woman of his acquaintance. He viewed her as a strong, phallic, political figure. Two of her women friends happened to be present. "As I looked at one woman she seemed to waver, as if to say, 'Yes, I'm looking at you,' or as if I frightened her, or to show sexual feelings on her part. I don't know how much is projected."

"Suddenly I have an association with [sic] a dog who was sniffing something interesting, but was shouted at by his master and had to run away—but slowly—circ— circous— circuitously— peripatetically— I come back to the dream. There were a number of rubbers in the sewer which had inflated until they looked like big pale fish. They wavered and were buffeted against the screens. They were lascivious, though cold and white." In the process of association he tells of a poem he had written which ends with an image of his cousin, a pale nun, an image staring heavenward.

"Circ— circuitously" make a word image for the whirlpool of waste which flushes the young man back through the manhole to a world which is more sensual, more visual, one in which images may portray the ending of consciousness. In this Alice-in-Wonderland transit, his sexual wishes are unraveled, and simplified, very much as they would be in the actual synthesis of a dream. In fact the patient lets go of reality in a momentary way, loosens his reflection, and devolves upon the sensory world of his dream formation.

He re-emerges with some new material and some new conclusions. He interprets his attempts at making his girl friend the scapegoat for his fear of sex by "exiling her, dropping her into the sewage." His fecal associations lead to the birth of his brother and a wish to drop him into the toilet. He also reports that his mother says his father was afraid to have sex, that he had to be coaxed. He tries momentarily to make fun of the analyst's reconstruction that the fantasy of giving birth to his brother was tied to an enema which his mother gave him soon after the birth of his brother. He had retained his feces for several days.

> I read a case history of a boy who had a tremendous expulsion of feces after analysis. I was trying to make fun of you and lessen the impact of what you said. I was trying to say it's just a joke. In being inside this manhole my girl friend becomes a child who is in danger of falling into this river of shit. It is as if I play a game that she is on the inside and the outside. But the sewage flows out of the station. So I am saying that you are right. The man in the dream has a big bottle full of red brown fluid. I laugh at myself, not really, it sounds like a description of my father's penis [and the enema bottle].

There is a question in his mind about how his girl friend exists in her own right: can she be manipulated like words on a page, or like feces by the anus?

> It reminds me that my scratching in the book is very retentive. When I think of writing for publication, I get the words out in telegraphic style. But the book is something I can write and retain. I'm the only one who writes in it. It's all mine. I expect myself to want people to read it, but I seldom do. In this way I can write all I want. It stays in me. The idea of putting something out stifles me. As though, as a man I'm doomed to constant abortion. All my creations end in the toilet bowl.

This young adult creator manifests a regressive response to castration anxiety, in which the regression leads to an anal degradation rather than a successful creative response. He sees his girl friend as a bisexual figure, not of inspiration, but a threatening of his own bodily integrity. At the same time that he tries to "drop her," he develops a writing block. In his regressive defense he degrades the woman and his writing to the status of fecal objects, which, after they are deposited, return to torment him. Even the power of his "father/analyst," which he wishes to pre-empt, is degraded to a urinary/fecal flow of words, which finally becomes so viscous it must stop.

THE CREATIVE USE OF LANGUAGE

There are many examples of the adult writer returning to the margins of early language formation for novel modes of expression as many such devices can exploit the mode of language wielded with an omnipotent will by the two-year-old. The aggressive reality-altering devices of imitation, mockery, burlesque, ridicule, parody, satire, sarcasm, and so on originate in the two-year-old's attempt to wrest control of objects through the use of language. The very belief in the efficacy of language to denote the object concretely comes from the identification of language in this period with concrete objects. Then too, the purposeful alteration of syntax exploits the knowledge that syntax was once a discoverable process, learned through the imitation of those persons who first employed the powerful phrases that became introjects in the young child's mind.

Autonomy, exercised as internal narration, forms the basis of the two-year-old sense of identity. As the adult creator elevates internal narration to the status of a guide to the immediate outpouring of literary production, we are reminded that the prototype for internal narration is the formulation of a sentence, which is itself a single unit of thought. For the creator, uttering a sentence is a basic act of creativity. Besides the usual criteria, the sentence uttered must fulfill the aim of affirming the identity of the creator as one whose business is literary creation. We shall explore some examples of literary creation which reveal their origin in the two-year-old period of life.

First, though, we would like to propose that the sentence is a basic act of natural creativity, comparable in this period to the production of a transitional image in the preceding period of life. We recall that Freud defined an act of judgment as determining whether an image jibed with reality according to the criteria of goodness and trueness. This reflective act was carried out to insure that the discharge process did not proceed without the means of satisfaction at hand. Judgment limits primary process. The formation of synthesized language into sentence structures is what Freud called secondary process. Freud stated that thought is trial action. Thought produces a second limit on the discharge process, pending the decision that satisfaction is available.

Thus, for this era, a sentence is the natural neuropsychological structure which brings the separate components of consciousness into a single harmonious synthesis. In a sentence a subject acts upon an object, and the subject and object are linked in such a way that the sentence is a statement of social significance. The integrated subject and object of experience are held in conjoint linkage by reflection, according to those rules of internal narration which makes the sentence a vehicle of communication. The criteria of social significance determine which of a universe of possible sentences comes into full reflective conscousness. These sentences convey a sense of autonomy and identity as narrator to the three year old. Now we would like to explore some literary applications of these notions.

Dylan Thomas — A Poet of Sound

Dylan Thomas's poetry is fixated to an anal/auditory construction of the world. In it, mastery of language is possession of experience. Springing from a nexus of memorial-visual reconstruction/evocation and preoccupied by commands to consciousness, its subjects are awakening, maintaining consciousness, refusing to give up awareness. Descriptions of the poet's achieving and maintaining autonomy reinforce syntactical experiments which evoke remembered experience. This poetry asserts the magic of human nature.

Thomas's syntax is often ambiguous about the acted and the acted upon. The subject and the object often have a dual frame of reference.

"Poem in October"

Thomas's sentences form in the act of creation. They are permeated with sensous imagery not yet absorbed into the secondary process. Take his "Poem in October." It is the celebration of his thirtieth birthday and an evocation of the sense of awakened life in the two- or three-year-old Dylan. Moving from pictures of the sleeping town, to images of awakening, to a sense of his identity pervading the world, the poet finds his identity sung by all the birds around. He leaves the sleeping town and ascends in the hills outside until he looks down on the small town in the rain. There, up on the high hill, looking down, celebrating his awakened consciousness of self, Thomas sees the weather change. As the cold rain of October turns 'round to the warm sun of summer, Thomas is brought back to the experience of a young child with his mother who feels the life charge in everything he sees.

The essence of the poem is the re-experiencing in his thirthieth year of this sense of new vitality in consciousness. The sound of life brings consciousness of new identity on his birthday. He awakens to "The knock of sailing boats," his identity blends with the living imagery of the day. His language reflects the blending of self and object.

"A springful of larks in a rolling cloud" evokes a spiral of language working on itself as he rises above the valley of town and clouds and birds into the high hill of reflection where he finally listens:

> To the rain wringing wind blow cold
> In the wood faraway under me.

"The rain wringing wind" mixes back upon its own syntax as the wind is both the object of the rain's *wringing* and the subject. The rendition of sounds repeating in the syntactic ambiguity evokes the formation of language.

The center of the poem is the weather's turning around. This is the moment when the young child emerges affectively out of memory, bringing Thomas to tears. The compass of the poem turns on an alteration of an idiom. At the top of the hill looking down he says,

> There could I marvel my birthday
> Away but the weather turned around.

Thomas is changing and interrupting the idiom of "whiling away." One whiles away time to pass time, especially when one is a child inside the house when it is raining. But in this case the child is liberated. The rain stops:

> . . . and the blue altered sky
> Streamed again a wonder of summer

Turning the weather around also turns the idiom around. First one marvels rather than whiles, and then one is free. Taking an idiom and altering its expected course is a way of taking the introjected phrases of the aggressor and autonomizing them. It makes Thomas free to change the course of language; it made the young child free to take language over and to wrest fresh consciousness from it.

Thomas alters another idiom as the child springs up in him:

> And the twice told fields of infancy
> That his tears burned my cheeks and his heart
> moved in mine.

The fields of nature permeate Thomas's idiom, and the tale is told twice, once by the young child and once by the adult poet. Here Thomas tells the joy of discussing the attachment to life in nature and the joy in identifying that life in song:

> Where a boy in the listening
> Summertime of the dead whispered the truth of his
> joy, to the trees and the stones and the fish in the tide
> and the mystery sang alive still in the water and singingbirds.

With the last phrase Thomas returns to himself *still* feeling the magic of his own singing and his own being sung. He repeats the idiom:

> And there could I marvel my birthday away but the
> weather turned around. And the true joy of the long
> dead child sang burning in the sun.

The return to the turned idiom emphasizes the difference between the adult reflection from the vantage of 30 years and the child's joy in fresh experience. But the joy is repeated in the language. The mastery of the language and of idiom gives a sense of control over nature, as if the poem itself had turned nature around:

> It was my thirtieth year to heaven stood there then
> in the summer noon,
> Though the town below lay leaved with October blood.
> O may my heart's truth still be sung
> On this high hill in a year's turning.

"Do Not Go Gentle Into That Good Night"

In Thomas's poem, "Do Not Go Gentle Into That Good Night," raging against the dying of the light is more than an expression of resistance to death. The accreted experiences which symbolize or parallel those of the man who must resist dying explicate the refusal to give up consciousness. From this it appears that Thomas declaims against the trauma in every stage of life which threatens the maintenance of reflective consciousness, for each stanza employs a rage for expression to counter the yielding of the light that animates consciousness.

The rage invoked has its roots in the two-year-old's refusal to let the vision of the primal scene blind him and take away his words. This rage is a mania of identification with the aggressor. Thomas appears fixated on the formation of language as the means to find poetry with which to resist the ultimate necessity of giving up the blessing of consciousness. In the final stanza he evokes the power of the aggressor to fix language in its magical command of consciousness.

> And you, my father, there on the sad height,
> Curse, bless, me now with your fierce tears, I pray.
> Do not go gentle into that good night.
> Rage, rage against the dying of the light.

Each stanza of the poem takes the dying of the light, the visual image, and forces it to remain illuminated with the form of feelings. It is a poem about wresting autonomy from the extinguishing forces of reality. It is an assertion of narrative identity. In all this it recapitulates the inevitable experience of forming language aggressively, making syntax come into being through the force of repetition and so molds reflection into an enduring structure for the maintenance of consciousness. Another image of October, extinguishing consciousness, brings Thomas to recreate the world in words.

"Especially When the October Wind"

> Especially when the October wind
> With frosty fingers punishes my hair,
> Caught by the crabbing sun I walk on fire
> And cast a shadow crab upon the land,
> By the sea's side. Hearing the noise of birds,
> Hearing the raven cough in winter sticks,
> My busy heart who shudders as she talks
> Sheds the syllabic blood and drains her words.

In this stanza, Thomas, caught by the force that extinguishes consciousness, at his mother's side (the sea's side) holds onto consciousness through his evocation of the world in words. His voice is given over to the female muse, the bird. Yet it is a raven, carrier of death's syllables, that becomes his muse for the poem.

> Shut, too, in a tower of words, I mark
> On the horizon walking like the trees
> The wordy shapes of women, and the rows
> Of the star-gestured children in the park.
> Some let me make you of the vowelled benches,
> Some of the oaken voices, from the roots
> Of many a thorny shire tell you notes,
> Some let me make you of the water's speeches.

In this second stanza Thomas extends the voice of his muse bird to all of nature. He is allowed to create everything that exists as he composes his language. The expression "some let me" is an invocation of the aggressor, purveying reality in the invocation. It is also an ominous note sounding once again the danger of losing that essential voice.

> Behind a pot of ferns the wagging clock
> Tells me the hour's word, the neural meaning
> Flies on the shafted disk, declaims the morning
> And tells the windy weather in the cock.
> Some let me make you of the meadow's signs;
> The signal grass that tells me all I know
> Breaks with the wormy winter through the eye.
> Some let me tell you of the raven's sins.

In this third stanza reflective continuity is imaged in the clock. Again there is invocation of the source of permission to make poetry and to remain continuously conscious.

> Especially when the October wind
> (Some let me make you of autumnal spells.
> The spider-tongued, and the loud hill of Wales)

With fists of turnips punishes the land,
Some let me make you of the heartless words.
The heart is drained that, spelling in the scurry
Of chemic blood, warned of the coming fury.
By the sea's side hear the dark vowelled birds.

In this last stanza, the tantrum breaks through. The fist of turnip punches through the mother earth, and the poetic voice is dark with fury at mother's love lost. One wonders if Thomas's loved "hump of Wales" may be the child's *wail* of furious poetry creating mother in the strength of its utterance.

AUDITORY SCHEMES OF LANGUAGE

Alliteration and assonance, formally known as schemes of repetition, are devices used by poets for achieving the effect of poetry. The search for similarity in sound does more than this, however: it is involved in the regressive portion of the creative process in which the writer searches for new combinations of experience with which to solve particular creative problems.

Entering into the flow and form of language construction through the search for sound, and rhyme, and rhythm, the artist plumbs the neuropsychological origins of language formation. Through renewing contact with the phonemes, articulemes, and morphemes of language base, the writer immerses himself in a special kind of primary process search. Associations made on the basis of similarity in language constructions escape the rules of secondary process logic, forming new and otherwise unavailable connections.

In this way the process is like the formation of dreams. Just as in the formation of dreams, the phase of regressive search for poetic experience maintains reflective purpose. Reflective order is maintained through the necessity of satisfying special formal or syntactical metric requirements in arranging the language. In addition to this reflectively objective requirement, the poet also imposes a more subjectively reflective requirement that a certain problem of meaning be resolved in the formation of the new language that constitutes the work.

Ulysses *by James Joyce*

There is a good example of the regressive descent to language formation in James Joyce's *Ulysses.* It is a good example because it is self-describing, both illustrating and commenting on the process of the descent to the verbal underlayer. The passage occurs, memorably, at the very moment when Joyce carries Stephen out of the ordinary social world, down into the intrapsychic world of his flow of consciousness. Thus the passage has the formal significance of a departure from ordinary modes of creative communication. Joyce was able to describe the creative process in a more intrapsychic way, leaving it to his audience to supply the ordinary social link.

Schemes of Repetition: Alliteration and Assonance

EXAMPLE

> Stephen closed his eyes to hear his boots crush crackling wrack and shells. You are walking through it howsoever. I am, a stride at a time. A very short space of time through very short times of space. Five, six: the *nacheinander.* Exactly: and that is the ineluctable modality of the audible. Open your eyes. No. Jesus! If I fell over a cliff that beetles o'er his base, fell through the *nebeneinander* ineluctably. I am getting on nicely in the dark. My ash sword hangs at my side. Tap with it: they do. My two feet in his boots are at the end of his legs, *nebeneinander.* Sounds solid: made by the mallet of *Los Demiurgos.* Am I walking into eternity along Sandymount strand? Crush, crack, crick, crick. Wild sea money. Dominie Deasy kens them a'.
>
> > *Wont you come to Sandymount,*
> > *Madeline the mare?*
>
> Rhythm begins, you see. I hear. A catalectic tetrameter of iambs marching. No, agallop: *decline the mare.*

The "ineluctable modality of the audible" becomes the long poem of *Ulysses.* Joyce shows us the associative process of his creative self—Stephen—in the process of forming auditory connections. We notice the detached reflective self-observation maintained during the whole process of plumbing the sound modality. Joyce declines the nightmare of primary fusion. He declines to let go of his self-observation and let his words lead him into a primary visual world.

Schemes of Words

The anal child introjects language composed largely of commands and repetitive, rhythmic utterances. Command— and language generally—is most easily taken in when it is heavily cadenced. One thinks of drill sargents singing cadence to troops and of the ease with which rhythmic poetry can be memorized. In the anal auditory period the beat and prosody of language are welded by the aggressive drive. The phonetic aspect of the process is perceivable in schemes of word and schemes of repetition.

The orthographical schemes occur most often in poetry— although they do occur in dialect writing and other prose fiction. They depend either on the addition or subtraction of sound or syllables or on the alteration of sounds. When not used comically, experimentally, or in dialect, the schemes of words are used deliberately to fill out meter in poetry. They appear most often as deliberate archaisms.

EXAMPLE

Silent Noon

Your hands lie open in the long fresh grass,—
The finger-points look through like rosey blooms:
Your eyes smile peace. The pasture gleams and glooms
'*Neath* billowing skies that scatter and amass.
All *round* our nest, far as the eye can pass,

Are golden Kingcup-fields with silver edge
Where cow-parsley skirts the hawthorne-hedge.
'Tis visible silence, still as the hour glass.

Deep in the sun-searched growths the dragon-fly
Hangs like a blue thread loosened from the sky:—
So this winged hour is dropped to us from above.
Oh! Clasp we to our hearts for deathless *dower,*
This close-companioned inarticulate hour
When twofold silence was the song of love.

—*D. G. Rossetti*

The schemes of words, especially as they exist in poetry, seem to us to originate in the neuropsychological predisposition for rhythmic order. Their frequent archaism points to the primitiveness or ancient history of the predisposition.

THE INJUNCTIONS OF CRITICISM

One aspect of criticism is related to what we call the reflective function of internal narration. Internal narration describes the premier synthetic function of identity during the anal/auditory period. Internal narration is a flow of reflective speech employed to keep track of ongoing experience. The central anxiety of this period is that the synthetic function of internal narration will be overwhelmed by frustration-induced rage. The neutral but forceful commands of the superego are instituted in this era of life. Statements such as "wake up," or in a dream "you are dreaming," or "watch out"—commands to full consciousness—show the basic force of internal narration.

"An Essay on Criticism" by Alexander Pope

There is an aspect of criticism that is rooted in such injunctive narration. Alexander Pope's "An Essay on Criticism," his masterpiece of heroic couplets, gives enduring aphoristic testimony to the relationship between the critic and the poet. We are saying that the relationship between the critic and poet which Pope is concerned with recreates the relationship between the internal narrator and the formation of basic sentences directly from experience: "A little learning is a dangerous thing;" "Fools rush in where angels fear to tread;" "To err is human, to forgive divine." Pope's aphorisms lend injunctive instruction to what we accept in society as a basis for common conscience. Pope is devoted to articulating principles by which sentences are to be formed from experience.

As we have been arguing, reflection is formed throughout life in a series of layers. The first layer institutes beauty and truth. The layer of reflection which arises in the era under discussion makes originality and conclusiveness into permanent institutions. In his essay Pope argues for a modest acceptance of the givens of nature. Nature inculcates critical principles from above, as it were, and Nature gives the writer the talent to bear witness to his experience through the form of his expression. It is Nature which, through "grace," facilitates the ability to bring the senses into expressive conjunction with language, and it is Nature again, which brings the muse to bear as a kind of intermediary, presiding over the motive to enlarge upon that very same Nature.

Pope, in other words, has a theory of mind which accords with a theory of the nature of the common reality. The force of Pope's argument is that one must, either as critic or writer, accept the givens of Nature. For to attempt to appropriate these givens as one's own leads to inevitable failure and disjunction with nature. It is a conclusion based on an appropriate resolution of the conflicts of the anal/auditory period of development. It implies an understanding of the limitations of autonomy, of the limitations of personal power of verbal expression, and it implies an understanding that one cannot in one's personal identity usurp the power vested in the reality of nature.

Pope's heroic couplets have a form well suited to convey the cadence and command that form the aggressive intonation of the superego. These couplets exemplify a kind of "father-form" which can be instituted in reflection and which provides the context for ordinary syntax. In this way, introjected language comes to have a permanent organizational function. Introjected language is thus the underlayer for logic, and the basis for the so-called secondary process organization of thinking.

> Those Rules of old discover'd, not devis'd
> Are nature still, but nature methodiz'd.

As we have already implied, this stage of life contributes a whole layer of creative alternative. The aggressor in this period is institutionalized as the source of commanding language formation:

> Thence form your Judgment, thence your maxims bring,
> And trace the muses upward to their spring;

Pope proceeds to trace the connection to the muse and to nature through the great father figures of literary criticism in the past, Virgil and Homer. Then the interface between the reflective, critical power and the source of writing is imagined as occurring through the mediation of the Graces, allied to the Muses. We may take this as a comment on the connection between reflection and the origin of language in experience.

> Musick resembles Poetry, in each
> Are nameless Graces which no Methods teach,
> And which a Master-hand alone can reach.

Besides chiding the critic for hubris, Pope will give some positive rules for the conduct of good criticism. We may take these rules as a description of the working relationship that develops between the reflection of the anal/auditory period and the experience of this period as it is guided by language. The critic must expect originality:

Then, at the last, and only couplet fraught
With some unmeaning Thing they call a Thought.

The critic must expect authenticity:

The Sound must seem an Echo to the Sense.

The critic must expect evocation:

The pow'r of musick all our hearts allow.

Chapter 5

MAKING BELIEVE: THE PHALLIC MOTHER

Play Age—The Phallic-Oedipal Period— Three to Four-and-One-Half

The oedipal development seals early childhood identity at the same time that it forms the underlayer of adult identity. Just as the nature of the oedipal resolution helps determine future syndromes of neurosis, psychosis, and character disorder, so it also plays an important role in determining the evolution of the creator's syndrome. Our consideration of the roots of artifice leads us to say that by adolescence the creator's muse is heir to the oedipal identification with the phallic woman. The creator's muse will then be given the illusory, fetishistic organ which graces the bisexual composite of this era. This imaginary organ forms a basal construct in the generation of the creator's symbols. Metaphor and symbol are species of language that attain the potential for intrapsychic communication in the oedipal era. We mean to explore the ramifications of this statement in the present chapter, and to illustrate it in the consideration of literary material.

The newly percipient, reflective identity of the oedipal child develops in a process that can be compared to the transformation of images in a microscope. If the elementary experience of the oral/visual world is taken as the basic field of reality, grounded in the stuff of sensations, then the drives acting as the substage light of the microscope bring the basic reality into initial visibility. The primary sensation reaches its highest degree of organization, illuminated at a peak of intensity, in the neuropsychologically conceived experience of the primal scene. The anal/auditory period synthesis of language becomes the close lens which focuses the image of concrete experience. The synthesis of the oedipal period makes another lens, an objective lens which transforms the concrete experience of the preceding period. These new representations of experience become the basis for later, adult language.

The identity synthesized in the oedipal period accomplishes the mental work of distinguishing what is real and what is fantasy. This reflective function can be termed "reality testing." The oedipal child's play builds a range of fantasy roles which his reflection distinguishes from actual representations of the child and of others in the child's world. Reality testing organizes the various role representations into a limited set of relatively enduring identity possibilities.

It is our thesis that the future creator maintains a stronger than ordinary belief in the possibility that an identification with the phallic woman can bring fantasy into the real world. The future creator begins to build an alternative persona which embodies the capacity of imagination to create new productions, new works in the real world. Eventually this persona will develop into the writer's muse. Just as the fetish is the imaginary organ of the future muse, so the chimerical monsters of the creative child's play may be said to be endowed with a special eye for the imaginary.

The oedipal creator maintains his alternative, imaginative identity as a reserve against complete resolution of oedipal conflicts. The future creator is left with an enduring sense of being an imposter since the identity of pretense prevents a normal closure of the oedipal era. But the corollary to this failure to end the oedipal era is that the identification with the phallic woman keeps the channels to earlier periods of intrapsychic integration open to an unusual degree.

NEUROPSYCHOLOGICAL CONSIDERATIONS

During the oedipal period of development, the child heavily invests his consciousness in subjective wishes for pleasure. He uses his whole body as an instrument of his imagination, especially in the pleasures of childhood masturbation. This new emphasis comes about because of neuropsychological advances in this era. On the subjective side of the equation, there appears to be an increased libidinal investment of the functions of the phallic zone, especially the function of urination. Excitement comes to be discharged through release of the sphincters which control micturition. On the objective side of the equation, body representation comes into a new kind of neuropsychological prominence. The child comes to experience the whole body in space as an instrument which carries out a full range of play activities. The whole body becomes a stereognostic instrument capable of embodying postures which express the ongoing relationship to an extended spatial sense of the world.

During the play age era the function of speech undergoes a further evolution along lines made possible through expansion in the associative areas of the brain which coordinate and form speech. The expansion consists of a neurological maturation of those "supramodal" areas of the brain which associate data of experience which are no longer tied to the immediate concrete sensory basis of experience. These maturations make possible what Vigotsky (1965) called the "egocentric speech of childhood." This term refers to a speech pattern in which the child formulates a continuous stream of speech which expresses his ongoing action and intentions as he plays. This private speech, though it may be verbalized aloud, does not purpose to communicate to another child. Rather it is an ongoing recorder of the planning and intentions which, along with fantasy, constitute the essence of the child's play.

Other people at this time are experienced in terms of their sexual characteristics. Not only the primary, but the secondary sexual characteristics are used as the basis of categorizing other people into their roles. In fact, every quality that can be perceived, every aspect of character or personality, is related to the sex of the person. The fantasy life which extends the self empathically into the variety of roles and characteristics perceived in other people centers on sexual qualities of the object. This is the time when the adult male genital takes on its extraordinary luster, when the female genitals pale by comparison, and the pubic hair or some associated object develops a new compensatory significance. Castration anxiety comes into prominence during this era, centering not only on fears for the genitals but also on fears for the maintenance of the whole body image. For it is the whole body which comes to unify the sense of a self-representation which can effectively deal with reality.

There should be no doubt that oedipal conflicts are the important organizer of experience during this era. Sexual wishes are experienced toward each parent, and toward each parent there is a wish for exclusive sexual engagement, with hostile wishes to be rid of the other parent. It is the fear of retribution which lead castration fears into such prominence.

Now the masturbation fantasy, which is critical in the development of the person prone to the creator's syndrome, is the bisexual fantasy of the phallic woman. The imaginary representation of a person endowed with sexual characteristics of both sexes appeases the castration fears and allows childhood masturbation to go on unimpeded. The bisexual fantasy leads to a fixation on the belief in imaginary triumph over the facts of reality. In taking on composite characteristics, the oedipal child feels invulnerable. The sense of future greatness is engendered in this special fantasy.

Reflection takes on the important function of reality testing during this era. Fantasy, as a mode of thinking which accompanies masturbation and play, includes possibilities which may have access to realistic fulfillment, and other possibilities which can lead to bodily harm or to activities which may lead the child into difficulty of other kinds. It is the function of reflection to distinguish between what accords with the facts of reality and what may proceed solely on a fantasy level. To this end, reflection can mobilize a whole new kind of defense, called repression, against those fantasy derivatives of wishes which lead to the threat of castration or loss of bodily integrity.

If reflection always organizes identity (meaning the relatively enduring patterns of mental synthesis that determine the flow of consciousness) then during the oedipal period reflection organizes identity in terms of sexually defined social roles. In his play, in his stream of consciousness, the child accentuates one or another of these possible roles. What is known as selective identification becomes possible during this era. This consists of identifying the self with one characteristic of a particular object, and through an assemblage of such partial identification, various composites can be tried out. The selective identifications of this era supersede the total identifications of the earliest oral era and the identification with the aggressor of the anal era. This means that the child begins to have the ability to control the directions of his own development, since the identifications with important adults are not so complete or inevitable as they were in the past.

OEDIPAL DEVELOPMENTS IN THE WOLF MAN

We have referred to the fact that the oedipus complex transforms the neuropsychological outcome of the primal scene. To illustrate this we will now recall how Freud understood the oedipal transformations of the Wolf Man's primal scene experience.

According to Freud the primal scene is a universal construct equal in importance to the oedipus complex in determining the nature and course of psychic life in the individual. Whereas the primal scene sets concrete reality into a verbal context, lays the foundations of the psychic world, and stimulates the construction of that world, the oedipal resolution produces a transformation of the concrete world of reality, making a representational mental world in its stead. The oedipal transformations do more than make metaphor of the primary world of experience, they reorganize that primary world so that much of it remains accessible only to imagery and dreams and symbols.

We would like to suggest that the onset of the oedipal wishes reorganizes the primal scene as witnessed and fantasied, so that the revived scene is made to conform to a dynamic of oedipal identification. During the oedipal phase—and we shall focus here especially on the maturational process in male children—the feelings of urination begin to organize the phallic zone according to a new, powerful, and intense wish to discharge the erotogenic excitement which (under the pressure of a physiological and neurological readiness) is pressing for immediate expression. In this, it seems to us that the quantity of libidinal wish, experienced as masturbatory impulse, exceeds the capacity of the system of identification-with-the-aggressor to contain or neutralize.

Consider the breakthrough of the oedipal drives and their derivative wishes in terms of the kind of identification employed. At least on paper the Wolf Man derives almost of all his identity from his famous dream:

> I dreamt that it was night and that I was lying in my bed. (My bed stood with its foot towards the window; and in front of the window there was a row of old walnut trees. I know it was winter when I had the dream and night-time.) Suddenly, the window opened of its own accord, and I was terrified to see that some white wolves were sitting on the big walnut tree in front of the window. There were six or seven of them. The wolves were quite white, and looked like foxes or sheep-dogs, for they had big tails like foxes and they had their ears pricked like dogs when they

pay attention to something. In great terror evidently of being
eaten by the wolves, I screamed and woke up. (S. E. vol. XVII,
p. 29)

Having related the dream, the patient, SP, remarked that
it took him some time before he arrived at a conviction that the
dream was only a dream.

SP produced this dream on the eve of his fourth birthday.
He was terribly excited. The next morning, Christmas, was to
bring him a double load of presents. The child was stimulated
to such an extent that his dreams (which are usually the guardians of sleep, safety valves, psychic situations allowing for safe,
regressive, hallucinatory gratifications while the paths to active
discharge are cut off) failed to contain and structure the excitement. Evidently, during the wolf dream—and on account of a
confluence of wishes and an age-appropriate masturbatory impulse—the drive pressures built to such a pitch that the child's
sleep was disturbed, and under the weight of the traumatic
dream, SP produced a new oedipal identity synthesis.

The predominantly anal child of the evening had been
hoping for a large gift from his father, a present attached to the
Christmas tree, a really gratifying wish fulfillment—as Freud
surmised, a baby. But these excited early oedipal wishes were
at this time only capable of expression in the context of the
child's overriding identification with his chronically suffering
mother. We surmise that his excitement exceeded the capacity
of this masochistic identification channel. The child's wishes
were stronger than could be born by the structure which made
him the masochistic recipient of his father's anal sadistic gifts.
And, overcome by drive pressures, the child broke into a new
waking form of reflective consciousness.

Structurally, we may think of the opening window as describing a regression to the primal scene. The dreamed opening
of the window represented both the exposure of the infantile
scene and the hypnopompically imaged opening of the child's

eyes. And, beyond this, Freud saw that the dream was in itself a psychic event making memorable both the immediate extension of the Wolf Man's libidinal development and his entry into the oedipal phase. As such, Freud discussed the dream's role in his patient's genetic development:

> We have now carried our account down to about the time of the boy's fourth birthday, and it was at that point that the dream brought into deferred operation his observation of intercourse at the age of one and one-half. It is not possible for us completely to grasp or adequately to describe what now ensued. The activation of the picture, which, thanks to the advance in his intellectual development, he was now able to understand, operated not only like a fresh event, but like a new trauma, like an interference from outside analogous to the seduction. The genital libidinal organization which had been broken off was reestablished at a single blow; but the advance that was achieved in the dream could not be maintained. (S. E. vol. XVII, p. 109)

The dream reorganized the entire primal scene to make it conform to the oedipal dynamic established under the auspices of the dream. The dream embodied a fresh current of drive energy, capable of opening the channel which was to synthesize the oedipal identifications. But the Wolf Man's was an instantaneous kind of psychological, neurological advance, lasting psychologically only long enough to be experienced both as a trauma and as a castration threat requiring a reorganization of the defenses and a perfection of the defensive maneuvers that materialized in the wake of the threat. Analyzing this material, Freud discovered that castration threats, taken with equanimity at an earlier date, will, when revived under oedipal duress, acquire the freshness of new trauma. And so, the wolf dream revived and (with the aid of a recollected threat by his nursemaid Grusha to his penis when he micturated in front of her) hypercathected SP's old, infantile observation of the penis's disappearance during intercourse. For, when in treatment the Wolf Man came to produce his associations to the tree image in the dream, he brought it out that the tree was bleeding, wounded.

In addition to his wolf phobia, SP developed a phobia about the swallow-tailed butterfly. As Freud tells it, early in his analysis the Wolf Man told his doctor that during a period of severe four-year-old's naughtiness, he had been chasing a large butterfly with pointed wings, which, as it settled on a flower, suddenly filled him with intense anxiety.

Now the Wolf Man told Freud that he associated butterflies with women, with Grusha, seeing in the fluttering V of the butterflies' wings the opening and closing of a woman's legs. It came out finally that in Russian "Grusha" means pear. The Wolf Man has associated the yellow stripes of the pear with his nursemaid's name. Apparently, the Wolf Man also identified himself with winged creatures. He produced for Freud a memory of tearing the wings off of a wasp ("espe," in Russian pronounced "SP") in an act of ritual self castration. Hence the castration anxiety in watching the suggestive movements of the yellow striped butterfly.

The patient produced more memories and associations. He remembered "Grusha . . . kneeling on the floor, and beside her a pail and a short broom made of a bundle of twigs; he was also there, and she was scolding him or teasing him" (S. E. vol. XVII, p. 91). This memory represents Grusha as a phallic woman. Freud had come to understand phallic woman symbolism long before this, and in a letter to Fliess he delightedly pointed out the meaning of the witch's broomstick.

And so, in later life, the Wolf Man found himself compulsively and exclusively attracted to scrub women, women habitually in the *a tergo* position. SP fell in love on sight with a rear view—the castration being, presumably, invisible from that angle and the defect supplied by the scrubbing brush. The Wolf Man, moreover, identified himself heavily with women in that position, but he was gripped by an equal and opposing castration anxiety. Apparently his identification with an image of his mother as castrated left the patient with a sense of personal castration, as signified in the mutilation of the wasp. In his love habits, the patient identified himself with the woman at once intact and castrated.

Now we must suppose that the view of the woman's genitals in the primal scene would take on organizing significance when the boy fell under the sway of castration anxiety. The point is that anyone's sense of doubt about what is real is engendered not only in denial of the primal scene but also, in the oedipal period, by the questions of the mother's real and fancied anatomy. The Wolf Man did not clearly distinguish the castrated from the noncastrated representation of his own mother's intrapsychic image. He remained permanently doubtful about her genital makeup. Because of his remaining unresolved identification with his mother, he believed he could identify himself with the phallic mother, but he also believed he could be castrated.

This brings us to another detail of the wolf dream. If one looks at the Wolf Man's drawing, one sees that the bushy foxes' tails are accentuated and repeated in defense against castration: the busy foxes' tails represent the father's phallic endowment. The child wishes to identify himself with his father's endowment, even to multiply it in order to defend himself against a castrated representation of himself. The castration anxiety subsumed an earlier, primary fear of losing consciousness, of being swallowed up. Many is a kind of defense against none.

With regard to the inherent bisexuality of the oedipal period, Freud says:

> The homosexual attitude which came into being during the dream was of such overwhelming intensity that the little boy's ego found itself unable to cope with it and so defended against it by the process of repression. The narcissistic masculinity which attached to his genitals, being opposed to the homosexual attitude, was drawn in in order to assist the ego in carrying out the task. Merely to avoid misunderstandings, I will add that all narcissistic impulses operate from the ego and have their perma-

nent seat in the ego and that repressions are directed against
libidinal object cathexes. (S. E. vol. XVII, pp. 110–111)

In the Wolf Man's case we can see an oedipal age condensation of the male and female representation into the form of a
phallic woman—who also represented both partners in the
primal scene—came to be a suitable libidinal object, sought in
reality.

Oedipal Era Revisions of Language

As we have been saying, the ontological evolution of childhood thinking leaves residues which adult reflection projects as
species of schemes and tropes. In the attempt to classify these
schemes and tropes we have come to understand that they each
have a place in the normal scheme of intrapsychic development.
The oedipal period contributes some major species to adult
modes of reflective thinking. Insofar as these speech figures
reach back to their ontological origins, they convey mental
organizations of the past to adult thinking.

The tropes of the oedipal period exemplify a reordering of
language which was formed in a concrete, denotative sense
during the preceding period. This is a Chomskian notion, for
the representations and categorizations of the oedipal period
have a potential for a multitude of meaning according to the
context they are used in. Synechdoche and metonomy are species which make the transition from single, concrete denotative
meaning to multiple, potentially connotative meaning in the
oedipal period. Farther into the oedipal period metaphor and
simile come into play as tropes which transform the basal
meanings of concrete meanings buried, or not so buried, within
the speech pattern of metaphor or simile.

In this period of what we would term secondary revision
of language, effortful expansion of the connotation of words

increases the possibilities of figurative language. We are suggesting that in this stage of life a libidinal kind of effort of reaching for means of identifying needs in the selective properties of objects expands the usefulness of language. Words standing for objects can thus come to take on secondary elaborations connoting a whole array of physical properties. There are at least two tropes which originate in this activity of enlarging the capacity for intrapsychic communications.

SYNECHDOCHE AND METONYMY

Synechdoche is a trope in which a part of an object or a genus or a whole class of things is made to stand for the whole. In metonomy an attribute or closely related notion represents the thing meant.

Synechdoche: "Is this the face that launched
                 a thousand ships?"
                 — *Christopher Marlow*

Metonymy: "The pen is mightier than the
                 sword."
                 —*Edward Bulwer Lytton*

Synechdoche substitues a part of the concrete object for the whole concrete object. In this example the oedipal period need to maintain the integrity of the whole body can be counted on to give the trope its effect of eliciting an affective response in the reader. As is often the case, the imagery of the figure is derived directly from the ontological origins of the trope itself. The reader will notice the last aphoristic example of metonymy describes the impulse to expand meaning and to give it a phallic thrust. The libidinal thrust is evident in the following tropes, which seem to embody the phallic sense of increase and decrease in the subject's effect on the spatial world.

HYPERBOLE AND LITOTES

Hyperbole is emphatic and essentially truthful exaggeration. Litotes is understatement, not for concealment, but for effect.

The Road Not Taken

Hyperbole: I shall be telling this with a sigh
                  Somewhere ages and ages hence:
                  Two roads diverged in a wood, and I—
Litotes: I took the one less traveled by,
                  And that has made all the difference.
                  —*Robert Frost*

Betraying his sense of greatness, Frost's modesty charts his life's direction in spatial terms.

METAPHOR AND SIMILE

Metaphor reenacts the transformation of early concrete perception of objects into representational experiences of people. It would, afterall, be correct in saying that oedipal representation is a metaphor for the whole of previous intrapsychic experience. In this developmental period, thinking is liberated from the necessity of stimulation by the presence of the object. And so, the transformations from the earlier periods to the representational period produce a new kind of sentence which represents a multiplicity of basal sentences. Roughly speaking, metaphor and simile are comparisons between objects in some ways alike and in some ways different. A well-functioning metaphor comments on or informs our apprehension of one or both members. The difference between metaphor and simile is this: in metaphor the comparison is implied, in simile the relation to the concrete or basal object is still expressed.

Metaphor: My life went up in smoke.

Simile: Old Men Admiring Themselves in the Water

I heard the old, old men say,
'Everything alters,
And one by one we drop away.'
They had hands like claws, and their knees
Were twisted like the old thorn trees
By the waters.
I heard the old, old men say,
'All that's beautiful drifts away,
Like the waters.'
                              —*William Butler Yeats*

Metaphor and simile reduce a representational statement—"My life lost all its meaning"—to a concrete, experiential antecedent—"went up in smoke." In this, the base or concrete antecedent must be capable of generating any number of representational statements, such as, *my life lost all its value, I lost all my dreams, I was destroyed by the loss of my lover, everything I had disappeared swiftly into nothing.*

IRONY

Irony is a complicated device rooted in the oedipal era. It is complicated because, to use irony one must undertake an extended false identity. Irony presupposes an imposture. The one who employs irony undertakes an identification with the voice of the imaginary self. It is a way of pre-empting the whole channel of creativity for one's realm of discourse. Irony also presupposes that there is a reader or listener who is sympathetic to the intended meaning. There is, in this assumption, the original creative assumption of a mother who will attend to the created reality, giving it truth through her attention.

In irony, the thing said is the opposite of the thing meant.

> For Brutus is an honourable man;
> So are they all honourable men.
> —*William Shakespeare, Julius Caesar,*
> (Act III, Sc. ii, 88–89)

Irony is used to destroy false postures and meanings. The speaker takes on a false posture and, in enunciating it, reveals its shoddiness. In irony, conclusions reached on the basis of represented evidence must be false ones. In assuming the false posture, the speaker or writer exposes the falsity in a maneuver deriving from oedipal mode identification with the phallic mother.

Enough meaning is transferred to the false representation that in it the falsity becomes apparent and significant enough for reflection to judge it false.

NEUROPSYCHOLOGICAL CONSIDERATIONS IN THE ORIGIN OF THE CREATOR'S LANGUAGE

We have been commenting all along on the self-conscious side of creator's language. It seems that many figures of speech are descriptive of their own construction. Our thesis about this phenomenon is that it is an outgrowth of, and an aspect of, a special variety of language which is peculiar to creators. We contend that the creator's alternative to normal identity commands and organizes a special variety of language, which, like ordinary language, is accreted through the life cycle of the individual.

We have noted that alternatives which structure the creator's identity are formed during each stage of the life cycle during periods of trauma. Intense trauma, as we have noted, produces an objectification of self and a formation of significant identity accretion. The figurative language tendency of the creator maintains access to earlier channels of neuropsychological and intrapsychic integration.

Language in general has two surfaces. One is directed toward the intrapsychic formation of communication between different functioning parts of the mind—and brain—and the other is directed as communication toward some significant other person or persons. Creative language bears a special tension in that the intrapsychic-directed portion is fully solipsistic, speaking in full voice to its own construction—as in poems dedicated to their own writing, or in the formal structures of literary work which are directed toward their own ontogeny. The outward-directed portion of creative language, meanwhile, carries the provisional voice which only an audience can verify as valid communication.

This leads us to address the question of how symbols develop their significance to writers. It seems appropriate to take the question up in the present chapter because the concept of fetish, which is central to the creative person's avoidance of resolving the oedipal dilemma is tied into the origin of symbols. The symbol is a species of intrapsychic thought which can be used to account for experience in which the concrete referents are missing. Since the creator's syndrome is based on a series of avoidances of trauma through special means in each stage of life, the symbol, which condenses such avoidances, has great importance to the creator.

In speaking about symbols we are not referring to mythologized symbols that have come to have a meaning to mankind, but rather to symbols that develop in an individual in response to various kinds of trauma. Thus we are speaking of personal symbols. Of course, personal symbols often turn out to be quite similar in different individuals—an argument in favor of the universality of those developmentally important experiences which are full of trauma and of the common ways of responding to such trauma.

One principle we have been emphasizing in this regard is that trauma produces a neuropsychologically determined response of moving out of experience and into reflection. In reflective consciousness, then, one responds to trauma with the defenses that are available according to the genetic stage of development that has been reached.

In the earliest stage of development the response to unfulfilled yet pressing need is the production of a hallucination which can lead to mental pain and trauma if left to develop. Reflection in this case can only marshall the gravest of defenses, namely, the blotting out all consciousness. A little later in development, during the era of transitional thinking, one produces an image of the object in response to trauma; and if this does not lead to the appropriate action for gratification to ensue, then one reflection blots a portion of experience in what may be called the defense of denial. Later, anal stage frustrations invoke the use of sound figures in reaction to frustration. Images and denial, sound figures and reaction formation, and later symbols and repression, are thus intimately and organically linked.

We are asserting in this argument that certain species of reflective thinking (figurative language, schemes-tropes, symbols) are residual ways of referring to traumatic experience, for in psychic life it is as important to be able to refer to those experiences that have given rise to trauma as to be able to refer to those experiences that have given rise to pleasure. Thus writers develop a facility with the language that originated in response to trauma at the various levels of development.

Put in another way, images, or figures or symbols all cover over some discontinuity in experience. The facility in dealing with the integers of these negative experiences may be referred to as the writer's talent. As we have said, the person with the creator's syndrome is optimistic about the eventual outcome of dealing with trauma through his creative products. For the writer of literature, images, and figures and symbols form part of the basic language skills necessary to his productions. There is a tendency for repetitious use of images and symbols in the writer's repetoire, because the person with the creator's syndrome is continually trying to master a past trauma. Every bit of creative language made in response to trauma is spawned as just a single production in a focus capable of continuous production. Image after image is cast out of an original mold, each image being a negation or inversion of the original traumatic experience.

We are implying that creative language presents to our reflective consciousness a kind of awareness of what is missing in our experience. The illusion that something exists in reality, or can be made to exist, is a compensation that enters into the formation of the structure of our thought. Through his use of image, figure, or symbol, the creator is made aware of what is missing in reality while simultaneously the language used is, in itself, a substitute formation, a prototypical symptom, a holding action against the expected imposition of frustration by reality.

"Astrophel and Stella" by Sir Philip Sidney

Taken in this way, poetic language is a symptomatic expression of a compromise between what is not allowed in experience and what is allowed using the creative means of expression. Indeed, we are not surprised to find poems describing such constructions. The following passage is from Sidney's "Astrophel and Stella," a series written to the muse, Stella, and imaged in response to poet's deepest and most essential need. The poem is a product that attempts to answer that need on all levels.

Who will in fairest book of Nature know,
  How virtue may best lodged in beauty be,
  Let him but learn of love to read in thee,
Stella, those fair lines, which true goodness show.
There shall he find all vices overthrow,
  Not by rude force, but sweetest sovereignty
  Of reason, from whose light those night birds fly;
That inward sun in thine eyes shineth so.
  And not content to be perfection's heir
Thyself, doest strive all minds that way to move,
Who mark in thee what is in thee most fair.
So while thy beauty draws the heart to love,
  As fast thy virtue bends that love to good:
  "But ah," Desire still cries, "give me some food."

(verse 71)

The night birds appear as a symbol, a harbinger of desire. A reference to satisfied desire. At the same time they fly away from reason and flow out of reason. The night birds act ambiguously, as symbol of the muse's scope. "Astrophel and Stella" is a poem that appeals to the muse to remove trauma on many levels.

PATHETIC FALLACY

The pathetic fallacy describes a literary understanding of the effect of trauma in producing a particular kind of literary figure. The notion of pathetic fallacy is Ruskin's, and in the chapter 12 of *Modern Painters* he says, "All violent feelings have the same effect. They produce in us a falseness in all our impressions of external things." (Harold and Templeman, 1966, p. 815) This is a good description of the denial and displacement produced by trauma. According to Babette Deutch (1962), pathetic fallacy is "a phrase coined by Ruskin to characterize the false impression of things produced by violent emotion. It is found in lines that inappropriately ascribe human feelings to nature." (Deutch, p. 106)

The pathetic fallacy is to be distinguished from empathy, an awareness, more intimate than sympathy, of the feelings of another person and, more narrowly, of the feelings that something not sentient might be supposed to have. Thus Shapiro writes of "A Cut Flower":

Yesterday I was well, and then the gleam,
The thing sharper than frost cut me in half.
I fainted and was lifted high. I feel
Waist deep in rain. My face is dry and drawn.
(Deutch, p. 106)

Although the pathetic fallacy runs to personification it actually has wider application as a prototype for the formation of images, figures, and symbols. Ruskin used his understanding of this mechanism to form the basis of literary judgments. In itself P. F. is a comment on the state of mind that enters into the formation of literary devices. To quote Ruskin:

I believe these instances are enough to illustrate the main point I insist upon respecting the pathetic fallacy—that so far as it is a fallacy, it is always the sign of a morbid state of mind, and comparatively of a weak one. Even in the most inspired prophet it is a sign of the incapacity of his human sight or thought to bear what has been revealed to it. (Harold and Templeman, p. 822)

A symbol, then, can be seen as an object that exists in nature and is suitable to represent the feelings that the pathetic fallacy means to avoid—and to evoke. Now artists often symbolize their muse as birds, butterflys, and other winged creatures. A combination of reality, anatomy, and mental tendency seems to favor this symbolism. Then, too, there is historical antecedent for this particular symbol.

The mature artist's trauma overlies a number of earlier ones. That trauma that calls up the pathetic fallacy of a bisexual muselike creature naturally overlies the earlier trauma of discovering the absence of a female genital. At an earlier stage of life, this traumatic perception was met with a strong need to obliterate the child's "knowledge" that his mother had been castrated. The perfect, uncastrated mother had always been the child's perfect audience. Coming upon the need for a source of response and inspiration, the artist summons up his archaic memories of the transitional mother. At the same time, he attempts to repair another negative in experience. The perfect audience-inspirer mother has been deprived of a part of her anatomy and so is imperfect. So she is revived in the person of a phallic mother or phallic mother representation, and thus the negatives in experience are repaired.

Paradise Lost *by John Milton*

Invoking the Heavenly Muse, Milton, in the first book of *Paradise Lost* asks for a special sort of aid:

> And chiefly Thou O Spirit, that dost prefer
> Before all Temples th' upright heart and pure,
> Instruct me, for Thou know'st; Thou from the first
> Wast present, and with mighty wings outspread
> Dove-like satst brooding on the vast Abyss
> And mad'st it pregnant: What in me is dark
> Illumine, what is low raise and support;
> That to the highth of this great Argument
> I may assert Eternal Providence,
> And justify the ways of God to men.
>
> (I:17–26)

Here the images of bird and muse are utterly compounded, which is a matter of particular importance. The image of the brooding bird comes directly from the first book of Genesis. There, God is first seen as a bird brooding on the waters. In the notion of impregnation the Holy Spirit is identified with the muse. The effect of the invocation is to join the notions of male God, female muse, impregnating, and female nurturing (that is brooding, which is sitting on eggs). The blended sexuality is inherent in the biblical imagery. Milton has simply intensified it. In his labor of intensification, he has deliberately used the word *brooding*, which is the word that appears in the ancient texts. For their own reasons, translators choose to depict God as hovering or moving on the waters. However, in the original, God broods.

Chapter 6

MAKING BELIEVE: THE CREATIVE FETISH

The child whose personal fortunes are involved in the creator's syndrome is redeemed by it. This child believes that gratification is expression. Neurological precocity and the luck (or casualties) of mothering have begot in him a deep and primal optimism. This optimism, engendered in scenes not unlike those leading to psychosis, narcissistic fixation, and perversion, is easily but necessarily linked to unaverted fixation and perversion.

Creative narcissism develops this way: in infancy, the creative person averts psychosis by performing some act capable of turning the tide of maternal cathexes. Originally, this child's mother demands that her infant exist as a narcissistically gratifying extension of herself. Performing a number of special acts and so exceeding her narcissistic demands, the infant completes a maneuver destined to establish his separate being in the mother's mind. Through performance he liberates himself. But the infant may avert a major disaster only to be beset by a more manageable, personal difficulty, a narcissistic fixation originating in this early reversal of the cathectic tide.

The relation between the creator's syndrome and the possibilities of perverse oedipal resolution is the subject of this chapter. The creative resolution is not perverse, although it is possible for the creative person to resolve matters in a way that is perverse. The creative resolution of the oedipal problems has much to do with a group of possibilities Phyllis Greenacre (1971 [1957] vol. 2, p. 479–504) has recognized as the *collective Alternates.* "Collective alternates" describes the oedipal youngster's creation of a group of imaginary identities. Greenacre's idea is that if the child is himself unable to defy the incest taboo, if the child in his own person must abandon incestuous wishes, he may be able to gratify himself under cover of fantasy. His productions—imposters and false selves—are created out of a composition of parental qualities and exhibit mixed sexual characteristics.

Although in creative people oedipal developments serve the same functions as they do in normal people, they serve creative needs as well. Ordinarily, during the oedipal period the gains of the preceding periods are consolidated. Childhood sexuality effloresces in masturbatory patterns of fantasy. The child fashions choices of sexual identification. Conscious reflection develops into the mental constituent generally known as the self-observing function of the ego. In the present context, it seems more suitable to call this subjective function and its twin objective critical correlate the reflective function. Setting the stage for the spurt of intellectual development that will occur in the latency period, this function is central in the organization of reliable memory.

But in the creator's syndrome, the child makes a provisionally normal resolution of the oedipal conflicts. This apparently normal resolution orders his everyday relations with his parents. The male child renounces his wishes toward his mother. The female child transfers her wishes from her mother to her father. As for negative oedipal strivings, the creative child usually resolves to renounce homosexual wishes.

Thus while the creative person has renounced manifestly oedipal behavior and with it a portion of libidinal attachment to his parents, he has not renounced his devotion to certain mental representations of the phallic mother. As Phyllis Greenacre pointed out, the creative child does not relinquish the positive and negative Oedipal attachments. Instead, he maintains them all. By alternating these, as he has alternated transitional objects, the potentially creative child avoids the normal shattering of the Oedipus complex. At the same time of shattering, most people renounce specific fantasy about their parents. The creative youngster renounces neither playfully imagining fantasy nor the specific pansexual fantasies originally connected with infantile masturbation. Instead, he plays out his fantasy by identifying with the desirable aspects of the composite parent. When the self-identification is complete, the fantasy is then available to artistic expression, for it no longer has obvious reference to fantasies of breaking the incest taboo.

Devotion to these representations bears an obvious, perhaps misleadingly obvious, resemblance to the devotion of the fetishist. The creative devotion is syndromatic, devotion to a fetish perverse. The point, which must be firmly grasped, is that fetishism is the prototypical defense against castration anxiety. It alters the child's representation of reality to allow him to maintain masturbatory, sexual, fantasy behavior.

"The Artist of the Beautiful" by Nathaniel Hawthorne

The devotion to mental representations of the phallic mother, which is characteristic of the creator's syndrome, has another purpose. While the creative person may have passed through a stage of extreme castration anxiety and phallicized his image of his mother as a defense against his fear, in his creative being he endows a mental representation with attributes from both parents. The result is that in the creator's

syndrome, the phallic mother is a composite, a well-differen-
tiated representation who might alternately be known as the
"pregnant father." Consider this sentence from Hawthorne's
"The Artist of the Beautiful":

> Can the philosopher, big with the inspiration of an idea that is
> to reform mankind, believe that he is to be beckoned from this
> sensible existence at the very instant when he is mustering his
> breath to speak the word of light?

This syndromatic composite parent differs from the fetishist phallic mother or phallic woman. First, it is highly un-
likely that the creative child ever conceives directly of this
figure. Instead, imagination produces a special kind of imaginary person with whom the creative child may associate himself
in fantasy. The meaning of these persons is available only to an
adult's reflection. The creative child's alternative to the resolution of the oedipal complex puts a fetishistic imprint on his
reflection. The superego of the creative person is therefore more
permeable to possibilities that do exist in reality.

There are several fruitful comparisons to be made between
the significance of the fetish object and the significance of the
composite parent. The fetish object is a token of the fetishist's
requirement, of his insistence on his right to affirm in fantasy
the existence of a condition which he recognizes as impossible.
The creative child's composite parent is the expression of a
similar requirement. The creative person insistently produces
figures of speech and fantasy that affirm his right to endow one
kind of body with the sexual attributes of another. The figure
of a man pregnant with ideas, as in the quote from Hawthorne,
is perhaps the most familiar. The composite parent, like the
fetishist's phallic woman, derives from the fetishist's use of one
or many transitional objects. But the creative person's composite figure does not mediate between his own subjectivity and the
reality of sexual situations; it mediates between subjectivity and
the realm of the imagination.

Nathaniel Hawthorne's short fiction is well stocked with references to such composites: "The Artist of the Beautiful," one of the more famous short bits ("Ethan Brand" is another), turns on the narration of a piece of intrapsychic history, immediately preceding and deliberately building up to one young man's self-identification with the phallic mother.

"The Artist" is a fictionalized description of Hawthorne's conscious understanding of the peculiar relation between the artist and the object: "When the Artist rises high enough to achieve the beautiful, the symbol by which he makes it possible to mortal senses becomes of little value in his eyes, while his spirit possesses itself in the enjoyment of reality."

Briefly, this is the tale of a watchmaker who endows a clockwork butterfly with spiritualized life—or a representation of it. The butterfly is a wedding gift for Annie Danforth, née Hovenden, Owen Warland's ideal lady. Warland has served his apprenticeship under Peter Hovenden, Annie's father. Annie's father and her husband, Robert Danforth, are the praiseworthy watchmaker's opposites. Between them they divide the negative qualities of worldliness, pragmatism, materialism, common sense, and brute strength. Annie, whose limitations are known to Warland—she is highly intuitive but lacks corresponding intelligence and sensitivity—is not so much Warland's Beatrice, as she is his Laura. For Annie is not the kind of woman who abets fantasies of her own ethereality. The narrator, who is both more intellectual and more verbal than the taciturn Owen, seems to disapprove of Annie more as an object choice for Warland than as a person. Her elevation is a raising of Dulcinea to the pinnacle of courtly love. Annie is of the earth, a woman the narrator and Owen will find almost physically unfit for her role as object of veneration.

> "Go Annie," murmed he; "I have deceived myself, and must suffer for it. I yearned for sympathy, and thought, and fancied, and dreamed that you might give it to me; but you lack the *talisman*, Annie, that should admit you into my secrets. That

touch has undone the toil of months and the thought of a lifetime! It was not your fault, Annie; but you have ruined me!"

How does a wish for the phallic woman or composite
parent enter into this tale of a frail, impotent seeming child-man
who, after three attempts succeeds in perfecting a toy? To answer this question, we must explore the meanings of the toy.
The toy is given as a wedding gift and destroyed almost
immediately by the child of parents incapable of appreciating
its beauty. This is the fourth and final breaking. The first three
acts of destruction leave Owen groveling, shattered, in a state
of deep regression. After one disaster he takes to drink, to
riotous living. He "made proof of whatever show of bliss may
be found in riot. He looked at the world through the golden
medium of wine." Recovery comes through the agency of a
magnificent butterfly who recalls him to his obsessional contemplation. On another occasion the artist becomes ill after the
destruction of the butterfly. Given that the butterfly is introduced quite late in the story, and that the story is painfully
overwritten, it appears that only our sympathy with the dynamics of phallicization can justify the tension we feel on Owen's
and the butterfly's account.
For whatever we may feel about Owen, who is a rather
repulsive child-man, remarkable chiefly for his puniness, his
agile fingers, his alternating fits of fantasy and lugubriousness,
and his passion for real as well as imagined butterflies, he
compels attention. There is something uncanny about our interest in his illusional activity. How, we wonder, are we so involved in the fate of a man who has made a little machine whose
very beauty is not described until the end of the tale. When we
do see it it is:

> Nature's ideal butterfly . . . realized in all its perfection; not in
> the pattern of such faded insects as flit among earthly flowers,
> but of those which hover across the meads of paradise for child-
> angels and the spirits of departed infants to disport themselves

with. The rich down was visible on its wings; the luster of its eyes seemed instinct with spirit. The firelight glimmered around this wonder—but it glistened apparently by its own radiance, and illuminated the finger and outstretched hand on which it rested with a white gleam like that of precious stones. In its perfect beauty, the consideration of size was entirely lost.

Apparently, at a certain point for us, as always for Owen, the butterfly has ceased to be a machine. In answer to Annie's amazed question, "Is it alive?", Owen replies,

"Alive? Yes Annie, it may well be said to possess life, for it had absorbed my own being into itself."

In exchange for the gift Owen receives Annie's blush, her first sexual response to him. Her response, however, is tinged with contempt. As well it may be, for she is married to a man of iron. Danforth's large hands stand in contrast with Owen's delicate fingers. His brawn is compared to Owen's childlike body. Owen is not a sexually functioning man. The butterfly he brings to Annie, however, is a sexual object. And it is phallic. This delicate machine responds to a touch. Its ability to flicker and grow dim and radiant are phallic attributes.

At first Owen's ability to relinquish the butterfly and face its destruction in the fist of Annie's "child of strength" presents something of a problem. On reflection, though, we realize that Owen has come to participate vicariously in a family reunion and that he suffers there a vicarious mutilation. We realize also that Owen has made Annie into a mother figure. He visits her only after she has become a matron and produced a child. He comes as a child to the fireside of the man of iron. Only one seen as a father could have such large hands and be so overwhelming to a little boy.

For what is is worth, we will add that there are two father figures present. Peter Hovenden, the intolerable authority figure, is the second father in the house of the ironbound Danforth. Owen has been Hovenden's apprentice, his "half-son," if you will.

The vicarious mutilation is an act of ritual castration. The notion of ritual castration is, as Freud tells us, intimately bound up with the oedipal boy's mental representation of a phallic mother. This image is destroyed when the reality of female genitalia is described or shown to him.

In the essay on "Fetishism" (1927) Freud writes, "For though no doubt a fetish is recognized by its adherents as an abnormality, it is seldom felt by them as the symptom of an ailment accompanied by suffering." (S. E. vol. XXI, p. 152) Witness Owen Warland. In his case, suffering is not typified by the butterfly. Instead, suffering is felt to come from the outside, from his relations with the world. He does not want to give up and is unable to give up his preoccupation with the butterfly, his gift for Annie. For if the boy could give up the idea of existing without this endowment, then, as Freud observed in his paper on Fetishism, "his own possession of a penis was in danger." (S. E. vol. XXI, p. 153) The fetish object "remains a token of triumph over the threat of castration and a protection against it. It also saves the fetishist from becoming a homosexual, by endowing women with the characteristic which makes them tolerable as sexual objects." (S. E. vol. XXI, p. 154) Moreover, the fetishist may have feelings other than reverence for the object. Remember Warland's idealization and then berating of Annie's image. Recall that he destroyed the butterfly at the time of Annie's engagement.

"In many cases he [the fetishist] treats it [the fetish] in a way which is obviously the equivalent to a representation of castration. This happens particularly if he has developed a strong identification with his father." (S. E. vol. XXI, p. 157) The point is that the father is seen as the castrater of the mother. A boy identifying with the castrater might both reverence the fetish and wish to reenact the scene of primal castration. This describes Warland's treatment of the butterfly quite well.

At the family party Owen profers the phallic machine in its hand-carved box as a gift for use. He hands it over in the spirit of "better late than never." (How else would a boy fantasize the belated endowment?)

In the giving, the butterfly becomes an imaginative phallus, a fetish object. Warland is endowing Annie with an imaginative phallus. Remember the talisman (man's tail, perhaps?) that Annie lacked. Remember that the butterfly has been thrice shattered before achieving perfection. Surely this is an allegory for a refusal to accept the mother's body image which precedes the imaginative solution: creating a composite image as a figure for self-identification. How else can we explain this: "He knew that the world, and Annie as the representative of the world, whatever praise might be bestowed could never say the fitting word or feel the fitting sentiment."

Remarkably, the artist, like the fetishist, can let the object go; the created object, like the fetish object, is almost a spare part. The source of these objects is inviolable and produces an endless supply. This is the only reasonable explanation for the anxiety we feel for the mysterious butterfly, an anxiety all out of proportion to the glories attributed to it.

We are caught up in Owen's castration anxiety and in Hawthorne's making of the composite figure. Since there has been a successful identification with the composite figure, the fate of its external representation no longer matters. "When the Artist rises high enough to achieve the beautiful, the symbol by which he makes it possible to mortal senses becomes of little value in his eyes, while his spirit possesses itself in the enjoyment of reality."

This sentence, which ties together symbols from above and below, also (1) binds together the notions that the product is expendable and that it represents certain of the creator's reflective intrapsychic integrations, and (2) confirms our suspicion that the creative product recapitulates the process of its own development. The phrase "possesses itself in the enjoyment of reality" admits of such a psychological interpretation that it may be taken retroactively as a description of the mental process of fantasy and creation, for the phrase "possesses itself in the enjoyment of reality" is genetic in character. It describes the satisfaction of the infant who has achieved a profounder reality in the creation of a transitional object, the satisfaction of oedipal resolution, and the satisfaction of having created a product of known cultural worth. At the oedipal level, this phrase has its origin in masturbatory fantasy.

This object, the butterfly, bears destruction, as does any specific representation of the phallic mother, because the mental integration, the internalization of the composite image, is indestructable. This being so, the creator possesses himself with the enjoyment of his new, successfully creative potential, including his newly created faculty for creation mediated by the phallic mother. This is his reality.

These identifications of self with phallic mothers or composite images surface in fantasy and play like a troop of hermaphrodites perfumed with libido, representing the various possibilities of associative self-expression and gratification. "The Artist of the Beautiful" revolves around this phase of experience, carefully describing the creation, endlessly pointing toward her, pondering the quality of the creator's need for her, but never revealing her in action. Rather than fantasize about her, Hawthorne leaps from her genesis to her function in structuring mental organization. The specific fantasy seems to be covered by the general amnesia we throw around most early sexual fantasy, admitting, as we do, its existence but resurrecting it rarely, and often with pain.

Thus in the creator's syndrome, the phallic mother comes to stand for a whole tribe of sexual possibilities. These imagined possibilities, originally available to all, evade the censorship of the oedipal prohibition by proliferating a whole range of imagined sexual gratifications, attached to the phallic mother and detached from the actual parents. These syndromatic fantasies, connected with the phallic mother, and incompletely detached from experience with the parents, are cherished secretly; the normal fantasies of sexual congress with the parents are more sharply repressed. The syndromatic fantasies defy the incest taboo; in them the phallic mother comes to stand for possession by and of the mother, by and of the father.

If it should happen, however, that the artist comes close to recreating the intrapsychic genesis of this phallic mother, then he will seem to shy away from depicting overtly oedipal fantasies, because in this sort of representation, the artist would have to depict the very oedipal fantasies that existed before his self-identification with the composite parent. For this the incest taboo will be too compelling. Thus, when Hawthorne describes the genesis of Owen's (and, by extension, his own) self-identification with a phallic mother, he avoids portraying Annie as Owen's mother. Instead, Hawthorne describes Owen's placing Annie on a pedestal, his desire to create the ideal object for her, his renunciation of her at the time of her engagement to the large, fathering, Danforth, and his triumphant creation of the ideal object. When Owen's self-identification is complete, Warland no longer needs to create objects for Annie. Having already identified with her as a composite parent, he is able to produce ideal images for his newly identified creative self. He has thus successfully altered the meaning of the butterfly. It was a phallus for Annie. It becomes an object whose significance is derived from within. The phallic woman, the lady on the pedestal, the composite parent has become the creative self.

"Feathertop" by Nathaniel Hawthorne

When she has been internalized, the phallic mother functions as a muse. Travestied, she is Mother Rigby in Hawthorne's "Feathertop." "Feathertop" was to be Hawthornes' farewell to tale writing. His tale is the child of two impulses. One is a drive toward self-mockery. Mother Rigby is a travesty of the author's creative self. The other is an urge to express ambivalence, that is, to excoriate works for which Hawthorne still harbored tender feelings. Thus Mother Rigby's dismissal of the empathic scarecrow, Feathertop. In this context, "Feathertop" is a self-parody, a play on "The Artist's" symbol making.

Briefly, Mother Rigby, decides to make a scarecrow. She erects one of phallic symbols. His backbone is her broomstick —which, as Freud so enthusiastically observed, is "the great Lord Penis." (S. E. vol. I, p. 242) He is dressed in tatters and brought to life by Mother Rigby, who is a great smoker. Her pipe is maintained through the agency of her familiar, Dickon. "Dickon," she cries, "a coal for my pipe!"

> The pipe was in the old dame's mouth when she said these words. She had thrust it there after filling it . . . but without stooping to light it at the hearth. . . . Forthwith, however, as soon as the order was given, there was an intense red glow of smoke from Mother Rigby's lips. Whence the coal came, and how brought hither by an invisible hand, I have never been able to discover.

The coal, taken presumably from the neighborhood of Hellmouth, is thrust into Feathertop's mouth, and the scarecrow is commanded to smoke. The phallic puppet, with his feather crowned pumpkin head and Master Rigby's old clothes, is transformed into a regular beau. Mother Rigby, who can barely contain herself, sends Feathertop on a mission.

In his glowing phallicism, which is maintained only through constant smoking—if the pipe goes out Feathertop will grow dim and eventually "die"—Mother Rigby's creation is sent off to seduce Pretty Polly Gookin. Her father has gotten himself into some kind of Faustian involvement with Dame Rigby. Polly is the unconscious forfeit.

At first, Polly is flattered to be courted by so fine a gentleman as Feathertop. She has nearly yielded him her hand in marriage when disaster strikes. With a great 'oh my,' the narrator points to a magic mirror, strategically located. Polly sees Feathertop as a man of trash. Her vanity is shriveled, her virtue saved, and Feathertop, who is not a bad sort, goes home in discouragement and pain.

Now, it happens that Feathertop has served two masters, Hawthorne and Mother Rigby. These two compose two varieties of authorial self-identification. At an upper level Feathertop is Hawthorne's allegory for the tales preceding the present one.

> There it stood—poor devil of a contrivance that it was!—with only the thinnest vesture of human similtude about it, through which was evident the stiff, rickety, incongruous, faded, tattered, good-for-nothing patch work of its substance, ready to sink in a heap upon the floor, as conscious of its own unworthiness to be erect. Shall I confess the truth? At its present point of vivification, the scarecrow reminds me of some of the lukewarm and abortive characters, composed of heterogeneous materials, used for the thousandth time, and never worth using, with which romance writers *(and myself, no doubt, among the rest)* have so over peopled the world of fiction.

But below this layer of literary self-criticism, Feathertop lives because Mother Rigby wills that he shall.

This willful old belle dame is, in her turn, phallicized by Hawthorne. Acting out the phallicism of her kind, Mother Rigby sets out to outdo other witches by seducing a young girl. Since Feathertop is her puppet, she will "know" Polly through Feathertop who gets his potency from her pipe. This pipe she will eventually take back from his strawy corpse. Rather than revivify him, at his demise, she puts the organ of his potency back in her mouth and calls for another coal. So Hawthorne, who has associated himself with the phallic mother will go on to write another romance. Hawthorne, like Mother Rigby, can always make another creature, can always endow a surrogate with potency. The surrogate, like Owen's butterfly (the name is an obvious pun on "own") will represent its maker's potency, will derive also from self-identification with the phallic mother, and will be disposable.

Chapter 7

THE CREATOR'S EGO

Latency—Age Four-and-One-Half to Eleven

There is no synthesized ego before latency. Latency welds disparate forms of consciousness. As is well known, the superego forms in the resolution and aftermath of the oedipal conflict. This resolution bonds reflective consciousness to experiential consciousness: reflection becomes a functional aspect of a centralized ego, the self-observing function. The sense of personal identity becomes a functionally compounded amalgam of subjectively purposeful intentionality and objectively defined cultural goals. Shame and guilt arbitrate this new sense of centralized identity.

The future creator fixates on the creation of this identity, and in addition believes that it is possible to create a world like the one that is being inculcated in him under the tutelage of society. The creative child of latency dedicates himself to particular extended fantasies: the family romance (indicating that he is descended from special and unusual parentage, part of some grander social purpose), or the fantasy of the birth of the hero (indicating some unusual talent and purpose in the life of the dreamer). These preoccupying fantasies produce the alternative and secret self of the latency age creator. He feels set apart by the degree of his belief in his special separateness from his peers.

NEUROPSYCHOLOGICAL CONSIDERATIONS

A shift in the neuropsychological ground brings on a latent period in the efflorescence of the instinctual life of childhood. The balance between the driven quality of experience and the neutral quality of reflection becomes equalized in latency. The equalization is accommodated, we think, through the neurological development of the so-called tertiary neocortex. This neocortex (which accounts for massive portions of the prefrontal areas of the brain) myelinates, matures, and then mediates between the driven experience of childhood and the socially inculcated reflection of latency. The sensory based information which informs experience, and the socially derived information —the cultural legacy—are smoothly meshed in the vast tertiary areas of neocortex, giving rise to a mental apparatus which, computer-like, supports a smooth and continuous integration and synthesis of time and space.

We think the sense of personal time is integrated in the sphere of the subject because the extended sense of purpose that orients the subjective sense of a continuity in identity during this stage of life is rooted in the tertiary areas of the dominant hemisphere prefrontal cortex. Analagously, the sense of personal space that comprises the social world is rooted in the tertiary cortex of the nondominant hemisphere. Just as the sensory basis of experience is integrated in the two hemispheres of reflection, so also are the driven origins of experience integrated in the two hemispheres. We theorize that the libidinal drive is integrated in the dominant hemisphere under the aegis of the function known as the ego-ideal, and that the aggressive drive is integrated in the nondominant hemisphere under the aegis of the function known as the superego.

The vast neuropsychological maturation triggers a synthetic fusing of the disparate neuropsychological systems resulting in the first permanent sense of unitary identity. Those separate systems of consciousness which we have been discussing—subject and object, reflection and experience—are joined in a new and complete apposition in latency which therefore deserves to be called the period of ego synthesis. For latency is the period in human life when the sense of permanent identity is formed, when the sense of memory becomes continuous, and when recollection responds to verbal cues.

In other words, the sense of mind as we know it as adults comes into a functional and recallable synthesis during the period of latency. The sense of time and space becomes continuously orienting during this era. The sense of identity which comes into enduring being is built on sediment of earlier childhood identities, and for the first time it includes a sense of future change. Time comes to have a subjectively conceived sense of development coextensive with the past and the future. The child's frequent concern with death at the onset of this age is more than the oedipal concern and fear, it is a sign of the recognition that the sense of identity, which has been attained with a feeling of great effort, can be lost. The anxiety over loss of ego synthesis becomes the over-riding anxiety of this era. A continuous panic ensues when desynthesis of the ego occurs in an adolescent or adult psychotic process.

The concept of space also becomes infinitely extendible during latency. The significance of space now extends beyond the three-dimensional sense of the body's sphere of activity to encompass first the neighborhood, and then a total geography of extended need fulfilling locations with their own organization, which must be learned. The spatial world comes to include an extended social milieu, the world of the father and the mother when they are away from home.

EGO-IDEAL AND SUPEREGO

The ego-ideal and the superego comprise the twin reflective functions that constitute morality. Morality is the overriding reflective function of this era comparable in importance to reality testing, internal narration, and judgment of earlier eras. Morality functions to preserve the identity synthesis of latency. The ego-ideal functions to regulate self-esteem and to preserve the sense of continuity in subjective identity. The regulation occurs via the ego's signal affect of shame, which arises in situations in which it is felt that there is not enough identity, or face, or esteem, or initiative, or effort, or maturation to perform successfully. There is a good example of shame morality expressed in Robert Herrick's poem, "The Scar Fire." It is a poem that expresses the moral force which must preserve overall identity, even if it means sacrificing libidinal aims.

The Scar Fire

Water, water I desire,
Here's a house of flesh on fire:
Ope' the fountains and the springs,
And come all to Buckettings:
What ye cannot quench, pull downe;
Spoile a house, to save a towne:
Better tis that one shu'd fall,
Then by one, to hazard all.

Professor J. Max Patrick, the editor of *The Complete Poetry of Robert Herrick,* says (1963) that a scar-fire is either "a sudden and dangerous fire or the fire alarm." We suggest that the *scar* in the title refers, also, to the scar that will be left if the "one" is made to fall or pulled down. Should the libidinal fire survive the poet's attempts to transform it into urine or sweat, we may suppose that the threat of scarring castration will be sufficient to dampen any hardy vestige of remaining ardor.

The superego comes to encompass the morality that determines the objective rules that govern the interrelationships in the social world. These objective rules, which are felt to exist outside of the mind, are represented intrapsychically by formulations, admonitions, and criticisms which, if breeched, give rise to a signal affect of guilt. The immersion in the social world which is so characteristic of latency accomplishes a kind of massive neutralization of the aggressive drive, and in this way puts a lid on the oedipal wishes.

Linguistic Considerations in Latency

In latency socially available symbols become available to language formation. As Freud said, this is the period in which culturally acquired information is transmitted to the school-age child and in which social authorities take on the authoritative aspects which had been ascribed previously to the parents alone. More, the experience of the social group of one's peers, club, or neighborhood bunch, intensifies the sense that one's aspirations or investigative motives are also shared and somehow derived from culture. The sense of objective self-observation is externalized, and attributed to the perfectability of group actions, such as jumping rope to time-honored patterns.

The idea of learning, of effortful connections between previously unconnected kinds of information, is applied to language development in this era. It is possible for the latency-age child to understand that there are different kinds of speech, that there is a grammar and a syntax which, even if it is difficult to structure into rules, is still present as a part of his own mind-structuring speech order, and is available for playful rearrangement. The latency child reflects on the experience of sentence arrangements that come to mind and fit in simultaneously with a set of rules which are certainly understood by teachers and other authority figures. This period engenders the sense of the mind's conscious structure as being composed of a part that is set off and capable of observing and criticizing, and is endowed with socially derived truth.

We tentatively put "anthemeria" forward as a scheme engendered in the developments of latency:

ANTHEMERIA

Anthemeria transforms one part of speech into another, for example:

> The thunder would not peace at my bidding—
> —*William Shakespeare*
> *King Lear,* (Act IV, Sc. iv)

The mechanism is engendered in verbal performance—in the playful alteration of the operative possibilities of syntax. The ability to imaginatively alter the use of parts of speech is rooted in the interaction between an imaginary and a real world of syntax, representing the creative alternative which was structured as one possible oedipal resolution. That it is a product of verbal performance indicates its generation in reflection. The device is a somewhat radical solution to expressive difficulties and therefore carries a sense of averted trauma—as is evident in this example—with its use.

LITERARY FORMS OF FIXATION

One assumption underlying our work is the notion that the creator's syndrome influences works of art through a fixation in the stages of creation which accompany the normal accession of identity in the life cycle. Now latency is the first stage in which a more or less complete mental world is created. This suggests that the creative person would retain some fixation to latency through the very fact that the creation of a mental world is endogenous to the creation of any work of art.

We would like to suggest also that fixation to particular stages of development can determine very much about the structure of a particular work, and even makes a contribution to the nature of the literary genre to which the work belongs. In previous eras of the life cycle we have seen that contributions to literature are made in the nature of literary kinds of language. For instance, we have seen that various schemes and tropes originate in particular eras of development, that symbols develop in response to oedipal kinds of trauma, that cadenced language originates in the rhythm that determines the introjection of syntax and so on.

The shattering of the oedipus complex in latency is really a transformation of the whole childhood organization of thinking. The primal scene which had been revised in terms of primary language formation and then remade to conform to the oedipal stage of life is transformed once again in latency. A new world is created in the latency, one that extends the primary and oedipal family to encompass the enlarged family of man, the community. The oedipal illusions of play and role formation is extended into a more realistic framework of peer groups dominated by rules and ideals that transform and sublimate the oedipal fancies.

There is a kind of literature or an aspect of it, which originates in the period of latency. Works of a new social order, the exploration of new and possible worlds, as in utopian works, take much from the transformations of latency.

New Atlantis *by Francis Bacon*

We would like to consider an example of the utopian literature to show how closely its construction parallels the syntheses of latency. We take *New Atlantis* by Francis Bacon as a prime example. As Freud shows in *Civilization and Its Discontents* (S. E. vol. XXI, p. 69), the buried city is an apt symbol for earlier modes of psychic integration. In replacing the old Atlantis, the *New Atlantis* evokes an image of a new society where an old one has been lost and buried.

The *New Atlantis* is a transformation of an old identity according to a new, logical, but visionary scheme. Bacon's utopia is presented in a fable. Now a fable is a device for extending a metaphor in time and space. It is also a device for bringing and transforming some sense of the past into the present as extended metaphor. This is precisely the work of latency. In fact, in a manner of speaking we may call this the inductive method. True, it is induction carried out without full conscious attention. But, like induction, it conveys experience of the past into a realm of new realization and conclusion. We should like to assert that this, Bacon's preferred mode of explanation, is the means by which the latency-age child transforms and sublimates the formal organization of his earlier modes of thinking. It is, neuropsychologically, a means of conveying tertiary revisions of experience to tertiary forms of reflection.

So we set off on a voyage with Bacon. It is a voyage of exploration recalling the finding of America, still mythologized in the seventeenth century as a land sprung up in place of the old Atlantis. We are born again, saved through our arrival, as one arrives in life's journey at a new stage—a new social order.

How do we come to know this new social order? The sequence of details in Bacon's fabled utopia follows the same sequence of discovery natural to the latency-age child. First we come to know the superstructure of the land. Like a threatened latency child going to school for the first time, we come to know the social structure, the rules and regulations, and the name of the place. It is Ben Salem. We recall that in latency the name of a place is steeped in social significance. The name conveys the whole history of the place and it conveys a sense of its possibilities. It is only later, after latency, when we learn that a name may convey more, or much less. We need to know the origin of the authority that steeps the place in its order and regulations in order for our induction to take hold, in order to know the basis for propriety in our actions in this new neighborhood of ours. So Bacon tells us of the founding Christian miracle that gave rise to the social order. It was a miraculous cylinder of light, we learn, cyclonic, and hidden from this world except to the true believer, the disciple of Christ.

Latency is the time of life when religious doctrine replaces the authority of the developmental experience of father. This cylinder of light is a nice symbol, because it acts as a channel to the past. It condenses the primary world where miracles, the creation of reality, did occur, before the resolution of the primal scene, with the ultrabright luster of the phallic endowment. Once we can believe the symbolism of the miracle of light we can delimit the world of infancy and early childhood, bringing it into the authority structure of the present. That is what Bacon does in the construction of his utopia. In fact the true believer allowed into the funnel of miraculous light on the sea offered the following prayer:

> Lord God of heaven and earth, thou hast vouchsafed of Thy grace to those of our order to know thy works of creation and the secrets of them, and to discern (as far as appertaineth to the generations of men) between divine miracles, works of nature, works of art, and impostures and illusions of all sorts.

The reference to the impostures and illusions serves to bind the oedipal period fantasies, and to bring them also into the channel of availability, as works of art.

Given the prayer, the laws follow; and following the laws the history of the place and its manner of inculcation are made clear. God created the house of Salomona, the center of the light which illuminates Ben Salem. The verbal similarity binds the sense of the place to the name of the one who was given the light of the laws. Then the elder who has been relating the history of Ben Salem gives an interpretation to Bacon's protagonist: "We maintain a trade, not for gold, silver, or jewels, nor for silks, nor for spices, nor any other commodity of matter, but only for God's first creature, which was *light,* to have *light* (I say) of the growth of all parts of the world." Now this is an interpretation of the transformations of latency. The infantile and early childhood drives are transformed so that the world can be grown into.

The next stage in the entry into the world of Bacon's utopia is the description of the ceremony of the feast of the family. It is a ritualized rendition of the earlier giving of the laws. In this case the father of the family presides over the ceremony at a time in his life when 30 of his offspring are alive and beyond the age of three. It is a kind of family circle honoring the procreation of the father. This is myth making and ritual making. As a ceremony it has the effect of making social myth out of the earlier symbol of procreation. Its relevance to our understanding of latency, however, is that it orders authority from God, to the community, to the family in the community.

This fabled ceremony must remind the modern reader of Freud's *Totem and Taboo.* Indeed, the next part of the story deals with the lack of incest. But the theme of the identification with the community through the identification with the power vested in the father has roots in the advent of latency, an element neglected by Freud in his consideration of the subject. The point we wish to make is that the formation of ritual to support the mythology underlying social structure is a natural outgrowth of the period in latency when reflection has been socialized and is capable of constantly transforming, sublimating, and rechanneling the earlier experience of childhood.

Finally, the transformations of latency are summarized and codified through the inculcation and tutelage in the actual practices and structure of the society. It is much like going to a school to learn the complete knowledge and practices of society. One of the fathers of Salomona's house tells the protagonist of the very ideal and wonderful achievements of his culture. It is a divination of secrets and codes—precisely the organization that is sought and codified in secret societies, clubs, and gangs.

God bless thee, my son; I will give thee the greatest jewel I have. For I will impart unto thee, for the love of God and men, a relation of the true state of Salomon's house. Son, to make you know the true state of Salomon's house, I will keep this order. First, I will set forth unto you the end of our foundation. Secondly, the preparations and instruments we have for our works. Thirdly, the several employments and functions whereto our fellows are assigned. And fourthly, the ordinances and rites which we observe.

We shall not enter into a description of these givens, except in a summary way. The protagonist is told of the preservation of social life, of the use of space and of materials, of the means to harness nature. He is told of the means to effect living things to improve commerce, of the experimental method by which this is carried out, of the inductive method which supports science. He is told of the means of manufacture. He is told how the teaching facilities are based on an elaboration of each sense, and beyond the education of the senses how the body's energy and locomotion are augmented. He is told of the various performing arts and how they are used for the edification of the senses. In essence he is told how platonic ideals can be translated into the realm of real life. He is told of the roles which are possible for individuals in this society. Bacon's utopia is a description of the ideal feelings that attend the whole gamut of latency experience and reflections.

THE CREATOR'S SYNDROME IN LATENCY

The latency-age creator (five to 11) identifies his mind as it comes into continuity with the created alternates—the work of art. The future literary creator identifies his mind imaginatively with the text, objectified as The Book. Books are taken as an example of minds fixed and in function. Hence the mind is taken as an instrument of artifice, an extension of fantasies vastly elaborated during this period. The latency-age creative child is secretive. His imagined text-fantasy is his secret. The illegitimacy of his strivings produces a barrier and conveys a sense of solitude to the child. He reserves his creativity from his family and from his peers, and the creative fantasies become a compensation, secretly held to buffer the detached sense of participation and lack of satisfaction in the new social world.

The genre of the autobiographical essay illuminates this period in the life history of the creator, for most autobiographers believe that their importance lies in the history of their own creator's syndrome. An examination of autobiographical essays finds the sense of their ontology extending back into the latency. It is a common heritage of creative individuals that they strive to create their own significance and to escape from the normal resolution of the oedipal period. That is to say, they attempted to render the circumstances of their existence as self-made and self-legitimized. The details of their childhood existence are molded into stories about the development of their alternative identity as creator which veil the givens of their circumstance. This is, of course, the essence of the creator's syndrome, optimistically to set forth a work, be it an elaboration of fantasy or a story, which will compel an audience to legitimize it, and in legitimizing it to give satisfaction to the creator. Thus the work of the creative autobiography is to set forth the imposture as the author as gradually credible, to himself and to his later audience.

The autobiography of the artist, like his other works, focuses on the growth of the creator's syndrome as it is generalized in the particular individual. It is because of this provisional quality that the creative person may elaborate intimate details of his life without invading the privacy of his personal life.

The Words *by Jean-Paul Sartre*

A prime example of the genre is *The Words* by Jean-Paul Sartre. Because of a fact of his personal history—the death of his father soon after his birth—Sartre's autobiography exemplifies the plasticity of reality in the latency-age experience of a future creator. The lack of belief in the father's supremacy during this age, which belief is a natural outgrowth of the resolution of the oedipus, leads to the abnormal latency age belief in the excessive mutability of reality, of time and space during the latency. To be more specific, we contend that Sartre's feeling of objectified impostership during his latency is directly related to a failure to model his own objectified self-image on the image of a father who is contained within an ordinary social world. Sartre's comprehensive exploration in *St. Genet,* of Jean Genet's latency-age identification as a thief suggests the intensity of Sartre's own fixation on latency identity. The social designation as creator or genius compels quite as much future objectification of identity as the social designation as thief.

Sartre's *The Words* has a translucent quality. The man looks back at his origins in latency with a kindly, semi-neutral, totally observant retrospection. His searching gaze penetrates far enough into the latency child that the reader has a sense of the boy's origins always illuminating a smooth, inviting, latency-age consciousness. From his old man's vantage, Sartre manages to associate into the boy's mind in a series of episodes which are tied together by the organic principle of the growth of the young writer. The reader's empathy is invited up to the point where the reader might develop the wish to possess totally the young man as a child of the reader's own consciousness, and at that point the episode breaks off with something like an intellectual threat. It is the common caveat of the creative writer, that he cannot be possessed completely through his work, because, after all is said, it is a fiction.

In the beginning of the autobiography, when he is tracing the origins of his grandparents and his parents Sartre has an ironic, even humorous voice. The irony is always present throughout the autobiography, but it tends to disappear in proportion to the closeness with which the old man allows himself to really assume the voice of the child as his own once again. Of course, all reflective devices, irony included, protect the user from the effects of old traumas. It is a maxim, perhaps, that no one transcends one stage of life, entering into the next, without some sense of relief: "I'm better out of it." Sartre masters his object, the boy-creator-in-the-world, but to the extent that the boy felt himself to be totally objectified as a creative performer dependent on the observer for his existence, is threatened with extinction of his identity.

This is Sartre's existential problem. Such self-objectification in latency is the dilemma of that particular character disorder we have been naming the creator's syndrome. We think Sartre would have agreed with us in this contention, because it is only through maintaining some provisional sense of the alternative, creative identity that the creative person protects himself from the psychotic process that would be induced through entering completely into the created character and losing touch with the world.

The death of Sartre's father, besides setting up a spate of organizing fantasies activated through each stage of Sartre's life, lent itself to a particular kind of latency which was to be the main avenue of Sartre's exploration of himself. The normal latency child finds himself objectified in terms of the father's authority. Sartre took the grander authority of his grandfather as a more omniscient reflection model under which he established the category of the self-as-creator. And he felt that he possessed his mother, since there was no father to possess her; she was his playmate, sleeping in a twin bed next to him through his latency.

The danger in this kind of situation is the fantasy that the father who is dead, will nevertheless exert himself, destroying the usurper at the exact moment of total possession of the mother, which happens to be the same moment that the young creator identifies completely with the self of his imaginary hero. Thus the identification with the reality of the father is to be complete in the death of the son.

This explains the tension which is ever present in the autobiography between the self striving to become the complete creator, and the self which must in all humility acknowledge that he is only pretending, only an imposter. We would like to explore these themes through a series of quotes from the work, taken from the chronological sequence of the book itself. The quotes will be taken from the 1964 Fawcett edition of *The Words*.

> In 1904, at Cherbourg, the young naval officer who was already wasting away with the fevers of Cochin-China, made the acquaintance of Anne Marie Schweitzer, took possession of the big, forlorn girl, married her, begot a child in quick time, me, and sought refuge in death. (p. 9)

> There is no good father, that's the rule. . . . Had my father lived, he would have lain on me at full length and would have crushed me. (p. 11)

> Command, obey, it's all one. The bossiest of men commands in the name of another—his father—and transmits the abstract acts of violence which he puts up with. (p. 12)

He goes on to describe his grandfather's adulation of him in public. His grandfather admired his own generosity as it was manifested in his poses with the child. Only the grandmother, Louise, saw through the tableau which these two put on, so admired by Anne Marie.

> In point of fact, Louise had seen through me. She openly found fault with me for the hamming with which she dared not reproach her husband: I was a buffoon, a clown, a humbug. (p. 21)

He goes on to make the statement of the nascent creator:

> Am I therefore Narcissus? Not even that. Too eager to charm, I forget myself. After all, it doesn't amuse me very much to make

> mudpies, to scribble, to perform my natural functions: in order
> for these to have value in my eyes, at least one grown-up must
> go into raptures over my products. (p. 25)

Sartre continues his saga of provisional identification with
an object in the world defined by others. But here the intermediary is the book. It is the experience of being the audience,
somehow validating the object, which if it could be produced
by him could also be validated by some other audience. In this
experience the story-book becomes a whole possible mind, even
a set of two minds communicating, even a whole, provisional
social world. It is an ordinary experience, made extraordinary
because it is speaking the language of the creator's syndrome,
for the first time, to one who comes to find that that is his
natural language. It is like greeting an unknown friend.

> I was bewildered: who was telling what, and to whom? My
> mother had gone off: not a smile, not a sign of complicity, I was
> in exile. And besides, I didn't recognize her speech. Where had
> she got that assurance? A moment later, I realized: it was the
> book that was speaking. Frightening sentences emerged from it:
> they were real centipedes, they swarmed with syllables and let-
> ters, stretching their diphthongs, made the double consonants
> vibrate. Singing, nasal, broken by pauses and sighs, rich in un-
> known words, they were enchanted with themselves and their
> meanderings without bothering about me. Sometimes they disap-
> peared before I was able to understand them; at other times I
> understood them in advance. . . . Someone began to ask ques-
> tions. . . . It seemed to me that a child was being questioned. . . .
> But that child was not quite I, and I was afraid to answer.
> Nevertheless I did. My weak voice faded, and I felt myself be-
> coming someone else. Anne Marie, with her blind extra-lucid
> look, was also someone else. It seemed to me that I was a child
> of all mothers, that she was the mother of all children. (p. 29)

Then came a great discovery. He himself, through a special
exertion of his pretense, could become the audience to the
creative mind impostering as book. He learned that his own

reflection was capable of giving objective being to the scope of pretended self. He learned how to read. Rather, he discovered reading.

> I then became jealous of my mother and resolved to take her role away. I got my hands on a work entitled *Tribulations of a Chinese in China* and went off with it to a store-room. There, perched on a cot, I pretended to read. My eyes followed the black signs without skipping a single one, and I told myself a story aloud, being careful to utter all the syllables. . . . I went through every page of it, one after the other. When the last page was turned I knew how to read.
> I was wild with joy. They were mine, those dried voices in their little herbals, those voices which my grandfather brought back to life with his gaze. (p. 30)

He learned a truth of artistic creation which took him 30 years until his maturity to unlearn. He learned that the province of created words was as real as what he came across in his own experience. It was the necessary fiction.

> There I would take real birds from their nests; would chase real butterflies that alighted on real flowers. Men and animals were there 'in person': the engravings were their bodies, the texts were their souls. (p. 32)

He felt himself in the company of illustrious authors and their characters. *T. W.* demonstrates how Sartre developed perspective on this necessary illusion.

> What I have just written is false. True. Neither true nor false, like everything written about madmen, about men. . . . I realized later that we can know everything about our attachments except their force, that is, their sincerity. Acts themselves cannot serve as measuring-rods unless one has proved that they are not gestures. (p. 43)

He goes on about his puzzling and paradoxical sense of imposture.

> I would turn to the grown-ups, I would ask them to guarantee
> my merits. In doing so I sank deeper into the imposture (p. 52)

> I escaped into the family play-acting, twisting and turning, flying
> from imposture to imposture. I fled from my unjustifiable body
> and its dreary confidences. . . . I'm a dog. I yawn, the tears roll
> down my cheeks, I feel them. I'm a tree, the wind gets caught
> in my branches and shakes them vaguely. I'm a fly, I climb up
> a window-pane, I fall, I start climbing again. (p. 58)

He enters into an impassioned explanation about why he
had to start writing himself. It begins with an apology for his
pretenseful avoidance of resolving the questions of authority in
his life, and ends with an explanation of why he had to write
in order to be reborn of his own intentions. He must turn the
imaginary child who exists in the forbearance of his adults into
a self-created child who exists through his own efforts.

> Since nobody laid claim to me seriously, I laid claim to being
> indispensable to the universe. (p. 69)

He recounts this in a parable. He finds himself aboard a
train without a ticket. He does not question the authority that
demands the ticket, nor does he question that he has no ticket
of conveyance. Instead he pleads a higher authority which requires that he be given passage for the good of mankind.

> The train, the ticket collector and the delinquent were myself.
> And I was also a fourth character, the organizer, who had only
> one wish, to fool himself, if only for a minute, to forget that he
> had concocted everything. . . . feminized by maternal tenderness,
> dulled by the absence of the stern Moses who had begotten me,
> puffed with pride by my grandfather's adoration, I was a pure
> object. . . . In order to escape the forlornness of the creature, I
> was preparing for myself the most irremediable bourge as soli-
> tude, that of the creator. . . .
>   Everything took place in my head. Imaginary child that I
> was, I defended myself with my imagination. When I examine
> my life from the age of six to nine, I am struck by the continuity

of my spiritual exercises. Their content often change, but the program remained unvaried. I had made a false entrance; I withdrew behind a screen and began my birth over again at the right moment, the very minute that the universe silently called for me. (pp. 70–71)

At the beginning of his writing Sartre felt he had found a new form of imposture, the cloak of plagiarism. His first work as a latency-age child, like the first dream in analysis, or the first production of any stage of life bears witness to the dynamics of the epoch. Sartre's first work bore the name *For A Butterfly* and it was really dedicated to that portion of the muse, the fetish portion, that protects young heroes from the sure destruction and anxiety which the elaboration of their oedipal fantasies in their own print would surely bring.

Hardly did I begin to write than I laid down my pen to rejoice. The imposture was the same, but I have said that I regarded words as the quintessence of things. Nothing disturbed me more than to see my scrawls little by little change their will-o-the-wisp gleam for the dull consistency of matter. It was the realization of the imaginary. . . . The first story I completed was entitled *For a Butterfly*. A scientist, his daughter, and an athletic young explorer sailed up the Amazon in search of a precious butterfly. (p. 87)

He tells how he had plagiarized the whole thing from a quarterly magazine and he comments wryly about the plagiarism:

If, as is commonly believed, the inspired author is other than himself in the depths of his soul, I experienced inspiration between the ages of seven and eight.

We see the young Sartre cloaking his identity by escaping into reflection, or by segregating the identity of the imaginary hero from himself and reflecting on that.

> The collector of butterflies and his daughter, who had been separated by a stroke of fate and were then aboard the same ship without knowing it and victims of the same shipwreck, clung to the same life-buoy, raised their heads and cried out: "Daisy!", "Papa!" Alas, a shark was on the prowl for fresh meat; it drew near; its belly shown in the waves. Would the unfortunate pair escape death? I went to get the volume "Pr-Z" of the Big Larousse, carried it painfully to my desk, opened it to the right page, and, starting a new paragraph, copied out, word for word, "Sharks are common in the South Atlantic."

Of course the young Sartre did not know that his plagiarized tale contained the nucleus of his past history, mother and grandfather thrown back together, and so on.

> As author, the hero was still myself; I projected my epic dreams upon him. All the same, there were two of us: he did not have my name, and I referred to him only in the third person. I fashioned for him, by means of words, a body that I made an effort to see. This sudden "distancing" might have frightened me; it charmed me. I was delighted to be him without his quite being me. He was my doll. . . . In order to save his fiancée and future father-in-law, the young explorer in *For A Butterfly* fought the sharks for three days and three nights; in the end the sea was red. (p. 91)

> By writing I was existing, I was escaping from the grown-ups, but I existed only in order to write, and if I said "I", that meant "I who write." (p. 95)

Sartre describes identifying his purpose in writing with the high ideal goal of saving mankind, of preserving its thought. It was a sacred kind of order. Thus his latency reflection came to be identified with symbols of religious necessity. In the background his grandfather lurked as the essence of the judgmental reader who validates the essential reflective and religious purpose of the writing. It is a function in latency mental organization to identify the individual conscience with the values of mankind which exerts an order on the organization of reflection and hence of identity. The bisexual portion of the reflective religious order became symbolized as the holy ghost. And the symbol of the holy ghost is a bird, an extension of the necessary butterfly, or the necessary angel.

> The product of that amalgam was the Holy Ghost, patron of the arts and letters, of dead and modern languages, and of the Direct Method, a white dove that gratified the Schweitzer family with its apparitions, that fluttered on Sundays, over organs and orchestras and perched, on working days, on my grandfathers' head. (p. 111)

> The day that I discovered Chanticleer, a knot was formed in my heart, a tangle of snakes that it took me thirty years to disentangle: thrashed, lacerated and bleeding, that rooster finds a way of protecting a whole barnyard; his song is enough to put the hawk to flight, and the base throng showers praise on him after having jeered at him. . . . Chanticleer would be me. It all looked simple: to write is to add a pearl to the Muses' necklace. . . . It did not occur to me that one could write in order to be read. (p. 112)

With this statement Sartre recalls that it was not until his maturity some 30 years later that he cured himself of the creator's syndrome enough to truly address the common concerns of mankind. He goes on to tell how he began to enjoy some respite from his latency-age creator's syndrome. The solitary and friendless child finally found friends, and the importance of the centralizing creative organization receded for a while. But first, Sartre brought his latency fantasy of future greatness as a writer to its very central essence. He showed the grandiose identification of the latency child with the notion of adult identity.

> The Holy Ghost and I held secret meetings. "You'll write," he said to me. I wrung my hands: "What is there about me, Lord that has made you choose me?—"Nothing in particular."—"Then why me?"—"For no reason."—"Do I at least have an aptitude for writing?"—"Not at all. Do you think that great works are born of flowing pens?"—"Lord since I'm such a

nonentity, how could I write a book?"—"By buckling down to it." (p. 116)

> I could appear to the Holy Ghost as a precipitate of language, could become an obsession to the species, could in short be other, other than myself, other than others, other than everything. I would start by giving myself an indestructible body, and then I would hand myself over to the consumers. I would not write for the pleasure of writing, but in order to carve that glorious body in words. . . . When the work was done . . . Around 1955, a larva would burst open, twenty-five folio butterflies would emerge from it, flapping all their pages, and would go and alight on a shelf of the National Library. Those butterflies would be none other than I. (p. 121)

The butterfly was the symbol of Sartre's latency age identity as a future creator.

Chapter 8

LOVING THE MUSE

Adolescence—Age 11 to 21

Sexual identity is realized in adolescence. Sexual awareness is engendered in the prelude to, during, and in the aftermath of falling in love. The work of adolescent identity formation includes formulating functional genital expectations. This requires a revival of and working through of feelings toward the oedipal love objects, a transferring and then sublimating of the old affections to new and extrafamilial objects. The adolescent bisexual alternative, which is enormously intensified in the future creator, is a normal stage and variant in this process, for this is the age of sexual idealization. Genital oriented fantasies of ambition, conquest, and romance charge all intimacies with supernatural affection and dread. The creative adolescent is prone to condense and unify his wishes and fears. Freud, for instance, revived and inflamed his childhood passion for Gisela. We quote Eissler (1978) in his article on *Creativity and Adolescence.*

The sexual excitement during the railroad trip home is evident
from Freud's reaction to a 12-year-old girl whom he described
as having the head of an angel and a face so neutral that it
possibly might turn into that of a boy. But most important, we
learn Gisela's nickname, "Ichthyosaura," meaning an aquatic
reptile of dinosaurian proportions, that is, in man's imagination
a fear arousing beast. (p. 471)

In further evidence of Freud's adolescent pursuit of the
sexual phallic composite, Eissler goes on to cite Freud's adolescent dissection of hundreds of eels determining, as he did, that
the eel is a bisexual creature. Future creators fall in love with
a bisexually conceived person who comes to have the inspiring
and trauma-reducing qualities of the muse. The muse is built,
as we see in the case of Freud, on the oedipal phallic woman,
and therefore must literally be perceived as containing the fetish
equivalent of the bisexual genitals.

We can surmise, then, that the future creator does not give
his love entirely to the object. Instead the love object functions
as an alternative to a real person in the world. The love object
of the future creator person is, in adolescence, experienced as
the inspirer of works and personal revelation. If the normal
prototype of adolescent love engenders a sense of sexual identity, then the love of the muse engenders the wish to produce
works to love, representations of the muse which act as an
intermediary to the real world.

In sum, muse consciousness refers to the adolescent experience of complete identity between the love indwelling in the
intrapsychic world and everything that exists in the extrapsychic world. The creator loves whatever exists and wishes to
capture that experience in his work.

INTRAPSYCHIC CONSIDERATIONS

In adolescence there is a new surge of libidinal current,
accompanying the new physiologically induced genital compe-

tence. The surge redirects the focus of reflective consciousness to the subjective side of mental life. The adolescent is filled with initiatory urgency. The adolescent wants to bring his love objects right into the center of his own subjective experience. The conflicts which this wish for intense intimacy engenders release the regressive creative process, which functions to restructure personal identity throughout adolescence. The adolescent must reshape his own objective self-representations so that they encompass the new body with its genital competence and a mind with the capacity to fall in love.

The era of adolescence is suffused with a consciousness of love. As Freud says in his paper "On Narcissism" the state of falling in love is one in which the subject feels that love and the conditions for self-esteem are poured into the object of love. (S. E. vol. XIV, p. 100) The subject is dependent on that object for a feeling of return of love. This all makes for a radical transformation of identity in adolescence.

Those feelings of mutual love engender prolonged states of empathy, and maintenance of empathy becomes the precondition for the maintenance of mental synthesis, which is to say the maintenance of sanity. Therefore object relatedness becomes a mandatory condition of mental health. The major conflict that revolves around the introduction of sexualized empathy concerns the shift of feelings of love from members of the immediate family to some chosen persons outside the family. The prototypical conflicts have to do with the adolescent's sense of reluctance to grow up and to move out of the family to satisfy his conditions of existence and mental balance.

Primal scene and oedipal interests are shifted from family onto members of the adolescent's own generation. The danger experienced in this shift is loss of identity. Heretofore, identity had been circumscribed by the family's relationship to the prevailing culture. The loss of this stabilizing influence combined with the sense of loss of identity in falling in love threatens the sense of stability of the intrapsychic world—hence the intense fears of separation from the family and the reluctance to accept the conditions of growing up.

Creative identity in adolescence is characterized by love for the muse. The idealized yearnings of the adolescent creator find satisfaction in the long-haired, long-limbed text. The work is the supernatural, bisexually condensed object of satisfaction. It is equated with the life of imagination in adolescence. Relating to the work is an alternative to the normal conflicts revolving around love of some particular person. The muse figure becomes the organizing focus for the sexual metaphor of adolescence. The work takes on the significance of compromise formation, which is necessitated by the bisexual identification of the creative person. The creative person falls in love with the muse. She belongs to him, and she belongs to the world. The provisional bisexual identification of the creative person is cemented in the love for the muse, the love of creating, subjectifying the world.

LINGUISTIC CONSIDERATIONS (THE LANGUAGE OF LOVE)

The extended sexual metaphor, the language of love, is the natural expressive voice of adolescents. The intense preoccupation with genital orgasm and the accompanying fantasies require a major revision of the reflective surface of consciousness in order to avoid an immersion in trauma-inducing actions. The substitution of the language of sexual metaphor for acting out gives the adolescent a safe field for testing the possibilities inherent in relationship. When the sexual metaphor on both sides becomes identity, that experience is an introduction to the communication of love. It is a prelude to genital action. Reflection is suspended when communication is complete. Extended metaphor melts.

Reflective identity is sacrificed for the identity experienced with the beloved. Adolescent language is an invitation to love. Many late adolescents consciously imbue their own voice with significance of pleasure—they hear their own voice as one continuous love song. Closely allied to this technique for seduction is the attainment of a new rhetorical scheme—the rhetorical question. "Do not ask what it is, Let us go and make our visit," Eliot says. The rhetorical question is a powerful device for subjectifying the world. It is an insistent request for the audience to enter into the subjective world of the speaker's pleasure.

Rhetorical questions are questions asked not for the sake of concrete answer, but for the rhetorical effect of leading the listener into the speaker's world.

EXAMPLE

> How many roads must a man walk down
> Before people call him a man?
> How many seas must the white dove sail
> Before she can sleep in the sand?
> —*Bob Dylan*
> "Blowin' in the Wind"

Dylan invites the listener to contemplate his own struggle to find an authentic identity as a creator.

"Leda and the Swan" by William Butler Yeats

Some of the most powerful literary figures in the English language are attained when eroteans are coupled with the questioner's identification with the muse. Yeat's "Leda and the Swan" demonstrates this mechanism. As a composite figure, Leda-and-the-Swan has the significance of the muse figure which dwells in and animates the work. It is the composite image which the speaker identifies with in the process of forming the poem. At the end then, when the speaker wonders, "Did she put on his knowledge with his power, Before the indifferent beak could let her drop?" the question asks whether the poem itself achieves its climax. It asks whether the fusion of the poet with his muse was complete. The answer to the question can only lead one in to the omniscient pose of reflection when it is structured by such a creative identification.

Leda and the Swan

A sudden blow: the great wings beating still
Above all the staggering girl, her thighs caressed
By the dark webs, her nape caught in his bill,
He holds her helpless breast upon his breast.

How can those terrified vague fingers push
The feathered glory from her loosening thighs?
And how can body, laid in that white rush,
But feel the strange heart beating where it lies?

A shudder in the loins engenders there
The broken wall, the burning roof and tower
And Agamemnon dead.

Being so caught up,
So mastered by the brute blood of the air,
Did she put on his knowledge with his power
Before the indifferent beak could let her drop?

The first two questions are rhetorical, the last questioning takes on the power of these rhetorical questions before the poem can drop to a conclusion.

THE CREATOR'S SYNDROME IN ADOLESCENCE

Between the ages of 10 and, say, 21, the creative person comes to a consciousness of his creative expression. In some material form—literary, scientific, philosophical—the muse becomes available to reflection.

Probably, most creative works exist in the normative, museless condition, for, as one would expect, composite figures are characteristic of works about creativity and/or reflections on the origin (usually in the self) of creative production. The appearance of the muse in a work is revealing. It is a sign of the "creative" and "normal" selves' achievement of mutual access. These selves are distinct until, during an intense adolescent experience of epiphany, they enter into a conjunctive relationship.

THE EPIPHANIES OF ADOLESCENCE

James Joyce called any sudden revelation of the nature of experience an epiphany. Adolescence is the most common period of epiphanies, though Joyce did write epiphanies for older people. In *Dubliners,* for example, older people experience epiphanies. But the habit of epiphany is Joyce's; it is a habit originating in youth: the prototypical example of an epiphany is Stephen Dedalus's experience with the birdlike woman, his muse.

The muse enters the creator's syndrome as a complete alternative identity in the epiphany of the creator's adolescence. There are two sides to the consciousness associated with the muse. The first is musing—a generalized reflection on the creative relationship with reality. The second is the experience of the muse as a figure of intrapsychic inspiration who may be possessed in the real world. The muse takes on its full significance after an adolescent epiphany in which identity as a creator is realized after the appearance of the muse figured in reality. The creator identifies with the muse.

The epiphany occurs when, in a state of intense turmoil and unresolvable tension the adolescent suddenly finds his longing personified and embodied in the figure of the muse. The newly found image of love takes up residence—like a transitional object—with one foot in reality and the other in a newly synthesized reflective state of speculative romantic ardor. The appearance of the bisexual composite in reality gives this stage in the development of the creator's syndrome the fixity of a perversion, for the creator dedicates himself to recreating the experience of finding the muse figure. The creator wants to bring the muse experience back to life under the auspices of his work. James Joyce's *A Portrait of the Artist as a Young Man* is typical.

Portrait is the autobiography of an artist. Its adolescent epiphanies exemplify the intersection of normal and creative personality. In *Portrait* avatars of the muse facilitate the creator's search for perfect, illusory erotic pleasure. At the center of *Portrait* is an experience with a muse figure. Such experiences remained the focal points of Joyce's adult creativity.

Richard Ellman's complete and intimate biography, *James Joyce,* makes it possible for us to put *Portrait* into the context of Joyce's life. In it we see factors in Joyce's life experience and innate disposition which determined the nature of Joyce's creator's syndrome.

Joyce presented his experience and left it to the reader to develop a perspective on the experience. In other words, Joyce expected the reader to take on some of the synthetic function that had traditionally belonged to the author. Joyce's adolescent-style habit of rendering his experience as it flowed intrapsychically made it possible for other artists to display their experience closer to its genesis in the artist's consciousness.

Joyce's relationship to his audience is heavily overdetermined by his relationship to his father, a relationship which was fixed to the circumstances of Joyce's anal-auditory period of life. Here we will investigate *Portrait* as Joyce's fixations determine its composition.

James Joyce was the first surviving child of a 21-year-old, sweet-tempered mother and a 31-year-old father who welcomed the boy as the second coming of James's grandfather, who had died when his father was an adolescent. Another son, born about a year before, had not survived, so James was doubly welcome. The many children who came after James were not as welcome, since each one added a debit to the family's failing fortunes. Still, James was always treated with a special indulgence. He was to fulfill the father's unfulfilled and flagging ambitions. According to Ellman the Joyces were a musical family. James's father was said to have been a tenor almost unparalleled in the Ireland of his time. James inherited his father's famous tenor voice, the same sure ear, and the penchant for telling fabulous stories.

The combination of weak eyes and a strong aural disposition disposes a person to a particular kind of resolution of the primal scene trauma. James was disposed to take in whole phrases and rhythms in situations of intense stimulation. As a primal scene figure his father was often drunk, rollicking, singing, chanting—insistently possessing his wife with the strength of his voice.

James introjected his father's voice, rhythms, phrases, aphorisms and expletives, producing a whole mélange of intoned prosody with which to bind the overstimulation that filled his life: Joyce was able to tolerate a cacophony without hearing it as one. His special talent in discriminating elements of the aural world and binding vast amounts of introjected syntax lent itself to a fixation in the anal-auditory stage of life. Thus Joyce's anal fixation amounted to a strong identification with the phrase making of his irrepressible father. With this fixation it was inevitable that Joyce would retain a strongly ambivalent need for a father figure in his life.

Joyce's oedipal period and entrance into latency were heavily influenced by a newcomer into the family scene. Dante Conway joined the family after being jilted by a suitor who ran away with all her money. She undertook Joyce's early education with a mixture of fidelity and bitterness. She lectured him sternly on the perils of hell, and treated his interest in the five-year-old girl who lived across the street as if it were an indication that James would surely come to damnation.

Stanislaus, Joyce's ambivalently devoted, three years younger brother, tells a story about the six-year-old James's favorite game. James was the snake in the garden of Eden, sneaking around on the floor, while Stanislaus was Adam and sister Margaret was Eve. Joyce's phallic identification appears to have been based on a composite put together from his father and Dante. Dante taught him to fear the end of the world; thunderstorms were the warning sign. James developed a phobia for thunderstorms which lasted his lifetime. He could identity with the phallic Dante and his father as one unified composite with which to defend himself against the castration anxiety of the oedipal period. At the same time he could preserve his mother as the Madonna who was quiet and forebearing.

The same factors that disposed Joyce to take in a vast and rich concrete world of words disposed him to success in his latency. His talent for making easy language connections allowed him to stand out as a special student. Although he was frightened of the older children and his Jesuit teachers, and although he had a strong wish to submit to their authority, he did not. As he had done in the anal period of his life, he introjected the best and most intense of what his chums and teachers had to offer. He became something of a show-off for his peers.

Joyce's anal-aural fixation accounts for the accurate autobiographical detail in his novels. He held the introjected fragments of thousands of individuals in his mind, classified on the basis of how their speech sounded to him. He was able to draw easily from among these introjected personages, combining elements of one two or three into his created characters.

Just as his characters comprise an assemblage of introjects, so Joyce's construction turns on a loosely knit series of episodes. Key words carry the reader from one episode to another. Joyce condenses associative power into particular phrases, or words, as is characteristic of the anal-auditory stage use of words.

Joyce's creative problem, given the insistent anal/aural fixation, was to constitute an over-riding identity as a creator for himself. In part this was a problem of identifying the sources of authority within himself. This became a problem because Joyce's father was both an overwhelming figure and yet a fragmented one. Joyce could not thoroughly pattern his identification on the authority of his father though he certainly tried in the conduct of his ordinary life.

Joyce's solution to this problem was to find some external authority to be responsible for his creative life. Yeats and then Pound took on some of the guiding functions in Joyce's search for an avenue to his audience. An abstract audience was expected to put together the sometimes disparate nature of Joyce's prose, allowing Joyce himself to concentrate on the more intimate subjective aspects of his experience. But the main psychic avenue which allowed Joyce to constitute an identity for himself was the creative identification based on Joyce's love for the bisexual muse figure. Joyce's love for the muse brought him into contact with women. Otherwise he would have remained fixed to the image of the dirty cloacal woman, the prostitute split off from the presexual madonna. Joyce's devotion to the muse allowed him to explore the consciousness of women and to recognize his own female kinds of identification. The presence of muses in Joyce's work (Molly and her men, say) allowed Joyce to synthesize what would otherwise be an anal multitude of fragmented characters.

We have seen from *Portrait* that Joyce brought his identity as a creator into focus only after he became devoted to the muse figure. This devotion brought him into the possibility of experiencing the "Joy" contained in Joyce, his real namesake. Joyce's joy was in creating. *Portrait* is the story of Joyce's creation of his own identity as a professional creator.

THE CREATIVE SEQUENCE OF ADOLESCENT IDENTITY FORMATION IN *PORTRAIT*

Phase 1—Frustration in Latency

Joyce's anal fixation is clear enough, and clearly enough portrayed in *Portrait*. What interests us is the literary use the

anal fixation is put to, and the transformation of the anal prototype through the adolescent love of the muse. This transformation effects a change from an anal, disorderly character to the
identity of a creator.

The young Stephen is an orderly-disorderly boy, in constant turmoil over his impulse to submit to authority, to the
priests, or to the older boys. He resolves the first chapter in
Portrait, and the first phase of his identity transformation as it
is outlined in this book, by refusing to submit to authority. He
sets a certain obstinate standard of honesty for himself which
he will maintain despite whatever pain or terror, or even possibility of extinguished consciousness is set on him. In the first
chapter he gains autonomy and integrity.

Phase 2—Regression in Adolescence

In the second chapter the orderly and categorical resolutions of his latency are broken down by the genital urgency
which arises and carries him into a sense of his future identity
as a man in the world. He succumbs finally to the masturbatory
adolescent impulses and engages himself with prostitutes. Beset
with intensity he gives way to the epiphany of new consciousness. The way of this breakthrough is well paved with the lore
of his father's riotous conquests.

Phase 3—Primary Process in Adolescence

In the third chapter we see Stephen the future creative
hero quite vanquished by a return of terrorizing conscience. His
conscience speaks in the aural liturgical rhythms of the church.
Stephen re-experiences all of the pitfalls of tormenting, anal
conscience until he finally confesses his sins. The process of
suffering his torment also opens his mind to a sense of what is
eternal in life, a vista of future identity, and he becomes conscious of his responsibility to the future man he is becoming.

The resubmission to the anal prototype authority of the church does not, however, quench his longings for sexual freedom; not even the possibility of becoming a priest himself and wielding all the power of the church can quench his aroused adolescent longings.

At the height of his guilty torment he dreams of his own personal hell. It is a field of fecal demons come to torment him eternally with their issue of soft language. In the aftermath of this dream he confesses to a priest and feels that he has been forgiven.

Phase 4—Revision of Identity in Adolescence

In the fourth chapter his torment has given way to an obsessive-compulsive residue of symptoms. The anal disgust invades his senses, and he trys to accept these continuing signs of the Hell he might let himself in for if he succumbs to his feelings of arousal.

Approximately at this point Joyce arrested work on the book for a period of time. For at this point that it was necessary for him to remake his identity as a professional creator. Joyce's life had taken on the disorderly quality of an anal character who loses control of his destiny. His younger brother, Stanislaus, who lived with James and his wife, Nora, had taken of the authoritative role of the man of responsibility, earning money regularly and keeping emotional order in the house.

Resumed, Chapter 4 began the resolution of Joyce's stultified identity conflict. Joyce was able to mobilize his love and expressivity in the service of joining with the muse figure who is portrayed so clearly in this chapter. This resolution saved Joyce from submitting to the anal prototype so totally that he would have lost all possibility of creative expression. In the alternative guise of the muse prototype Joyce could come to look for women and men, jointly and separately, as sources of inspiration and of help. His voice was liberated.

Phase 5—Return to Reality: Adult Identity

The final chapter extends the resolution to become a professional creator into Joyce's adult life. In this there is a return to his present day reality. From the point of view of the creator's syndrome, the polemical last chapter is an assurance that Joyce knows his own literary voice and that he can use it and experiment with it. Through this work Joyce accepted the reality of his being an adult creator. The final structure of the work shows the phases of adolescent identity formation that every human being is bound to undergo in the creative sequence on the way from latency to adult identity formation.

A PORTRAIT OF JOYCE'S CREATIVE FIXATION

Joyce's *Portrait* is of a young man who resolves his adolescent identity crisis through the formation of an alternative identity as creator. Stephen Dedalus is an intense, talented, intellectual adolescent immersed in his discovery of the potential for genital satisfaction. He finds pleasure in intercourse with prostitutes. The pleasure is repeated over and over in masturbation. The intensity of this experience collides with Stephen's Jesuitical beliefs, and in a guilty act of contrition he confesses his sins and almost settles on a course destined to lead to an adult identity as a Jesuit priest. But this course, though it would appease his guilt and allow him to enter into an essentially homosexual, sadomasochistic relation to God-The-Father, denies Stephen the sexual pleasures of possessing a woman.

Unable to resolve this dilemma of adolescence, and traumatized during a Jesuit school retreat by an immersion in the pain and privation of an almost present Hell, Stephen retreats into a search for his roots in boyhood and early childhood. He experiences an epiphany, forming a new subjective sense of himself which is rooted in the image of Dedalus the fabulous artificer of antiquity. The voice of this great bird man of his mythic past fuses with his sense of poetical inspiration; Stephen sees a the bird-woman poised on one leg standing in water like a crane. Once entered into his mind this muse image of unsurpassing beauty remained as the eternal inspirer of Stephen's identity as a poet and writer.

In the epiphany of finding his new identity as a creator Stephen resolves the traumatic conflict of his adolescence. As the text shows, the bird-woman gives the poet in him a sense of a female soul wedded to a man's articulation. Stephen avoids the damnation which his guilt and his submissiveness require. He finds comfort and sexual gratification in possession of muse identity. This epiphany became the prototype for Joyce's adult creativity.

> Now, as never before, his strange name seemed to him a prophecy.... Now at the name of the fabulous artificer, he seemed to hear the noise of dim waves and to see a winged form flying above the waves and slowly climbing the air. What did it mean? Was it a quaint device opening a page of some medieval book of prophecies and symbols, a hawklike man flying sunward above the sea, a prophecy of the end he had been born to serve and had been following through the mists of childhood and boyhood, a symbol of the artist forging anew in his workshop out of the sluggish matter of the earth a new soaring impalpable imperishable being?
>
> His heart trembled; his breath came faster and wild spirit passed over his limbs as though he were soaring sunward. His heart trembled in an ecstasy of fear and his soul was in flight....
>
> His throat ached with a desire to cry aloud, the cry of a hawk or eagle on high, to cry piercingly of his deliverance to the winds....
>
> He would create proudly out of the freedom and power of his soul, as the great artificer whose name he bore, a living thing, new and soaring and beautiful, impalpable, imperishable.

Stephen walks up a rivulet away from the sea, feeling that his boyhood is over. He is alone and bursting with song.

A girl stood before him in midstream, alone and still, gazing out to sea. She seemed like one whom magic had changed into the likeness of a strange and beautiful seabird. Her long slender bare legs were delicate as a crane's and pure save where an emerald trail of seaweed had fashioned itself as a sign upon her flesh. Her thighs, fuller and softhued as ivory were bared almost to the hips where the white fringes of her drawer's were like feathering of soft white down. Her slateblue skirts were kilted boldly about her waist and dovetailed behind her. Her bosom was as a bird's soft and slight, slight and soft as the breast of some darkplumaged dove. But her long fair hair was girlish: and girlish, and touched with the wonder of mortal beauty her face.

She was alone and still, gazing out to sea; and when she felt his presence and the worship of his eyes her eyes turned to him in quiet sufferance of his gaze, without shame or wantonness. Long, long she suffered his gaze and then quietly withdrew her eyes from his and bent them towards the stream, gently stirring the water with her foot hither and thither. The first faint noise of gently moving water broke the silence, low and faint and whispering, faint as the bells of sleep; hither and thither, hither and thither; and a faint flame trembled on her cheek.

Heavenly God! cried Stephen's soul, in an outburst of profane joy.

He turned away from her suddenly and set off across the strand. His cheeks were aflame; his body was aglow; his limbs were trembling. On and on and on and on he strode, far out over the sands, singing wildly to the sea, crying to greet the advent of the life that had cried to him.

How phallic this muse-figure is: the emerald trail of seaweed fashioned as a sign upon her flesh seems to be a fetish.

In the aftermath of this experience Stephen goes to the university. At the university his mind is preoccupied with the development of his own personal aesthetic theory. It is clear that the aesthetic theory centers on and recreates the prototypical experience he has undergone in his own epiphany. The aesthetic theory becomes the basis for a whole reflective system which comforts Stephen in the privations and loneliness which are his lot as he sets out as a creator. Whenever he feels his theory may be destroyed by powerful arguments, he recalls the source of his very personal aesthetic, finding the original image of his muse still fresh and inspiring.

FIXATION TO EPIPHANY

While writing *Portrait*, James Joyce, the professional creator, used his work to screen the traumatic aspects of his life. Joyce wrote the first draft of *Portrait* when he was 21 during a visit to his family home after his mother's death. His father's decline and the neediness of his siblings must have touched Joyce. It is likely he covered his pain by setting to work on his manuscript, encouraged by his admiring brother Stanislaus, who actually suggested the title of the work. After the brief draft of *Portrait* was rejected for publication, Joyce set about revising it. Over the succeeding years it grew into an opus, *Stephen Hero*. But, like Joyce's adult life, *Stephen Hero* did not gell. Instead it remained the sustaining broth for much of Joyce's literary work, supplying the material for the later revisions of *Portrait* in addition to much of the material that ultimately went into *Ulysses.*

Joyce drank too much in his early twenties, and like his father before him, he spent too much time with cronies in bars. He was lost, living on the intensity of his experiences without putting together a life stable enough to provide him with a context from which he could synthesize his imaginative work. The solution to his dilemma came walking down the street, proud and tall, on June 10, 1904, in Joyce's twenty-third year. Nora Barnacle was Joyce's first effective muse representation.

For the adult creator a relationship with a mate is unusually problematic. Sometimes the mate is the outward representation of the muse. Then the artist may succumb to a temptation to possess his mate so completely as to drive her away. On the other hand, the mate is sometimes a transference object based on the artist's real mother or father; then the creative work becomes a rival to this relationship and a barrier to its continuity.

Joyce held Nora in a state of fluctuating significance. As a muse figure she was invested with bisexual significance, and she became a tormenting object of jealousy when Joyce connected her with male friends. As a mother figure Nora was expected to accept Joyce completely in all his childish, errant, unreliable ways.

In the thrill of sexual union with his muse figure, Joyce set back to work on *Stephen Hero*. But as Nora became more valuable to James, he saw her more and more as a mother. When she was a madonna, he had to stay away from her. To get away from the compelling tug of the maryolatrous religion of his childhood, James began his long odyssey, traveling with Nora to Trieste. Stanislaus followed, apparently moved by James's entreaties after the birth of his son. Joyce was not making a living. For some time Stanislaus supported the couple, while Joyce wrote erratically.

After a financially unsuccessful stay in Rome during Joyce's mid-twenties, the family returned to Trieste. Joyce developed rheumatic fever with severe iritis. He believed that he was dying, or if not dying, on his way to blindness. Frightened, he swore off drinking and resumed his work on *Stephen Hero*. At the same time Nora became pregnant with the girl who was to be called Lucia: light. Nora became bitter about Joyce's lack of support. Stanislaus was disgusted. James decided to return to Ireland, both to try to help along the publication of some works, and to re-establish his roots.

Still, in 1909 Nora was either Joyce's madonna or his muse. Early in the summer Joyce wrote to her: "O that I could nestle in your womb like a child born of your flesh and blood, be fed by your blood, sleep in the warm secret gloom of your body." (Ellman, p. 303) But while he was in Dublin, an old friend mischievously told Joyce that he had "known" Nora

before James and Nora had cemented their relationship. Lifted
to a pitch of acute jealousy and acuter longing, Joyce masculi-
nized Nora; she became his muse again. He wrote to her on
September 7,

> Tonight I have an idea madder than usual. I feel I would like to
> be flogged by you. I would like to see your eyes blazing with
> anger. I wonder is there some madness in me, or is love madness?
> One moment I see you like a virgin or madonna the next moment
> I see you shameless, insolent, half-naked and obscene. (Ellman,
> p. 296)

After his return to Trieste, Joyce invested Nora with another kind of reality. She was more than madonna or muse, she
became real.

Undergoing the problems of ill health, financial insecurity,
the birth of a child, the danger of losing his wife's and his
brother's affection, the perils of succumbing to alcohol, Joyce
turned back to *Stephen Hero*. He reduced its many chapters to
five descriptions of the development of the hero's identity.
Progress stopped again, though, apparently because his problems had been resolved for the time being. It had become necessary for Joyce to invest some other woman with the germinal
significance of muse. He found a Jewish girl, a student of his
who became his erstwhile muse as he finally wrote the bird-
woman into print and found his identity as a creator. Ellman
quotes Joyce's dream picture of his young student Amalia Popper: ". . . a little smooth naked body shimmering with silvery
scales. It slips slowly over the slender buttocks of smooth pol-
ished silver and over their furrow, a tarnished silver
shadow. . . . Great bows on her slim bronze shoes: spurs of a
pampered fowl." (Ellman, p. 354–355) Prototype for the bird-
woman this phallicized vision of Amalia Popper became the
basis for Stephen's aesthetic and literary consciousness.

WHITMAN'S EPIPHANY

Unlike Joyce, whose work is predetermined by an anal/auditory fixation, and who refuses the fusion of primary visual process, Whitman is a primal scene poet. Whitman's adolescent epiphany and discovery of voice is determined by primal scene imagery. His muse-bird speaks with the phallic disposition of the primal oral mother, which is the voice Whitman recollects in "Out of the Cradle Endlessly Rocking." Full of concern for beginnings, "Out of the Cradle" is a reminiscence, a rediscovery of the great moment when the child Whitman entered into first heartbreaking contact with his adult potential for poetry. Looking backward the grown poet intuitively rediscovers the child's transformations when certain feelings and possibilities in adolescence became a raison d'être.

> Demon or bird! (said the boy's soul)
> Is it indeed toward your mate you sing?
>   or is it really to me?
> For I, that was a child, my tongue's
>   use sleeping, now I have heard you,
> Now in a moment I know what I am for,
>   I awake,
> And I am already a thousand singers,
>   a thousand songs, clearer and more
>   sorrowful than yours,
> A thousand warbling echoes have started
>   to life within me, never to die.

Whitman wrote this poem after the death of his father, after Whitman had re-entered the family home as the head of the house, so that "Out of the Cradle" was written after Whitman had succeeded, if only by dint of physical survival, in supplanting his father. How very likely that the nature of events would prompt, in this least repressed of poets, a rediscovery and re-elaboration of the poet's notion of himself and the relation between his creativity and his sexual development.

Beautifully the poem begins with a return, a kind of controlled regression, to an earlier time, when the young boy became aware of the consanguinity of birth and death.

> Out of the cradle endlessly rocking,
> Out of the mocking-bird's throat,
>   the musical shuttle,
> Out of the nine month midnight . . .
> A man, yet by these tears a little boy again,
> Throwing myself on the sand, confronting
>   the waves,
> I, chanter of pains and joys, uniter of
>   here and hereafter,
> Taking all hints to use them, but swiftly
>   leaping beyond them,
> A reminiscence sing.

And so there is a reminiscence of the sea and of two birds who built their nest near the beach near Whitman's home. As it happened, the female bird, probably killed, once and forever failed to return to her mate and their four light-green eggs spotted with brown. For the rest of the summer the bird:

> . . . called on his mate
> He poured forth the meanings which I
>   of all men know.
> Yes, my brother I know,
> The rest might not, but I have treasured
>   every note,
> For more than once dimly down to the
>   beach gliding,
> Silent, avoiding the moonbeams, blending
>   myself with the shadows,
> Recalling how the obscure shapes, the
>   echoes, the sounds and sights after
>   their sorts,
> The white arms out in the breakers tire-
>   lessly tossing,

I, with bare feet, a child, the wind
    wafting my hair,
Listn'd long and long.

The listening boy recalls some moment of parental intercourse and hears in the sea "with angry moans the fierce old
mother incessantly moaning." In this way the bird becomes a
symbol onto which Whitman can project new and refound
subjective integration, for there is new mental integration, new
structuring, inherent in the recognition of the impossiblity of
oedipal gratification. So while the bird cries out for his mate,
the child cries:

O give me the clue! (it lurks in the night
    here somewhere,)
O if I am to have so much, let me have more!
A word then, (for I will conquer it.)
The word final, superior to all,
Subtle, sent up—what is it?—I listen:
Are you whispering it, and have been
    all the time, you sea waves?
Is that it from your liquid rims and
    wet sands?
Whereto answering, the sea,
Delaying not, hurrying not,
Whisper'd through the night, and very
    plainly before daybreak,
Lisp'd to me the low and delicious
    word death,
And again death, death, death, death,
Kissing melodious, neither like the
    bird nor like my arous'd child's heart,
But edging near as privately for me rustling
    at my feet,
Creeping thence steadily up to my ears and
    laving me softly all over,
Death, death, death, death, death.
Which I do not forget,
But fuse the song of my dusky demon and brother,

That he sang to me in the moonlight on
  Paumanok's gray beach,
With the thousand responsive songs at random,
My own songs awakened at that hour,
And with them the key, the word up from the waves,
The word of the sweetest song and all songs,
That strong and delicious word which, creeping
  to my feet,
(or like some old crone rocking the cradle,
  swathed in sweet garments, bending aside),
The sea whisper'd me.

And here, as clear as can be, is an image for the sudden conjunction of normal and creative selves. At last, the adult Whitman comes to a vision of the ache and sexuality of his fierce, old, widowed mother, longing for her dead husband. And so, in the man, the child's longing for his parent revives with the old force. With it is the endless realization of primal scene trauma, oedipal frustration, adolescent yearning, and reflection forcing the poet into a rediscovery of the creative resolution and identification with the phallic mother. And so a sort of muse is built up out of the phallic bird and the phallic and mothering sea, each bringing a lesson. The lessons are for the "normal" Whitman, and they are these: the poet is compelled to create as a way of expressing his wishes. These wishes have to do with the internalized object, the phallic mother, for the creative person keeps building the creative self as an object out of the intrapsychic composite parent (the phallic mother). The oceanic process of creating will continue till death, since only near birth and death is there the imagined satisfaction of complete possession by and of the mother. So only near in death will wishes cease to prevail.

In an epiphany, the sense of imminence is destroyed. The creator is privileged to perceive that "I am creating objects of value, now." The "I" of the present period, "now," seems "normal." The "I" of "creating" seems secret. The adverbial "now" forces on the creator a recognition of the ramifications of simultaneity. Returning to "Out of the Cradle," the repeated word "death" has another significance. It describes the end of consciousness, forcing on Whitman a perception of the value of "now." So there is a transcendence of the oedipally hungry man and by selves under the impulsion to create, now, since not to create is to be tending toward death, reflective entropy, seduced by the desire for the mother sea. Increasing reflection, and hence creation, produce an increment of subjective life.

This realization of simultaneity and the resulting fusion of the creative and normal "me," toward the conclusion of this period, forces the creator into a radical stance vis-à-vis the concensus opinion of external reality. This is like the first politicizing of reality (not necessarily the individual's ultimate stance), the stage during which normal and creative adolescents discover the disparities between the accepted social idealism and morality to which lip service is demanded, the actual morality, and the version of morality in which the adolescent has direct interest.

The frequently justified outrage and frustration of youth is mirrored in the creative adolescent's experience. The creative child emerges into adolescence craving an audience. His experience with his parents, with its root in the transitional period, has taught him that, by and large, satisfaction is available in proportion to his ingenuity and the audience (parental) response. The response is taken as a measure of ingenuity.

Before the thrill of union, the mental formulas for creativity must become accessible, the connections made and made easy. Now, if ever, the creative person learns to produce creative objects by using all the resources of his intrapsychic world, including those in the sphere of previously objectified consciousness. In this way he builds up, out of his normal and creative experience, a personal integration which he can present to the world.

With the possible exception of the child prodigy, the creative adolescent faces a great frustration in reality. He can find no truly appropriate audience until he comes to his own maturity. This frustration, like the frustrations at previous levels, compels the adolescent to take a reflective stance, to produce objects as solutions to the problem of frustration, and, with talent, to succeed in objectifying to the extent that honest appraisal of the created object produces the happy shattering of the state of imminence.

Chapter 9

THE CREATOR'S OBJECT: THE WORK
Adult Life—21 to 40

Adult mental life is characterized by a movement toward functional stability. Common work and common responsibility are the bases of the social valuation which take on the force of an organizing principle in the adult mind. The self-representation as an adult supersedes the childhood representations which held that adulthood was the province of the parents. Authority is now vested in a self-representation viewed as a more or less integral part of society.

In this connection, the social and political realities of the time become matters of great personal moment, whereas before they had been theoretical imponderables or distant structures of authority. The adolescent sense of efflorescence in personal identity gives way to the stable identity of the adult. Limits determined by career choices and choices of a mate are accepted more or less willingly as the responsibility of adult life. In this sense adult life is an era of binding structure formation, much like the latency limits to the oedipal period, or like the anal period limit to the primal scene efflorescence of the oral life of infancy.

The identity of adult life is oriented toward a maintenance of homeostasis, toward a personal continuity of identity, toward continuity and increase in family life, toward problem solving in the area of common work, and toward adjustment in the interaction and communication with other people. Thus it is a time when the adult accepts the givens of his own personality and evaluates them within the social framework. This more or less neutral objectivity about the givens of personal identity facilitates the hard and sometimes painful work of mutual adjustment and the development of satisfying mutual life. Personal identity in the adult comes to reside in self-knowledge, and self-knowledge provides a sense of continuity to the past.

It is our thesis in this chapter that the adult creator enters into a special creative state when he sets about to produce the created object. Although he feels a compelling, even an obligatory necessity to enter into this state, there is a voluntary aspect to it. The adult creator purposes to set aside his normal adult identity for a longer or shorter time to produce some created object which must function to solve some problem of his adult life.

For the adult creator the major problem is whether he dare undertake the life of a professional creator. To test this the work becomes supercharged with wishes that its social acceptance will validate the provisional professional identity of creator invested in the work. Applied to this period of life, Kris's (1952) concept of regression in service of the ego develops acute meaning. The creator decides to enter the creative process to try to make his identity as a professional creator real.

The creative process is not entered without a sense of peril and anxiety. There is the ever present feeling that one might not emerge from some regressive level which has been entered in the service of the creative purpose. Further, there is the risk that the work or works created will not be accepted by society. In entering the creative state the creator produces a breech in his normal adult reflective consciousness. The breach must be repaired by the work. The work must mediate between the creator and an audience, which in adult life comes to have permanent significance transcending the family of origin.

In adult creative life the muse is felt to reside in the work. To the extent that the work is accepted as a real contribution to social purpose, the creator feels that his identity as a creator is validated. When the creator enters the creative state he engages an alternative spokesman, an artificer. The spokesman may vary from work to work, or the spokesman may be elevated to the status of a continuing alternative to the creator's own identity. For instance, Stephen Dedalus remains Joyce's creative alternative in *Ulysses,* (though he shares this role with Bloom.) If this "voice" can be called the subjective alternative to identity in the creator, then the indwelling muse can be called the objective alternative to identity. Voice and muse structure the adult creative state in which disbelief is suspended voluntarily during the whole extent of the creative work.

In fact the galvanizing works of the adult creator are provided with a whole alternative set of all the major components of consciousness. The major characters in the work are endowed with their own subjectively reflective function by which they generate the work. In a completely parallel way the audience to which the work is communicating is represented within the work as an objective, reflective entity derived from the objective existence that has been granted to the muse. At an experiential level the characters of the work are endowed with effort and wishful energy. Again, in a parallel way, the muse figure of the work is felt to be an indwelling spirit in the work, speaking and spoken to. In this way the creator maintains a whole imaginative state which operates parallel to the ordinary state of reality consciousness.

The creator makes use of established genres to organize these components of the creative world of his work. Genre provides an external structure to aid in the synthesis of the work. It is in the nature of adult identity that work produced must have some meaning to the society. Even as society provides genres that help structure the creator's work, it also provides critics who must decide whether the work has social value, and whether it has aesthetic value in the sense of fulfilling or expanding the criteria of its intended genre.

The creator is peculiarly vulnerable to the requirement that his work be accepted by society. His work becomes the mediator of his social identity and his identity as an adult person. In this way the work functions like a relationship mediating between the creator and his social audience. The creator goes through much the same process in producing the work that the normal adult goes through in forming a new personal and intimate relationship. Since forming new and enduring relationships is the prototypical problem of adult life, we would like to explore this process to clarify the alternative function of creativity in adult life. First, though, we must extend our neuropsychological paradigm to describe the structure of consciousness in adult mental life.

PROBLEM SOLVING

We would like to begin with a consideration of the interrelation between reflection and experience in adult life, for the automatic shifting in the focus of consciousness is the essence of the stability that maintains order in the adult mind.

For the sake of clarity in this discussion, we define *realization* as the movement of consciousness from experience to reflection. Similarly we define *conclusion* in terms of the movement from reflective consciousness back to experiential consciousness. A conclusion marks the end of a period of reflective thinking signaling the return to experience. The transit we are describing between experience and reflection, and between reflection and experience is an ordinary event that occurs and shifts in brief instants or in longer spans. A person may spend more or less time in one mode of consciousness or the other over longer periods of time. We contend that these functional neuropsychological mechanisms operate under the aegis of the enduring pattern of adult identity.

REGRESSION IN THE SERVICE OF THE EGO AND TRANSFERENCE

Assume that the movement from experience to reflection is induced by anxiety or some other affective signal, whereas the movement from reflection to experience is triggered by the completion of a logical reflective process. Conclusion follows the rules of deductive logic, while realization follows the process of induction. If problem solving—conclusion making—does not yield to the innate syllogistic order of reflection, then a new mechanism is instituted to maintain functional stability.

This mechanism, already familiar from our discussion, is "regression-in-service-of-the-ego." Ernst Kris (1952) coined the term to refer to a creative process of problem solving. In essence it is a way of exploring the sedimented layers of chronological identity development in the past of the person's life cycle in the service of solving some otherwise insoluble present problem.

If regression-in-service-of-the-ego describes the special mechanism for making the transit from reflection to an extended and memorial form of experience, then transference is perhaps the proper term to describe the special mechanism for realizations that are founded as past experiences. Thus we are rediscovering the proposition that mental life has a regressive and a progressive movement. Viewing transference in this way —as a progressive current in the mechanism for solving problems of adult life—requires that we make a distinction between transference as a purely intrapsychic mechanism, and transference that takes on another person as the object of past experience.

Transference was a concept first elaborated by Freud to indicate the transfer of unconscious, repressed, infantile residues of conflictual experience onto later adult forms of consciousness. Then Freud elaborated this concept to include the transfer of such infantile experiences onto the expectations of the analyst during the course of psychoanalysis. Freud saw this as an expression of a natural emotional phenomenon which could be analyzed and used to provide the immediacy that makes the analysis become a vivid experience of emotional growth and realization. There are two steps in transference: One is the repetition of some past experience, the other is the reception of this experience into the realm of present reflection.

In the later sense in which Freud used it, transference becomes a meaningful phenomenon only in adult life. For before adulthood much of what falls under the rubric of relating is in itself a form of transference. It is not until adult life that the person is capable of reflecting upon the nature of his or her relationships and is capable of distinguishing the degree to which a relationship is defined by previous expectations. The reflective decision to go forward into a relationship that will take one in unknown directions is not possible until adult life.

A Quasi-Novelistic Account of Relationship

We would like to provide a quasi-novelistic account of mutual transference in a social situation in order to clarify these concepts. We hope to emphasize the relationship between reflection and experience in adult consciousness.

In this context transference is most noticeable as the configuration of emotional forces belonging to the establishment of a new relationship. As people develop experience in relating, they acquire some social veneer which allows them to put forward a kind of language capable of presenting their neutralized reflections of themselves. Thus when strangers meet in a polite atmosphere, there is apt to be a kind of topical conversation in which the shift of topics provides the main formal indications of the internal designs by which the conversants organize their respective intrapsychic worlds. These shifts may be occasions for a self-consciousness which at the same time occasions for consciousness of or curiosity about the other person or people.

These are potentially moments of openness in the social veneer. The mental organization that composes this veneer by which we begin to engage the stranger is the function we call the "observing ego." The social machine opens at some point of mutually identical reflective awareness, and this loophole in the facade may seem to either party an invitation to personal remark, either of inquiry or revelation. This social signal will either be met with reciprocity, or be recognized as an indication for a tighter renewal of a facade.

At moments of engagement the possibility for new experience begins. The mechanism for initiating new experience is tripped when each person suspends a reciprocating half of his reflective integration. The subjective component of one engages the objective component of the other, to make a whole reflective integration for each. In other words a feeling of identity is exchanged. The barriers can be easily reassembled because the parties exchange only social consciousness in this preliminary stage of communication.

During this period of reflective engagement each party begins to apprehend certain qualities of style, assertion, propensity for control, and inclination to dependency. Expectations of mutuality of interaction on the basis of these components of the reflective style begin to define the expected boundaries of new experience. This is the signal for the onset of mutual transference.

If the hypothetical strangers are young and inexperienced, or if they are seeking some major new interpersonal engagement, the interaction soon takes a new direction. Each person simultaneously accords a recognition to the transferential qualities of the other, indicating a kind of familiarity. It may suddenly flower in a joke, simultaneous impression (indicating the possibility of narcisstic coextension of perception), or frank gaze (calling up the whole sense of history of the search for satisfaction), or other common awareness—a similarity in sense of humor, say, or a common memory. This conclusion signals the beginning of searching conversation about the personal past.

The revelation of personal experience and background opens the speaker's recalled experience to the influence of the listener. The listener may merely confirm sympathy by relating analogous experience, or he may reinterpret the experience in a way which shows he reorganizes its essential components.

Such an alteration in the speaker's intrapsychic world can be better understood in the model of psychoanalytic therapy. If a patient has accepted an interpretation concerning the nature of the emotional components of an experience, then an alteration in the reflective set produces a realization of different emotions. This alteration is mediated by a temporary, total, reflective identity with the therapist, whose remarks are accepted as if they come from the speaker's own reflection. At the same time the therapist is experienced as if he were the revenant of the past experience.

This dual level identification *with* and *of* the therapist provides the necessary conditions for intrapsychic structural rearrangement. By this same mechanism a muse personage, granted new intrapsychic representation, can liberate hitherto repressed elements of past experience.

In this way phase-specific, organizing events such as the primal scene can take shape in the present reality. The patient invests the therapist, as the creator invests the muse, with a flexible and plastic array of qualities. For instance, the therapist or muse may alternatively and simultaneously be the mother and the father in the primal scene and an embodiment of the subject's own feelings at the time.

Let's assume that our strangers now on the point of intimacy with each other, have brought their relationship to a

similar transference. Expectations of intense repetitions of repressed central experience could lead to a neurotic enmeshing
in which each plays a part in the other's focal neurotic conflict.
However, if good will and maturity predominate, they will very
likely tell each other when they are treated in ways that do not
accord with what they ought realistically to expect. This may
be enough to bring each party back to a realization of the
other's presence. Subsequent interaction, perhaps love making,
may then be experienced as deeply satisfying. Each acknowledges and elaborates a shared intimacy. The two will develop
a love which exceeds the neurotic limits to transference.

Why do people resist this happy consummation? A tre-
mendous effort must be expended in forming any new relationship that is to go beyond the confines of past relationships. Each
new relationship must pass through all the old forms before a
new one can be constructed. This is the basis for the unfolding
of transference in analysis. Ultimately, the new person must be
granted a subjective existence differing from one's own and
from available categories of objects as well. Beyond the onerous
extent of this project, the person undertaking this venture
becomes, in a particular way, vulnerable. Every new relationship that is destined to transcend the boundaries of social facade
must pass through a stage where the new object alters the
existing pattern of identity structure. Resistance arises precisely
in reaction to the all-out effort needed to reorganize personal
identity. But it is only this effort that can attain the reward of
new experience, adding new pleasure to the exercise of reflective
consciousness on the immediacy of life.

LINGUISTIC CONSIDERATIONS

Adult Devices

The ideas of interpolation, asides, and momentary
breaches give rise to potential schemes of language.
It is important to understand that the schemes of this

period deal more with reflective order, which is to say with speech performance, than with experience, which is to say the generation of speech. Therefore the schemes have to do with the process for social communication rather than with the strictly intrapsychic communication in which the previous eras of speech figures find their roots. The *hyperbatons* or schemes of unusual word order—*anastrophe* (inverted word order) and *parenthesis*—and the schemes of omission—*elipsis, asyndeton,* and *polysyndeton*—force syntax to be individualized for reflection but still to be available for social communication. Breaches in the text, asides, and footnotes also reveal the tension between the adult creator residing in his state of creative identity, and his normal adult identity.

PARENTHESIS

Parenthesis is a syntactic interruption. A word, phrase, or clause is inserted into the running syntax. The writer editorializes within commas, double dashes, or parenthesis, so that one has the impression of being invited between cozy curved lines to hear the author's reflective judgment on the matter.

Example

> Now, culture admits the necessity of the movement toward fortune-making and exaggerated industrialism, readily allows that the future may derive benefit from it; but insists, at the same time, that the passing generations of industrialists,—*forming, for the most part the stout main body of phillistinism,*—are sacrificed to it.

> —*Mathew Arnold*
> *Culture and Anarchy*
> "Sweetness and Light"

We would suggest that Arnold—creatively—identifies himself with the portion in parenthesis, both as the reflective maker of the parenthesis and as an individual set apart from the stout main body.

SCHEMES OF OMISSION AND ADDITION

Elipsis (the omission of a word), asyndeton (the omission of a conjunction), and polysyndeton (the inclusion of an unusually large number of conjunctions) are devices for increasing or decreasing the energetic charge of the sentence. This is to say, they are schemes organized by reflection for the purpose of controlling the distribution of the psychic energy bound by syntax. This energy may be parcelled or controlled to draw the greatest impact from ideas.

> *Elipsis:*   "All turned out as expected"
> for
> "All turned out as had been expected."

As a concrete description of elipsis, the phrase describes its own "turning out" or exclusion of the words "had been," which, when they return to the phrase, make it "turn out" as had been expected all along.

Asyndeton and polysyndeton: with the *and's* left out, the following passage would be asyndetonic. Instead, it is a fine example of polysyndeton.

> In the bed of the river there were pebbles and boulders, dry and white in the sun, and the water was clear and swiftly moving and blue in the channels. Troops went by the house and down the road and the dust they raised powdered the leaves of the trees. The trunks of the trees too were dusty, and the leaves fell early that year and we saw the troops marching along the road and the dust rising and leaves, stirred by the breeze, falling and the

soldiers marching and afterward the road bare and white except for the leaves.

—Ernest Hemingway
A Farewell to Arms

The polysydeton of Hemingway's passage from a *Farewell to Arms* shows a quality of reflective energy distribution in the syntax which points, we think, to the neutrality of the energy at the disposal of his reflection. Increasingly, in adult thinking, reflection is able to employ its neutral energy to communicate socially in such a way that the communication is not prejudiced by the drive-related organization of experience. The aggression in Hemingway's passage, though implied, is neutralized by each *and* in the passage. The creative identity of the author may be seen to reside in, and to be concealed by, each *and* in the passage.

THE EXTENDED LANGUAGE OF LITERATURE

A study of adult life brings us to a discussion of genre. Genre is an organized structure which controls the form of a work of art. As an organized structure, genre has much in common with such ordinary forms of discourse as discussions, debates, chats, letters, documents, and so on. What is uncommon about planned generic discourse is that it always compounds an element from the realm of the imagination with elements from other forms of consciousness. Thus *genre* refers not only to a socially accepted medium for creative expression, but also to particular, structured forms of consciousness which created objects may display. Genres contain the social sanction of culture and criticism. The artist hopes that in relating his work in the medium of a particular genre he is entitled to have his work recognized as socially appropriate.

Besides this social function, the genre and related subsidiary mechanism have an intrapsychic function as well. Literary genre and literary devices allow the creative person to locate and express aspects of his experience in the service of creating the artistic object. In this the genre and devices act as structures for a limited regression in service of the ego, and for a limited transference. The genre or device structures the sense of provisional reality which the artist employs in the production of his work.

This brings us to a notion which has special relevance to a discussion of the adult artist. This notion is that all genres and devices contain in their organized reference to the realm of imagination a socially sanctioned sense that they will mediate the relation to some audience in reality. Like the muse who mediates between the god and the individual, the genre contains an inherent capacity to structure the artist's inspiration.

The genre is an open invitation to the artist to identify his own personal sense of provisional creative identity with the indwelling, social-mythological muse of the genre. In this way the genre becomes the mediatrix of the artist's relation to society. Thus if an artist writes immortal lines to the poem, he is by extension writing immortal lines to the indwelling social muse of the poem as well, and in this sense to the audience, with whom he feels he shares this common mediatrix.

We would now like to explore some of the major genres. The genres and literary devices appear to align themselves with particular areas of neuropsychological consciousness. Thus we see them as natural forms of language extended into the special realm of literature. Just as we have asserted that schemes and tropes owe their various origins to stages in neuropsychological development, so we also contend that literary genre and their subsidiary devices arise out of the creator's need for special adult forms of expression. Different creators are predisposed to different genres.

A Theory of Literary Analysis

We can project a small theory of literary analysis by simply considering that consciousness may be distributed by a work of art, as well as by an individual, into four areas of mentation. These are subjective-experiential, subjective-reflective (ego ideal), objective-experiential, and objective-reflective reflective (superego). The nature of the consciousness emphasized in the work determines which main genre structures the work. The types of consciousness and their corresponding genres are distributed as follows:

1. Subjective experiential—Romance
2. Subjective reflective—Comedy
3. Objective experiential—Satire
4. Objective reflection—Tragedy

In this schematic distribution, comedy and romance play on libidinal drive, while tragedy and satire emphasize the aggressive drive. Comedy and tragedy (reflective forms) are more inclusive structures which imply social consequences and significance. Romance and satire (experiential forms) draw more heavily on the intrapsychic sources of experience. Still, schematically we may pursue these broad divisions into their genetic sources to explain the economics of the effect which these structures play upon.

Libidinal Genres: Romance and Comedy

Romance implies a saga of action driven by libidinal need. We identify subjectively with the hero of the piece. Comedy plays upon the disparity between intended actions and their effect. Jokes and puns exemplify devices for the liberation of the libidinal in the affect of laughter. In comedy, the hero overcomes the barrier to sexual action, and in so doing changes the ideal structure of the society. Comedy depicts the effect of the adolescent young adult, marshalling libidinal forces to change the social forces that determine the focus of consciousness in society. The subsidiary devices of comedy ignite flares in adult reflection from the various stages of development. The buffoon is the comic purveyor of gestures, and he belongs to a primitive stage of semantic association. His antics draw one into the liberation of laughter from gesture. The self-deprecator, more anal, identifies with the aggressor in putting down the intent and the autonomy of the subject. The farcical impostor who stops action blocks oedipal and adolescent wishes whose masturbatory derivatives seem futile, and liberates the comic effect in that way. The reflective surface of comedy draws one into the subjective dilemma of the character at all levels of experience.

AGGRESSIVE GENRES: TRAGEDY AND SATIRE

Shifting to the objective and aggressive focus of consciousness we see that in tragedy, implacable fate, the externalization of the superego, imposes absolute order on events. The hero, operating at the limits of his moral authority, realizes finally, through the effortful neutrality of his judgment that no one can abrogate the limitations imposed by the natural order. Tragedy must end in the death of individual reflective consciousness for human tragedy is actuated by the attempt to circumvent the fates, which, for oedipal and neurological reasons decree that such attempts will end in failure. When objective representation of the self can no longer bind the impact of external events, the structure of human dignity must dissolve.

Another aggressive device is satire. Satire is a structure that deals with the folly of attempting to circumvent the misfortunes of experience. An imposture of the hero or narrator is an effective focus for the liberation of aggressive affect in the audience directed toward the hero. Indeed, in all genres imposture of central persons liberates libidinal or aggressive forces in the audience. The audience may laugh at or with the hero's imposture, depending on whether the imposture is structured satirically or comically. The agreement between the audience and the writer-performers allows the imposter to be infused with muse identity. Thus the imposter mediates between authorial consciousness and audience consciousness.

Now consider how all reflective-aggressive devices focus on the tension between the superego and the objective sources of experience. It is in the nature of aggressive imitation that it does some violence to the experience of reality. The violence to the structures that determine how we experience reality liberates artistic impact. The prototype of this is to be found in Freud's paper, "On Humor." (S.E. vol. XXI, p. 160) In this paper Freud argues that the source of the humorous affect is to be found in the relief that the terrible event is not really happening. In this sense humor depicts the worst of all possible events with the reflective acknowledgement that it is not really happening. The judgment that the perceived experiences is not true, releases possibilities of new experience. This is what Samuel Johnson meant when he wrote in his Preface to Shakespeare, "the delight of tragedy proceeds from our consciousness of fiction; if we thought murders and treasons real, they would please no more." (Tillotson, p. 1073)

Satire makes extended use of this tendency to enjoy unreality. Satire is an extended technique for downgrading authenticity. Someone's subjective intentions are portrayed as lacking true meaning. It is a way for the writer to project himself via his muse into the character of someone else, maintaining that the other person is no more authentic than his own deliberate artistic imposture. The moral, condemnatory tone in this is manifest in the portion of the technique which takes a whole socially condoned way of acting and shows that it is nothing more than an excuse for some form of infantile gratification. In making this clear the satirist takes a position of moral authority for himself and presumes to make judgments on the misrepresentation of others. In his "Epistle to Augustus," Alexander Pope comments:

> Hence Satire rose, that just the medium hit,
> And heals with Morals what it hurts with Wit.

Parody is another reflective device which plays for its effect on the disparity between the reflective function of judgment and the authenticity of the experience presented. It relies on the judgments fundamental to internal variation "Is it good" and "Is it true." Answering these questions of the writer points out the moral direction of his own composition. In parody there is some intention to injure through casting doubt on the authenticity of another writer's style. But of course doubt is cast at the same time on the authenticity of the style of the artist who is himself doing the writing. Thus self-parody is always a judgment of the writer's own worth. And in this resides a paradox, because one's artistic intent is always, in part, to present illusion. Thus the writer allows himself a moral position superior even to his own self-representation as writer. It is in this disparity that the affective impact of the device lies. The Henry Millers and the Norman Mailers are saved by their own superiority even to the narcissism of their styles. They are self-parodists in an age of self-parody. So they become satirists.

Parody announces a reflective superiority to the subject of ridicule. Its essence is the reproduction of the object in distorted form. Parody distorts style, which is the writer's vehicle for expressing his truth. In his Sonnet 62, Shakespeare provides us with a subtle example of the art of self-parody. It is also a comment on all the sonnets.

> Sin of self-love possesseth all mine eye
> And all my soul and all my every part;
> And for this sin there is no remedy,
> It is so grounded inward in my heart.
> Methinks no face so gracious is as mine,

No shape so true, no truth of such account,
And for myself mine own worth do define
As I all other in all worths surmount,
But when my glass shows me myself indeed,
Beated and chopp'd with tann'd antiquity,
Mine own self-love quite contrary I read;
Self so self-loving were iniquity:
'Tis thee (myself) that for myself I praise,
Painting my age with beauty of thy days.

In his book *Anatomy of Criticism,* Northrop Frye defines the ironic as a mode of literature in which the characters exhibit a power of action inferior to the ones assumed to be normal in the reader or audience, or in which the poet's attitude is one of detached objectivity. (Frye p. 34) In his definition of irony Frye focuses mainly on the "realistic" level of experience. As a reflective device, irony casts doubt on the meaning expressed. The superego takes on a tone of mild condemnation, of reproof. From the vantage of a false posture the writer casts doubt on meaning. He says in effect that the reality which he is describing is no more true than that he is really the muse. The effect of the device is in the disparity between the intended action and the sense of judgment that the experience, if true, is not also good. In T. S. Eliot's poem "The Wasteland," Tiresias combines the quality of the mildly reproving superego and the muse of indefinite sex.

I Tiresias, old man with wrinkled dugs
Perceived the scene, and foretold the rest—
I too awaited the expected guest.
He, the young man carbuncular, arrives
A small house agent's clerk, with one bold stare,
One of the low on whom assurance sits
As a silk hat on a Bradford millionaire.
The time is now propitious, as he guesses,
The meal is ended, she is bored and tired,
Endeavors to engage her in caresses
Which still are unreproved, if undesired.

Flushed and decided, he assaults at once;
Exploring hands encounter no defense;
His vanity requires no response,
And makes a welcome of indifference.
(And I Tiresias have foresuffered all
Enacted on this same divan or bed
I who have sat by Thebes below the wall
And walked among the lowest of the dead.)

Tiresias, reflective, incarnated by the body of the poem, is the muse.

The main point about reflection is its primacy must be renewed by continual reverification of the foundations of mental life. In considering reflective devices we are considering an interaction between the superego and the experiential structures that interact with it. An artist is someone who has developed a particular habitual way of dealing with trauma. For the artist the muse is the point of entry between the reflective world and the representational world. If Tiresias knows all about Oedipus he is privileged to make the mental descent from his knowledge to the experience of Oedipus, to all the experience of Oedipus. This is a prototype for the reflectively maintained intrapsychic descent through layers of experience. This descent is itself an allegory, often enough, of the journey into the underworld, where if one emerges with reflection intact, one also escapes with a sense of renewal.

AGGRESSIVE DEVICES

Reflective devices which use the muse to cast doubt on the reality of personal appearance re-enter all the genetic levels of development. Mockery makes a counterfeit of mature representation. Caricature assassinates character, without destroying the quality of recognition embodied in the representation. Burlesque attacks the qualities of recognition, taking them to the point of the ridiculous, almost making a cartoon of human figures. Finally, in the art of the mime, mimicry can reduce the meaning of gestures to the point of loss of human essence to image existence. In all of these devices there is a liberation of some aggressive energy from identity structuring the objective portrayal of subjective strivings toward reality. Here we have presented these devices in the order of their descent from the representational, to the figurative, to the imagistic.

THE CREATOR'S SYNDROME IN ADULT LIFE

The adult artist must reconcile his creative identity with his normal identity. In early adulthood it is not yet time for the artist to cure his own creative syndrome through a complete understanding of its nature; it is time to produce periods of resolution, however, through the production of works that have absolute socially sanctioned merit as real artistic objects worthy of existing in the world, as worthy as any other object. Attempting to accept the identity as an artist is a significant factor in the social life of an artist. This is one reason the adult artist seeks the company of other artists, even to the point of wanting to identify himself with some group movement in the arts. Such an identification with a group movement of other artists is to the social identity of the artist what genre is to the individual work. Indeed, the artist feels that he achieves some measure of respectability in society through the production of works sanctioned by a genre.

The work is the important thing. The work performs the essential economic function of reconciling the disparity between the normal and creative identities like a spark that equalizes the charge between two poles. For the artist, the work performs the economic function of bringing his creative self into the normal social world. For a member of the artist's audience, the economic charge is reversed: The work brings the normal social adult into the realm of the creative imagination, discharging affective charges which would otherwise threaten the stability of the adult integration of identity.

"The Love Song of J. Alfred Prufrock" by T. S. Eliot

For the creator, entering the threshold of adult life is like crossing a dread barrier. The thrill of union with the adolescent muse pales like a nun's expectations when she must enter the daily routine of her marriage to the church. The eternal epiphany of adolescence comes to an end when the creator contemplates his identity as an adult creator. T. S. Eliot's "The Love Song of J. Alfred Prufrock" is a poem describing the assumption of the alternative identity as a poet. Prufrock is for the poem the alternative identity as poet. The poem also contains an indwelling muse, functioning both as the object of inspiration and the audience which must understand the communication of the poet. The character Prufrock is full of irony, not only because he is aged, but because Eliot is aware of the imposture that makes Prufrock's search for love and communication inherently difficult. The sense of imposture in the poem relates to Eliot's sense that the mother he seeks to possess, both eternally and sensually, that the woman he wants to embrace from a position of adolescent shyness, is at the same time the indwelling muse of his work, inspiring it. The tension of the poem, which is resolved through the assumption of the ironic posture, is a product of the interaction of Eliot's unresolved oedipal conflicts with the resolution provided in the provisional identity as adult creator.

In "The Love Song of J. Alfred Prufrock," T. Stearns Eliot announces his debut as a poet of adult life. There is much in this poem that addresses the adolescent era identification with the muse who reorganizes the psychic life of the creative person; for Eliot, at the writing of his poem, was standing at the threshold of his entry into adult life, and he had not yet synthesized his personal identity as an adult poet. The poem is itself the signature of such synthesis in process. The late adolescent oedipal derivative concerns are much in evidence in the poem.

Eliot is aware that he subsumes his normal identity to that of Prufrock and that only through this imposture can he hope to be a successful poet. The inscription of the poem refers to Dante's Inferno, an imaginary place where tales may be told only under the condition that they may not be repeated. The bearer of the tales will lose his identity if the tales are brought into the real world. Thus Eliot is aware that he can resolve his oedipal turmoil only through the auspices of a work which can be a love song of Prufrock but not of Eliot. The love song with its ironic imposture carries the adolescent search for the means of expression of love into the imaginary realm of the poem. This realm is occupied by pursuit of the muse. The boy-adolescent-man-old man of the poem cannot hope to achieve a climax of love because he is destined to repeat the same search over and over through a life as a creator.

The love song is composed of an ambiguous pair questing the truth of self-expression. "Let us go then, you and I,"—"You and I" is simultaneously the subject and the variable object of the intrapsychic alternative identity of the creator. Eliot sets off on his quest, and his questioning, in the company of the "you" who is the poet and the "I" who is the writer. But once into the progress of the poem, "I" tends to become the song of Prufrock, and "you" becomes both the reader-audience and the muse whom Prufrock is courting.

Eliot begins by anesthetizing himself, putting his normal identity to sleep. (It wakes up in the end and the poet Prufrock loses consciousness.) Prufrock begins with images of time and space personified, the synthetic and personified components of identity. "When the evening is spread out against the sky like a patient etherized upon a table." To be spread out upon a table must also refer to the poem itself—the work in the beginning of its progress.

What is the 'overwhelming' question that Eliot asks? Evidently he asks whether the poem itself, and the poet, given his imposture, can succeed in producing an authentic work, much like the question, laden with irony, whether the oedipal child can hope to have his fantasy of sexual satisfaction ever brought out of the realm of childhood masturbation and into the realm of real satisfaction—understood performance. The yellow veiling images of time condense into the hallucinatory face of the poem, malleable enough "for a hundred visions and revisions." Finally the identity of the poem takes on Profrock's countenance: "With a bald spot in the middle of my hair—"

The vision of poetic identity sets off omniscient vision ("For I have known them all already") against the uncertainty of vision, and the terrible prescient vision of the critics endowed with Eliot's own critical faculties; "And I have known the eyes already, known them all—The eyes that fix you in a formulated phrase, . . . And how should I presume?" This is the question. How can the poet pretend to success when he knows with his own critical faculties that it is pretense that animates his search for satisfaction? It is the same presumption that leads the child to wonder at the possible satisfaction of his masturbatory fantasies and the adolescent to wonder if he can really love.

After a long preamble of questioning the work invokes the muse in a parenthesis.

> And I have known the arms already,
> Known them all—
> Arms that are braceleted and white and bare
> (but in the lamplight, downed with light brown hair!)

With this digression Eliot is ready both to presume and to begin.

> Shall I say, I have gone at dusk through
> Narrow streets,
> And watched the smoke that rises from the pipes
> Of lonely men in shirt-sleeves, leaning out of windows?

With this as a beginning, Eliot describes the actual experience that must be transformed if he is to be a poet. With this image of aging, without producing any work, Eliot sinks rapidly into the regressive phase of his poem.

> I should have been a pair of ragged claws
> Scuttling across the floors of silent seas.

These are the hands of Prufrock now, writing the love song. After this image of the primary process unconscious, the poem begins to rise back to the surface again. He must go on with it to a rendezvous in fantasy with the phallic woman of his dreams. His poem must come to a conclusion as much as one who goes to meet the woman in her room must proceed with the sexual activity despite feelings of impotence. One must accept the imagery of castration, total ineffectiveness, in order to proceed.

"Though I have seen my head (grown slightly bald) brought in upon a platter," he admits his fear. It is the fear that even the consummation will result in no communication. That is like the poet's death. If he gives his all and there is no response,

> If one, settling a pillow by her head,
> should say: "That is not what I meant
> at all. That is not it at all."

Would it have been worth while to have written the poem, to have made the advance?

Finally, to be a poet, Eliot, who now becomes Prufrock, as Yeats becomes Hanrahan, accepts his identity as a poet. He accepts his identification with the muse and what it means— that he shall be

> Full of high sentence, but a bit obtuse;
> At times indeed, almost ridiculous—
> Almost at times, the fool.

In taking on the identity of Prufrock he takes on the voice of pretense, which, if it would strive for immortality, still can never be fully satisfied. And he takes on also the proximity to the muse:

> I have heard the mermaids singing, each to each.
> I do not think they will sing to me.
> I have seen them riding seaward on the waves
> Combing the white hair of the waves blown back
> When the wind blows the water white and black.

Eliot demonstrates, really, the power of the muse to affect his voice, to make beauty through his identification with Prufrock. He must accept, however, in exchange for the grace of these voices, that as Prufrock there is no culminating satisfaction. With that Eliot awakens, comes out of his poetic reverie, leaves the sea of these phallic women, mermaids, sirens behind and foregoes, for the ending of his poem, the poetic voice.

> We have lingered in the chambers of the sea
> By sea-girls wreathed with seaweed red and brown
> Till human voices wake us, and we drown.

THE SOURCE OF LITERARY EFFECTIVENESS

Marshalling every shred of subjective and objective life, the great creators produce galvanic objects, objects that bring order and integration to diversity. They provide a new synthesis so complete that it is capable of detachment from the creator. The great teach us that anything may be objectified. The result is energy release (see Kris, 1952, Chapter 1, in passing). For the creator and audience, the object becomes a tool reducing mental work and functioning as an integer in a new synthesis. The celebrated first sentence of Jane Austin's *Pride and Prejudice* performs this economic function, is full of personality, and—being ironic, truthful, and utterly simple—it releases the energy needed in the author and reader to get through the novel, propelled by the reaction it generates:

> It is a truth universally acknowledged, that a single man in possession of a good fortune must be in want of a wife.

However, little known the feelings or views of such a man may be on his first entering a neighborhood, this truth is so well fixed in the minds of the surrounding families, that he is considered as the rightful property of someone or other of their daughters.

The galvanic object lives because the artist infuses it with the corporeal presence of his personal indwelling muse. In this sense every adult work contains an indwelling spirit, life breathed into it by the artist's muse. By offsetting human relationships against the muse relationship, the writer evokes the impact of truth in the reader. We recognize a special class of truthful account in the love sonnet. The sonnet, for traditional as well as formal reasons, provides the poet with two simultaneous and attractive opportunities. It allows him to display his ingenuity and, at the same time, offers an unparalleled opportunity for sating the internal audience while gratifying the outer "real" one.

"Shall I Compare Thee to a Summer's Day" by William Shakespeare

Consider for a moment poems on the order of Shakespeare's "Shall I compare thee to a summer's day?"—poems addressed to the writing:

Shall I compare thee with a summer's day?
Thou art more lovely and more temperate.
Rough winds do shake the darling buds of May,
And summer's lease hath all too short a date.
Sometimes too hot the eye of heaven shines
And often is his gold complexion dimmed;
And every fair from fair sometime declines,
By chance, or nature's changing course, untrimmed:
But thy eternal summer shall not fade
Nor lose possession of that fair thou ow'st,
Nor shall Death brag thou wand'rest in his shade

> When in eternal lines to time thou grow'st.
>> So long as men can live or eyes can see,
>> So long lives this, and this gives life to thee.

Sonnets on this pattern make up a subgenre. In Shakespeare's day, they were current enough to warrant the parody which begins "My mistress' eyes are nothing like the sun." These poems are love tributes, but curiously impersonal ones. Whether out of reticence, subservience to style, dispassionate desire to display ingenuity, or the necessity of production under the patronage system, these poems are traditionally tied together by strings of compliments more intrinsically beautiful than descriptive of any particular person.

"Shall I compare thee to a summer's day," in its extreme impersonality and deliberate attempt at the prototypical, magnifies itself and reduces the genre with the astringency of caricature. Because of the kind of information available in the text, we do not even know the sex of this poem's "thee." And Shakespeare has ingeniously altered the traditional compliments in such a way that he undercuts the conscious beauty of the first eight lines. The poem might read:

> Shall I compare thee to a summer's day?
> Thou art more lovely and more temperate ...
> Thy eternal summer shall not fade.

The object of this expense of ingenuity is a sort of practical joke, beautifully played and dramatic enough for anyone's taste. Shakespeare has deliberately subverted the poem's apparent purposes, which are pinning down the suitable but illusive pieces of a just comparison, and describing a worthy but unnamed person in order to immortalize him or her.

In fact, there are two purposes in current operation, the apparent one and another. At one remove, the poet pursues a difficult comparison, asserting that the poem's subject "thee" will become immortal since the poem will. "Thee" is the subject insofar as this unknown acts as a source of information. Syntactically, "thee" is the object, "I" the subject. At another remove the poet's purpose is different. Consider the line "When the eternal lines to time thou grow'st." Surely the "Thou" is the poem. The poet is addressing the poem. This is the reason for the subject's indeterminate sex.

All of which boils down to this: The personally unspecified subject of the poem functions as the poet's (secular) muse and the poem's indwelling spirit. The joke is that, whether the muse is the poem, its resident spirit, or simply the reader to whom the sonnet is dedicated, the rhymed couplet forces us to abandon all speculation and admire Shakespeare's ingenuity.

Chapter 10

THE CREATOR'S OBJECT: THE CREATIVE PROCESS

Later Adulthood

HAWTHORNE

If as we propose Keats and Whitman are primal-scene-fixated creators, and if Thomas and Joyce are anal-auditory-fixated creators, then Eliot and Hawthorne may be said to be oedipally fixated creators. Normand's (1970) biography of Hawthorne presents some of the biographical factors that predisposed Hawthorne to produce a strong fetishistic imprint in his works. The first factor is that Hathorne's father died of fever in Dutch Guiana when Hawthorne was four-and-one-half, the height of the child's oedipal period. This means that Hawthorne's belief in the efficacy of his masturbatory oedipal fantasies was intensified to an unusual degree. If his father could die, then the young and still helpless child was certainly in bodily peril.

The sense of bodily peril was affirmed when Hawthorne developed some affliction of his leg in his late latency, literally laying him up in bed for the better part of a year or two. Perhaps it was childhood rheumatoid arthritis, for if he had had rheumatic heart disease, that would explain Hawthorne's congested breathing difficulty later in life. It is clear from Normand's biography that Hawthorne's physical liabilities—and prowess —were mythologized. He was known as a tireless climber and hiker in college and after, which must mean that he was also a tired climber. Hawthorne must have been both overprotected by a mother fearful of losing him as she lost her husband, and also neglected by her as she retreated after her husband's death, leaving much of the raising of the child Hawthorne to her own extended family.

Hawthorne was afraid of contact with women. After college he returned to the family home where he lived somewhat monastically, writing, but not pushing too hard for publication. According to Normand the story is that Hawthorne would go for long night walks, where he would tryst with the fisherman's daughter who was reputed to be a mermaid. This myth contains Hawthorne's fetishistic view of the bisexual composite, and it screens Hawthorne's view of real women. Perhaps it is also a social screen to deny that an individual would practice masturbation.

Finally, after some small literary success, Hawthorne was pursued by a woman whom he had known as a child. Hawthorne declined her invitation but not that of her sister, Sophie Peabody. Sophie was reclusive like Hawthorne's mother, and also somewhat fragile in character. She had the outward appearance of one who must cover over some inner genital damage. In protecting her Hawthorne could repress his own fears for his genital intactness. She was enough like Hawthorne that together they could represent the image of one intact human being.

But getting married at the age of 38 meant sudden adult responsibility for Hawthorne. It became necessary for him to make a living. He had a child with Sophie, a little girl who has many of the characteristics of Little Pearl in *The Scarlet Letter*. Proud of his fatherhood, Hawthorne tried to devote himself to earning a responsible living. He parlayed his small literary reputation and an interest in politics into a political appointment at the Custom House at Salem. He gave up writing for the duration. But when the job fell through, and when Hawthorne's health gave some of its recurrent evidence of failing, he was up against a severe crisis. Hawthorne was in his early forties, and if he was ever to be a renowned creator it had to be now.

For Hawthorne, the writing of *The Scarlet Letter* made his identity as a mature creator. Without it he would have remained a lesser creator. Thus *The Scarlet Letter* is one of those identity-transforming works that moves the creator to a new stage of his life. Many writers have germinal works, written with a perfection owed to the flowering of their fixation in the efflorescence of a new period of identity formation in their life.

Hawthorne's introductory chapter to *The Scarlet Letter* contains the nucleus of his age-appropriate conflict as he entered into the mature period of creativity. The mature creator needs more than social sanction to be a creator, he also needs to feel that his efforts are actually transforming society. Thus Hawthorne was looking for a symbol of what was rendering him impotent to change society. If he could find that symbol it would operate as the talisman through his work. This is the social significance of *The Scarlet Letter*. Only after he finished the tale could Hawthorne go back and add the introductory chapter which states his social conflict.

"The Custom House Essay" in The Scarlet Letter by Nathaniel Hawthorne

The "Custom House Essay," which serves as an "Introductory" to *The Scarlet Letter*, is one of the clearest examples in English prose fiction of human frustration followed by creative regression-in-service-of-the-ego. Nathaniel Hawthorne wrote extremely openly about creativity and creation, about artists and their artifacts. His introductory essay is the sort that can never be detached from the body of the book. It is of chapter length, and while it has nothing directly to do with the main or subsidiary action of the romance, it has a great deal to do with its "real," imaginative, and "fictive" origins.

By way of introduction, Hawthorne describes his position in the Custom House at Salem, the conditions of his work, his relations with those who work under him, their ways, and his own unending distaste for the job. There is a certain amount of philosophizing and psychologizing, a certain amount of self-conscious direct address, a portion of eerily modern self-analysis in the third person, and an interpretation of the personal effects of family history. Only toward the end of the essay are we informed of the circumstance (fictional) under which the manuscript, which serves as a basis for the romance, was discovered.

While there is a good deal to say, in a literary way, about the effects of the essay as a frame for the tale, it seems more profitable under the circumstances to discuss the ways in which a personal frustration led to a scanning of the environment so that the scanning led eventually to the extended mining characteristic of regression-in-service-of-the-ego.

Hawthorne became the chief officer, the Surveyor, of the Custom House in Salem, Massachusetts through an act of political patronage. He remained in office for the four years of Democratic White House tenure preceding the election of a Whig President, Taylor. He completed *Mosses from an Old Manse,* wrote for it a mildly autobiographical preface, and entered the Custom House. On assuming office he developed a severe writing block. The commerce at Salem being at that time on the decline, though not falling alway completely, the Custom House was staffed by a group of feeble old men, retainers rather than workers, whose condition greatly resembled the condition of commerce at Salem.

The one pensioner for whom Hawthorne has any admiration is quite turned in on himself. Having no real power, surrounded by impotent old men, and leaning upon the patronizing arm of Uncle Sam, Hawthorne feels impotent. Unable to think of any material for fictive expression, the Hawthorne of the Custom House finds himself temperamentally unsuited to the task of expressing any truths which may present themselves.

In fact, writing has become painful. And since the Custom House is preternaturally dull, to relieve the tedium Hawthorne resorts to mucking about a second floor storeroom which serves as a kind of attic. This attic is compared, more or less consciously, to the human mind—the mind is described as the storehouse of untraceable memories. Hawthorne speculates that certain papers belonging to the time of the Protectorate must have been carried off to Halifax by the British army in its flight from Boston. The American papers that remain are as dull as the Custom House itself. As frustrated by the attic as by his writing block, Hawthorne regrets the absence of interesting documents, for he is fond of amateur history and archaeology and used to pick up arrowheads near the Old Manse.

Finally, to his relief and ours, the narrator hits upon something of real interest, some private documents of one Surveyor Pue, an officer who had received his commission from the British king. In the origin of his commission, Pue little resembles Hawthorne, who has received his from the Democratic party. Lying among these documents is the scarlet letter and some papers outlining the history of Hester Prynne.

Frustrated in reality and politically impotent, Hawthorne has begun scanning his environment for interesting objects. Unsatisfied by those present, he determines to write and falls upon a writing block. Frustrated again, he carries his researches into the realm of history, into a metaphor for mind, a storehouse of memory, and there finds material for a tale. This material is presented to him by the ghost of the magisterial Pue.

It impressed me as if the ancient Surveyor, in his garb of a hundred years gone by, and wearing his immortal wig,—which was buried with him but did not perish in the grave,—had met me in the deserted chamber of the Custom House. In his port was the dignity of one who has borne his Majesty's commission, and who was therefore illuminated by a ray of the splendor that shone so dazzlingly about the throne. How unlike, alas! the hang-dog look of a republican official.

In other words, a potent and phallic ancestor—and Hawthorne calls Pue his official ancestor—presents him with the material for a tale. This ancestor is clearly a father, for he is a man from the Protectorate. Clearly Pue resembles Hawthorne both in having held the same position, and in his capacity as amateur antiquarian. His documents are remnants of a time long preceding his own official tenure. In terms of the mental analogue, they arise from the deepest stratum of memory yet invoked. The surveyor's document tells of a woman, an adulterous mother, Hester Prynne. From this document Hawthorne fashions a tale with sources in the transitional and oedipal levels. Indeed, one of the ambiguous functions of the letter is transitional. It is little Pearl's (Hester's daughter's) transitional object; it has mediated her sense of reality. Oedipally, the tale is a probably unconscious allegory for the young son's struggle with incestuous wishes for his mother.

It seems that Hawthorne's was the first head to roll after the presidential election. The "decapitation" and Hawthorne's fascination with Pue's wig have, along with their several literary functions, the psychological function of describing a genital displacement. Moreover, there are two men in the tale, the emotionally weak minister, Dimmesdale, father of Hester's illegitimate child, and the scientific doctor Chillingworth, the youthful Hester's old and estranged husband. Chillingworth and Dimmesdale divide between them a young boy's—Hawthorne's—libidinal and guilty feelings about his mother and his jealousy of his dead father. Though to some extent fidelity is thrust upon her, Hester, like Mrs. Hawthorne, chose to remain faithful to a man she knows does not exist, a Dimmesdale potent in spiritual and human force.

The Scarlet Letter *by Nathaniel Hawthorne*

We saw earlier that the butterfly in "The Artist of the Beautiful" functioned as a fetishistic literary progenitor. The scarlet letter serves a similar function in the present story. Each character in the story plays a part in generating Hawthorne's identity as creator. Hester Prynne and her adjunct Pearl together serve as the indwelling muse of this work. Hester, the needleworker, like Lachesis spinning the thread of life, is imbued with the extraordinary means of creating vivid objects. Hester's status as muse is carried into the social realm as well. There, Hawthorne makes her into a signifier of the power of imagination.

Since he uses the scarlet letter as his personal symbol of contact with the audience, Hawthorne must see his audience as akin to Hester's social audience. For Hawthorne begins his tale with a magical rose bush containing a direct offering of the scarlet letter.

> Finding it so directly on the threshold of our narrative, which is now about to issue from that inauspicious portal, we could hardly do otherwise than pluck one of its flowers and present it to the reader.

Little Pearl animates the scarlet letter throughout the tale.

> But it was the remarkable appearance of this garb, and indeed of the child's whole appearance, that it irresistibly and inevitably reminded the beholder of the token which Hester Prynne was doomed to wear upon her bosom. It was the scarlet letter in another form; the scarlet letter endowed with life!

If Hester and Pearl are the objectified source of Hawthorne's inspiration in the book, then Dimmesdale represents the subjective source of the creativity. He is Hawthorne's alternative creator in the book. He is Pearl's father, and the scarlet letter is branded on his chest. Thus we see that the symbol of creative identity synthesizes Dimmesdale and Hester—in Pearl —into a single creative entity. Dimmesdale is the oratorical genius of the book. Thus he embodies the notion of the subjective generation of vocal meaning.

But the symbol of creativity cannot bring the two lovers together in reality. It only has the force to create the tale. For no sooner does Hester attempt to cast off the scarlet letter in order to go away with Dimmesdale, to have a real relationship, than the tale begins to move to a climax which prevents that reality. Old Chillingworth re-enters the scene like the return of the repressed [Father] avenger who cannot be denied. In this sense the tale is a scene of childhood masturbation carried out with the aid of the fetish object, which must finally be relinquished when the real world represented by the father is reestablished, for Chillingworth bars the way to the joint escape that Hester and Dimmesdale contemplate. Instead, the tale returns to the social reality of the day. All of the major characters of the tale are disposed of in some morally consistent way. Pearl goes on to thrive and Hester returns to her place as a stable, normal member of society. In other words, Hawthorne reaffirms his identity as a writer through the production of this adult work.

Hawthorne employed the creative process to remake his identity as an adult creator. As the work proceeds from (1) frustration in reality, to (2) regression, to (3) contact with the irrational core of the primary process, to (4) revision of the meaning generated in the core, to (5) a return to reality with new identity as a mature creator, the work itself carries the formal structure of the creative process into a structure of Hawthorne's adult identity as a creator.

THE THRESHOLD OF MATURITY

The Interpretation of Dreams *by Sigmund Freud*

In writing *The Interpretation of Dreams,* Freud remade his identity and established himself as a mature creator who had a unique place in society. Before writing *The Interpretation* Freud was frustrated in the work of adult creativity. He needed to establish publicly and for himself that his was a correct viewing of the human mind. We would like to examine *The Interpretation of Dreams* to see how Freud remakes his identity as a professional creator, to see how the creative process structures this change, and to see how the creative process of a creator on the threshold of maturity uses all the earlier prototypes for identity formation.

The Interpretation of Dreams, Freud's dream book, is strikingly like the dreams it is intended to explain. It has, as one of its features, a tendency to form structural analogues to transitional object making and dream formation. It follows a scenario of waking frustration, falling asleep, dreaming, movement toward awakening, and waking. This provides *The Interpretation* with a literary savor, and poses a literary problem. Is it, we wonder, possible to reconcile the primitive aspects of transitional object and dream formation with the intellectual and conceptual sophistication of *The Interpretation of Dreams?* We suggest that it is, that the transitionally patterned regression in the service of the ego will conclude in a new synthesis patterned on the genesis of mature emotional development. Seeing it, though, requires a fairly intensive reading of *The Interpretation.* In this case the creative pattern depends on taking emotional development as an intellectual model.

But of course *The Interpretation* is not a dream. It is an exercise in problem solving. And of course it is a creative product. It begins with the kind of frustration in reality easily transformed into a challenge and concludes with a successfully achieved solution. However "artistic" the essay, its form depends on Freud's drive toward solution, so the final product has that sparse elegance that we associate with economically performed equations.

As a creative product comparable to a dream, *The Interpretation* has this feature: Its manifest content (what it says) and its solution (what it proves) must have a certain coincidence. This is precisely because the latent thought or wish (to be able to communicate a scientific method for interpreting dreams) is that they coincide. Dreams are essentially wish fulfillments. As representations of gratification, they have the temporary effect of obliterating some portion of human frustration.

The Interpretation of Dreams is the fulfillment of the wish to write *The Interpretation of Dreams,* a fact that is less solipsistic than one would suspect. For, quite simply, the wish has attached to it latent thoughts of a scope wider than the simple desire to produce a book. Attached to the wish, synonymous with it, is a wish to overcome the censorship and an equal drive to enter into the unconscious and, like Orpheus, return firmly grasping the well-loved object of inspiration. It is as though Freud has taken the whole unconscious as his muse.

Phase 1—Frustration

The Interpretation opens with an invocation of frustration. Having summarized his intention in the space of one paragraph, Freud opens his first chapter, "The Scientific Literature Dealing with the Problem of Dreams" with

> ... by way of a preface a review of the work done by earlier writers on the subject as well as of the present position of the problems of dreams has made very little advance—a fact so generally admitted in the literature that it seems unnecessary to quote instances in support of it. (S.E. vol. IV, p. 1)

This hardly prevents Freud from giving instances, for

... in these writings, of which a list appears at the end of my work, many stimulating observations are to be found and a quantity of interesting material bearing upon our theme, but little or nothing that touches upon the essential nature of dreams or that offers a final solution of any of their enigmas. (S.E. vol. IV, p. 1)

Freud's intention, as we all know, is to

... bring forward proof that there is a psychological technique which makes it possible to interpret dreams, and that, if that procedure is employed, every dream reveals itself as a psychical structure which has a meaning and which can be inserted at an assignable point in the mental activities of the waking life. I shall further endeavour to elucidate the process to which the strangeness and obscurity of dreams are due and to deduce from those processes the nature of the psychical forces by whose concurrent or mutually opposing action dreams are generated. (S.E. vol. IV, p. 1)

A tall order.

There is something almost amusing about this ironic act of ritual obeisance, because, really, this chapter is interesting on account of Freud's picking out other people's focal ideas and his subsequent failure to integrate them into any necessary continuum of meaning. The focus dwindles. Initially, Freud builds up a tension of expectation and then is about to let the reader down hard, leaving a sense of failure of purpose. In point of fact, Freud has generated a frustration equal to his own, so that we come to empathize with Freud's need to synthesize— a need that compels the creative person to undertake his adventure.

The various sections of review achieve significance because they invite a search through the literature for clues to the relationship between dreams and mental disease. Freud ends the chapter in an expression of hope that his theory will establish this connection in a meaningful way. In fact, Freud has succeeded in demonstrating the generation of latent, dream inciting, or creative syndrome triggering thought. He has set himself the task of synthesizing existing material on dreams so that, at the end of the synthesis, he will be able to interpret and decode dreams. The (metaphorically) latent thought, born of frustration, is something like, "I wish I could understand how to interpret dreams; if I could understand how to interpret dreams, I would be able to understand neurosis and also become a 'professor extraordinary,' a coveted post, and achieve recognition." He would achieve new identity as a mature creator, recognized by his society.

At this point the latent thought branches off in various directions which have to do with the theories of Freud's predecessors. Each branching train of thought has buried within it a lively and vital connection to the latent thought. The result is a description of the prophetic sorts of dream analysis that bear strangely on the notions involved in Fredian dream analysis.

Phase 2—Regression

The parts of *The Interpretation of Dreams* that most resemble dreaming extend from Chapter 2 to Chapter 6. In the first stages of creation, analogous to the first stages of dream formation, Freud condenses theory, inviting us into a world of wishes and suspended critical judgment. Therefore, in the second chapter of *The Interpretation of Dreams,* Freud accomplishes a movement from frustration to a suspension of normal purpose. The release from normal purpose fires a vast scanning apparatus toward a transformation of the frustrating material. The great unanalyzed wish subtending the dream book and Freud's dreams within it is surely the wish to complete *The Interpretation of Dreams.*

However, Freud has more to say about critical suspension. Like the analytic patient, the reader is invited to subtract the self-critical attitude from the self-reflective function to achieve a relatively pure observation. The analysand's goal is self-observation. The reader is to observe Freud's mind. In analysis, adopting this attitude of self-observation, while the body is reclined and movement restricted, recreates the conditions of settling down to sleep. The analytic posture is intended to ease forward chains of thought which emerge without voluntary purpose. This is free association.

Freud underscores the similarity between dream formation and creative regression in a long quotation from Schiller.

> It seems a bad thing and detrimental to the creative work . . . if reason makes too close an examination of the ideas as they come pouring in—at the very gateway, as it were. Looked at in isolation, a thought may seem very trival or very fantastic; but it may be made important by another thought that comes after it, and, in conjunction with other thoughts that may seem equally absurd, it may turn out to form a most effective link. Reason cannot form any opinion upon all this unless it retains the thought long enough to look at it in connection with the others. On the other hand, where there is a creative mind, Reason—so it seems to me —relaxes its watch upon the gates, and the ideas rush in pell-mell, and only then does it look them through and examine them in a mass. . . . You critics, or whatever else you may call yourselves, are ashamed or frightened of the momentary and transient extravagances which are to be found in all truly creative minds and whose longer or shorter duration distinguishes the thinking artist from the dreamer. You complain of your unfruitfulness because you reject too soon and discriminate too severely. (S.E. vol. IV, p. 103)

Abjuring himself tacitly and inviting the reader to adopt this method, Freud presents a specimen dream, "Irma's injection," and plunges us into the very center of his life as of July 23 and 24, 1895.

The presentation has three parts: preamble, dream proper, and lengthy analysis. The text of the dream is included in full.

> A large hall—numerous guests, whom we were receiving. —Among them was Irma. I at once took her on one side, as

though to answer her letter and to reproach her for not having accepted my "solution" yet. I said to her: "If you still get pains, it's really only your fault." She replied: "If you only knew what pains I've got now in my throat and stomach and abdomen—it's choking me."—I was alarmed and looked at her. She looked pale and puffy. I thought to myself that after all I must be missing some organic trouble. I took her to the window and looked down her throat, and she showed signs of recalcitrance, like women with artificial dentures. I thought to myself that there was really no need for her to do that. She then opened her mouth properly and on the right I found a big white patch; at another place I saw extensive whitish grey scabs upon some remarkable curly structures which were evidently modelled on the turbinal bones of the nose.—I at once called in Dr. M., and he repeated the examination and confirmed it. . . . Dr. M. looked quite different from usual; he was very pale, and he walked with a limp and his chin was clean-shaven. . . . My friend Otto was now standing beside her as well, and my friend Leopold was percussing her through her bodice and saying: "She has a dull area low down on the left." He also indicated that a portion of the skin on the left shoulder was infiltrated. (I noticed this, just as he did, in spite of her dress.) M. said: "There's no doubt it's an infection, but no matter; dysentery will supervene and the toxin will be eliminated." . . . We were directly aware, too, of the origin of the infection. Not long before, when she was feeling unwell, my friend Otto had given her an injection of a preparation of propyl, propyls . . . propionic acid . . . trimethylamine . . . and I saw before me the formula for this printed in heavy type. . . . Injections of that sort ought not to be made so thoughtlessly. . . . And probably the syringe had not been clean. (S.E. vol. IV, p. 107)

Irma's injection is a "specimen dream of psychoanalysis" and is often taken as the first dream of the self-analysis. It is remarkably complete in the way first dreams (of analyses) are supposed to be. The first dreams of analysis are notorious for a comprehensive quality, being relatively inclusive statements of the central conflicts in the analysand's development. The reason (and this is a common psychoanalytic experience) is that resistance has not yet been systematically mobilized to counter the interpretive efforts which aim at uncovering the focal conflicts. Freud wishes at the outset that his solution to dream interpretation would be accepted.

Freud's endowing "Irma's Injection" with the comprehensive force of a "first" dream has reference to another dream of June 1900 (Freud 1950a, Letter 137), dreamed roughly five years after "Irma." As the editors of the standard edition have it, "Freud describes a later visit to Bellevue, the house where he had this dream. 'Do you suppose,' he writes, 'that some day a marble tablet will be placed on the house, inscribed with the words?—

> In this House, on July 24th, 1895
> the Secret of Dreams was Revealed
> to Dr. Sigmund Freud

At the moment there seems little prospect of it.'" (S.E. vol. IV, p. 121)

Clearly, the dream of the plaque stands as a screen for the entire experience. In addition to expressing an obvious wish, it recalls the wish to create the dream book, and with it a significant element of the dream, a verbal inscription or formula in heavy type. In the original dream, the chemical formula for trimethylamin appeared to Freud in heavy type.

> Trimethylamin was an allusion not only to the immensely powerful factor of sexuality, but also to a person whose agreement I recalled with satisfaction whenever I felt isolated in my opinions. Surely this friend who played so large a part in my life must appear again elsewhere in these trains of thought. Yes. For he had a special knowledge of the consequences of affections of the nose and its accessory cavities; and he had drawn scientific attention to some very remarkable connections between the turbinal bones and the female organs of sex. . . . I had Irma examined by him to see whether her gastric pains might be of nasal origin. But he suffered himself from suppurative rhinitis, which caused me anxiety, and no doubt there was an allusion to this in the pyaemia which vaguely came into my mind in connection with the metasteses in the dream. (S.E. vol. IV, p. 117)

Irma and Fliess, Freud's friend, are tied together under some such rubric as *bisexuality: Fliess/Irma.* Fliess, a Berlin nose and throat specialist had for years been Freud's most intimate friend. He was an eccentric with a group of theories about nasal infection, bisexuality, and critical periodicity (which had to do with numerical calculations), remarkable chiefly for their ostensible ability to predict the span of human life. He was also an ear, nose, and throat man of repute. In the dream Freud pits the good Fliess against the bad or foolish Otto and M. (Schur [1972], p. 8). This makes sense considering that Fliess is "the person whose agreement I recalled with satisfaction whenever I felt isolated in my opinions." (S. E. vol. IV, p. 117)

Fliess was quite definitely associated with theories of sexuality and bisexuality, so he is easily merged into the composite figure, Irma. Part of the effect of the analysis is a demonstration that Irma is the representative of a great host of dream figures. These include a governess with false teeth, a young, widowed friend of Irma's, Freud's wife, and Irma herself.

> Moreover the pathological changes which I discovered in her throat involved allusions to a whole series of other figures . . . they were concealed behind the dream figure of "Irma," which thus turned out to be a collective image with, it must be admitted, a number of contradictory characteristics. (S.E. vol. IV, p. 293)

The reference to pathology points to Fliess, who had examined Irma's throat. The sexual overtones are manifest. Even the examination through Irma's dress has a sexual coloration, being a sort of denial. There is a richness of complication. Bypassing several kinds of complications, two portions of the puzzle are outstanding. One, the triangle has a homosexual (bisexual) cast. Two, Irma, as composite figure, has the germinal significance of muse. Metonymically, she stands for the dream. She is, moreover, the source of Freud's inspiration. Surely the counter-transference has to do with Freud's com-

pelling need to make psychoanalysis work. He has tried
to force a solution on Irma.

Phase 3—Primary Process

With an inviting sense of necessity, the second chapter
concludes, "When the work of interpretation has been completed, we perceive that a dream is the fulfillment of a wish."
(S.E. vol. IV p. 121) And therefore the third chapter, "A Dream
Is the Fulfillment of a Wish," draws its imagery from the medi-
eval renaissance dream genre.

> When, after passing through a narrow defile, we suddenly
> emerge upon a piece of high ground, where the path divides and
> fine prospects open up on every side, we may pause for a moment
> and consider in which direction we shall first turn our steps.
> Such is the case with us, now that we have surmounted the first
> interpretation of a dream. (S.E. vol. IV, p. 122)

Clearly, this represents a deeper penetration into the dream
world. With logical consistency, Freud uses this chapter to
demonstrate his now famous principle that the motive force for
dreams is inherent in their tendency to represent some wish as
fulfilled. His muse has brought him into the realm of primary
process where all wishes may be imaged as fulfilled.

The editors append an appealing footnote:

> In a letter to Fliess of August 6, 1899 (Freud 1950a, Letter 114),
> Freud describes the opening chapters of this book as follows:
> "The whole thing is planned on the model of an imaginary walk.
> First comes the dark wood of the authorities (who cannot see the
> trees), where there is no clear view and where it is easy to go
> astray. Then there is a cavernous defile through which I lead my
> readers—my specimen dream with its peculiarities, its details, its
> indiscretions and its bad jokes—and then, all at once, the high
> ground and the open prospect and the question: "Which way do
> you want to go?" (S.E. vol. IV, p. 122)

The figure is traceable to classical and renaissance oratorical mnemonics, and poetry. It is vital to the construction of affectively reverberating chains of association to the reference. In poetry especially it recalls the great poems of the dream genre, "The Pearl," *The Divine Comedy* of Dante, *Pilgrim's Progress,* poems that have to do with mature walks of a special, figurative kind.

The fourth chapter of *The Interpretation of Dreams* accomplishes a deeper *pas* into the work of dreaming. The interest, for our purposes, lies in teasing out the various relations that link several varieties of content—all having to do with the process that interdicts simple wish fulfillment. Having established his correctness in the first three chapters, Freud is compelled to defend his discovery against criticism, giving as an examples wishes that are not represented in terms of obvious fulfillment. The idea is that distortion intervenes between the latent thought and the manifest content. The upshot is a more sophisticated statement about dream interpretation, accounting for the censorship and promoting the notion that the dream— or finished product—recapitulates the process of its own development insofar as it bears the stamp of production.

In sequence is a dream about an uncle of Freud's, a gentleman well endowed with a beard of yellow hair. Among other things, the dream has to do with two wishes—one, that Freud might be elevated to a professorship, and, two, that his discoveries be accepted. In the anti-Semitic Viennese society, Freud's Judaism seemed likely to nullify the possibility of either happy outcome. Freud's political meditation tends toward another meditation—on the political censorship. It turns out that the political and intrapsychic censorship operate on the same principles. Obviously, there are two agencies determining the shape of the dream (Vol. IV, p. 146), a wishful agency and a censoring one. The dream of the uncle with the yellow beard is a dream about dreaming. At least contextually it serves as a compositional function, being a dream about the agencies of dreaming. The subject of the chapter, censorship, has extended the formal requirements for manifest content into the matrix of dream synthesis. But here, censorship often refers to counterwishes or painful motives, and so wish and counterwish refer to the driven quality of dreams and of the unconscious.

Phase 4—Revision

The fifth chapter, with the dream of the "botanical monograph," moves toward awakening. During the relatively lengthy dream, work that precedes the transient business of representation, the latent thoughts, and dream-impelling wishes have access to affectively reverberating childhood memory. This contact is severed at the beginning of representation, which means that toward waking the complex that has achieved dream representation comes into contact with the censorship.

This is the beginning of secondary revision. And although Freud will only discuss this final, authoritarian, antianarchic revision in Chapter 6, he prepares for the discussion by informing these two chapters (5 and 6) with a certain formal, recapitulatory structure. In both chapters he dips into a set of childhood memories historically arranged, which is to say that the memories progress from early to later, from, say, anal developments to oedipal ones. This order moves consciousness toward waking and prewaking contact with the censor. Gradually the censor takes on political and social overtones of adult consciousness, so that the dream struggle of wishes against the censor takes fire in Freud's knowledge of Austrian political censorship and racial oppression (that is, the semioffocial anti-Semitism).

The chapter opens with a number of smaller specimen dreams pointing toward the pivotal "monograph." This is a dream about frustration and unlocking creativity. The dream of "the botanical monograph" is a specimen dream of allusion, of the ability to allude to an array of material. Such allusions are very like literary ones. In them an appropriate reference to an author's name or work may bring to bear a train of philosophical, literary, political, historical, social, emotional, and quite personal ideas. Not so simply, the dream is the efflorescence of Freud's wish to get over the difficult business of producing *The Interpretation of Dreams*. Freud narrates the dream as follows:

> I had written a monograph on a certain plant. The book lay before me and I was at the moment turning over a folded colored plate. Bound up in each copy there was a dried specimen of the plant, as though it had been taken from a herbarium. (S.E. vol. IV, p. 169)

One of the dream's less highly charged or indifferent sources has to do with the story of Frau L., a former patient. On one occasion this lady's husband neglected to bring her a gift of birthday flowers. Frau L. was inconsolable. This anecdote Freud

> ... had recently repeated to a circle of friends ... as evidence in favor of my theory that forgetting is very often determined by unconscious purpose and ... it enables one to deduce the secret intention of the person who forgets. (S.E. vol. IV, pp. 169–70)

This is precisely our point about recapitulation. Really, any product of subjectivity will in some way evince the mechanics of its creation. This idea is reinterpreted later in Chapter 6 in an ambiguous comment on the same dream:

> I had written a monograph; it lays before me; it contained colored plates, dried plants accompanied each copy. This reminds one of the peace that has descended upon a battlefield strewn with corpses; no trace is left of the struggle which raged over it. (S.E. vol. IV, p. 467)

In other words, there is no struggle, but vivid and obvious traces.

Bound into this framework are two experiences (day residues) from the preceding day, an indifferent and a stirring one.

The indifferent portion had simply to do with flowers. Cyclamen, the subject of a monograph glimpsed during the day, was Mrs. Freud's favorite flower. Under the circumstances, this observation had a low charge, but contained a self-reproach about not bringing her flowers more often. The comparison is presumably with Herr L.

More importantly, or more centrally, Freud had written a treatise capable of passing as a botanical monograph, a dissertation on the cocoa plant. The cocoa plant is the source of cocaine. Freud's experience with cocaine was a peculiar one. He published his dissertation in 1884 suggesting cocaine as an anesthetic. Soon after that, Freud's friend Koller, an eye surgeon, used cocaine as an anesthetic while performing glaucoma surgery, all of which ended in great frustration for Freud, who quite rightly believed that through his own oversight he had missed a chance at a discovery capable of releasing him from financial distress, a premarital difficulty. The topic of cocaine had embodied Freud's earlier pursuit of recognition. Freud also noticed the energetic impetus of cocaine, experiencing an analogue to a state of creative inspiration.

This dream covers the wish to succeed with a memory of a previous failure and refers back to the Irma dream. In that dream Freud refers to the death of his friend Fleishel, to whom Freud had recommended oral doses of cocaine as a temporary substitute for morphine.

One of the associations is almost funny.

> It had once amused my father to hand over a book with *colored plates* (an account of a journey through Persia) for me and my eldest sister to destroy. Not easy to justify from an educational point of view! I had been five years old at the time and my sister not yet three; and the picture of us blissfully pulling the book to pieces (leaf by leaf, like an *artichoke* [Freud's "favorite flower," as opposed to cyclamen, his wife's] I found myself saying) was almost the only plastic memory I retained from that period of my life. (S.E. vol. IV, p. 142)

This is a demonstration of the connection between dream content and childhood.

A dream element so small as "The book lay before me" calls up the following information:

> I saw the monograph which I had written *lying before me*. This again led back to something. I had had a letter from my friend (Fliess) in Berlin the day before in which he had shown his power of visualization: "I am very much occupied with your dream book. I see it lying finished before me and I see myself turning over its pages." How much I envied him his gift as a seer! If only I could have seen it lying finished before me! (S.E. vol. IV, p. 172)

This dream contains the latent thought, "I wish I could finish this book"—something Freud seems unready to admit. At the time of dreaming, March 8 or 9, 1898, Freud was still engrossed in the work of the dream book. As a result he fastens on the concept of overdetermination, which is necessary to explain other dreams, but not this one, and thereby avoids ascribing the genesis of this dream to any latent thought or to any wish at all. In the interpretation, Freud lays heavy stress on the word "monograph," which may be read "dream book" as easily as "dissertation on cocaine." Yet Freud concludes his analysis thus:

> I am prepared to find this explanation attacked on the ground of its being arbitrary or artificial. . . . Another indifferent impression of the same day—for crowds of such impressions enter our minds and are then forgotten—would have taken the place of the "monograph" in the dream, would have linked up with the subject of the conversation and would have represented it in the content of the dream. Since it was in fact the monograph and not any other idea that was chosen to serve this function, we must suppose that it was the best adapted for the connection. (S.E. vol. IV, p. 176)

Which is precisely right. One way or another Freud would have dreamed about the dream book. He might easily have dreamed in a context quite alien to his wife's favorite flowers or even Fleishel's tragedy (connected to cocaine and Freud's other attempt at significant discovery).

In the movement toward wakeful mastery of the technique of dream interpretation, Freud brings us into contact with his identification with Hannibal. In the dream giving rise to this association Freud is in

> . . . Rome once more. I saw a street-corner before me and was surprised to find so many posters in German stuck up there. I had written to my friend with prophetic foresight the day before to say that I thought Prague might not be an agreeable place for a German to walk about in. Thus the dream expressed at the same time a wish to meet him in Rome instead of in a Bohemian town, and a desire, probably dating back to my student days, that the German language might be better tolerated in Prague. Incidentally, I must have understood Czech in my earliest youth. . . . There was no lack of connection with my early childhood in those dreams either. (S.E. vol. IV, pp. 195–196)

All of this has to do with Freud's desire to see Rome and the inhibitions that kept him from entering that city. In untangling the allusions Freud writes,

> To my youthful mind Hannibal and Rome symbolized the conflict between the tenacity of Jewry and the organization of the Catholic church. (S.E. vol. IV, p. 196)

As readers of *Moses and Monotheism* know, Catholicism and literary censorship were, for Freud, nearly the same. Hannibal, who was ostensibly a Jew, came very near to conquering Rome, so for Freud,

> . . . the wish to go to Rome had become in my dream-life a cloak and symbol for a number of other passionate wishes. Their realization was to be pursued with all the preserverence and single-mindedness of the Carthagenian, though their fulfillment seemed

at the moment just as little favored by destiny as was Hannibal's lifelong wish to enter Rome. (S.E. vol. IV, p. 169)

And so Freud is brought to express in an anecdote the central wish to defeat the political censor, to defeat through shame the cowardly-authoritarian oedipal father, and the censoring agency of what we have come to call the super ego.

The following anecdote is about Freud's father. Jacob Freud seems to have been a lovable man, a beloved father, and like all fathers subject of a certain amount of oedipal rage.

I may have been twelve years old, when my father began to take me with him on his walks and reveal to me in his talk his views upon things in the world we live in. Thus it was, on one such occasion, that he told me a story to show me how much better things were now than they had been in his days. "When I was a young man," he said, "I went for a walk one Saturday in the streets of your birthplace; I was well dressed, and had a new fur cap on my head. A Christian came up to me and with a single blow knocked off my cap into the mud and shouted: 'Jew! Get off the pavement!' 'And what did you do?' I asked. 'I went into the roadway and picked up my cap,' was his quiet reply. This struck me as unheroic conduct on the part of the big, strong man who was holding the little boy by the hand. I contrasted this situation with another which fitted my feelings better: the scene in which Hannibal's father, Hamilcar Barca, made his boy swear before the household altar to take vengeance on the Romans. Ever since that time Hannibal had had a place in my fantasies. (S.E. vol. IV, p. 197)

Freud feels that the completed *Interpretation of Dreams* will be his passport to Rome.

The next dream in the series, the dream of "Count Thun" (Vol. IV, pp. 208–219), has principally to do with a wish "to amount to something." After a number of dream adventures Freud finds himself

Once more . . . in front of the station, but this time in the company of an elderly gentleman. I thought of a plan for remaining unrecognized; and then saw that this plan had already been put into effect. It was as though thinking and experiencing were one and the same thing. He appeared to be blind, at all events with one eye, and I handed him a male glass urinal (which we had to buy or had bought in town). So I was a sick-nurse and had to give him the urinal because he was blind. If the ticket-collector were to see us like that, he would be certain to let us get away without noticing us. Here the man's attitude and his micturating penis appeared in plastic form. (This was the point at which I awoke, feeling a need to micturate.) (S.E. vol. IV, p. 211)

The dream emphasizes wakefulness triggered by aggressive excretions such as urinating or moving the bowels in public —in front of one's parents—or with bed wetting. On one occasion, Freud answered the calls of nature in his parent's bedroom and was told he would never amount to anything. Part of the dream's force is in the reply, "Oh yes I will!" Therefore Freud helps his father, the old man of the dream who had unilateral glaucoma (Vol. IV, p. 216), to ease his own needs in public. The memory of the childhood scene is surely a scene of revenge.

What follows is curiously triumphant, as though Freud had somehow triumphed over the censor. Reading the context, the literally unnamed censor takes on the characteristics of the ubiquitous opponents of psychoanalysis. The transition from apology to assertion takes place in the course of a particularly physical dream. Gutted of a certain part of its substance, the dream reads,

I was riding on a grey horse, timidly, and awkwardly to begin with, as though I were reclining on it. . . . I now began to find myself sitting more and more firmly and comfortably on my highly intelligent horse, and noticed that I was feeling quite at home up there. (S.E. vol. IV, p. 229)

Analysis of this dream takes a somatic influence into account. At the time of dreaming, Freud was afflicted with boils, the ghastliest of which was "a boil the size of an apple which had risen at the base of his scrotum." The dream is a fine example of denial. In his misery Freud felt incapable of discharging his medical duties. "There was, however, one activity for which, in view of the nature and situation of my complaint, I should certainly have been less fitted than for any other, and that was—riding" (Vol. IV, p. 230). The dream has a sort of reassuring effect on the sleeper. Reassurance leads to discovery: Dreams are the guardians of sleep. The dream ensured sleep, over the insistence of bodily stimulation. Sleep, it seems, must be maintained through a balance of forces. The preconscious wish to maintain sleep, ever compromising with the latent thought and the unconscious wish attached to it. In this case the wish is to be in control of the material of the dream book. And, in fact, Freud *has* become master of the psychoanalytic material. Freud has been an expert, that is, an adult, not a child seeking knowledge. Such a person is surely entitled to his sleep and dreaming, particularly since these activities are undertaken for so commendable a purpose.

Now Freud has come to understand Oedipus:

> His destiny moves us because it might have been ours—because the oracle laid the same curse upon us before our birth as on him. It is the fate of all of us, perhaps, to direct our first sexual impulse towards our mother and our first hatred and our first murderous wish against our father. Our dreams convince us that this is so. . . . Like Oedipus, we live in ignorance of these wishes, repugnant to morality, which have been forced upon us by Nature, and after their revelation we may all of us well seek to close our eyes to the scenes of childhood. (S.E. vol. IV, pp. 262–263)

This, then, is the truth that has emerged from the analysis of dreams of retaliatory aggression.

In some way, the sixth chapter, on "dream work," traverses an undercurrent of affect governed by the same class of aggressive and sexual imagery that dominated Chapter 5. There is a summary quality to this chapter, as if Freud wanted to linger in his creative process for a while, before chancing the light of real social criticism. There is a primary process (prever-bal, associative) quality that pervades the exemplary material. The scientifically accurate theoretical statements are under-pinned with consciously selected examples of dream work, which, as is their nature, undo the abstract forms of thought and remake connections via condensation, displacement, and that necessity which pervades all dream work, the necessity to find suitable representation with deference to the requirements of the censoring agency.

The result is that there are a good many urinary, anal, and oedipal dreams—many of them incompletely analyzed because of Freud's modesty, all of which tend toward a destruction of the censor. There is a great spate of father dreams preceded by this interesting statement:

> Nor is it by any means a matter of chance that our first examples of absurdity in dreams related to a dead father. . . . The authority wielded by a father provokes criticism from his children at an early age, and the severity of the demands he makes upon them leads them, for their own relief, to keep their eyes open to any weakness of their father's. (S.E. vol. V, p. 435)

In this lexicon, censorship and the father are interchange-able. The emotional weight of the chapter is in the *Autodidasker* dream (Vol. IV, p. 298), a dream in which Freud saw this word and analyzed it into the obvious component of self-taught-author.

Chapter 6 is very definitely a preparation for Chapter 7, "The Psychology of the Dream Process." This statement has two quite interesting senses. One of them is that Chapter 7 has to do with the literal business of waking up. This is the obvious surface, the manifest, intentionally produced content of the chapter. The other has to do with one meaning of coming into conscious mental waking. Wakefulness is accompanied by an ability to recount experience in a logical manner.

And this is just what Freud does do in Chapter 7. He

details the relevant parts of his experience in dream analysis in such a way as to make them available to other people. In chapter 7 Freud produces a method for dream interpretation, so that the solution to his problem (which included certain unconscious drives, to overcome the censor, to fathom the unconscious, to overcome the Oedipus complex) is translated into a purer, more sublimated, logical, secondary process explanation.

Phase 5—Resolution

The final chapter, "The Psychology of Dream Process," is above all the chapter on methods. Its great significance lies in its opening and closing images. The chapter opens with a dream:

> A father had been watching beside his child's sick-bed for days and nights on end. After the child had died, he went into the next room to lie down, but left the door open so that he could see from his bedroom into the room in which his child's body was laid out. . . . An old man had been engaged to keep watch over it, and sat beside the body murmuring prayers. After a few hours' sleep, the father had a dream that his child was standing beside his bed, caught him by the arm and whispered to him reproachfully: "Father don't you see I'm burning?" (S.E. vol. V, p. 509)

The old man had fallen asleep and a candle had toppled over.

This dream, although not Freud's, is used as an allegory indicating that Freud is correct even if he encounters social resistance. It was told to him by a patient who, as Freud is at pains to assure us, had herself heard it in a lecture on dreams:

> Its actual source is still unknown to me. Its content made an impression on the lady, however, and she proceeded to "re-dream it," that is, to repeat some of its elements in a dream of her own, so that by taking it over in this way, she might express her agreement with one particular point. (S.E. vol. V, p. 509)

Presumably that point is that dreams have external origins. The patient's treatment of the material is not uncommon. In taking over the dream, she forced on it the shape of her own fantasy. If the wish were that dreams might have external stimuli and not arise from psychological sources, then in redreaming she quite neatly disproved her own theory—to Freud's amusement, no doubt.

Curiously, Freud was quite taken by this bit of third-hand dreaming. It is, surely, a memorable dream, perhaps the most memorable in *The Interpretation*. "Pity and terror," a very appropriate formula, takes light in such a context. Yet Freud is again at pains to assure us that his purpose is dry, scientific, and, in fact, anticathartic.

> The problems of dream interpretation have hitherto occupied the centre of the picture. And now we come upon a dream which raises no problem of interpretation and the meaning of which is obvious, but which, as we see, nevertheless retains the essential characteristics that differentiate dreams so strikingly from waking life and consequently call for explanation. It is only after we have disposed of everything that has to do with the work of interpretation that we can begin to realize the incompleteness of our psychology of dreams. (S.E. vol. V, pp. 510–511)

The idea is that the most powerful example in the entire essay serves a mechanical, not an evocative end. Its simplicity is used to underline a deficiency in dream interpretations. As Freud is telling us, dreams analyzed according to Freudian principles have no Freudian psychology to buttress them. There is no framework of fact and theory, medicine and neurology, capable of providing them with context. Chapter 7 is written to provide such a context.

All of which is terribly important, but none of this unalterable significance explains the painful beauty of the dream image. It is remarkable, however, that this dream represents a radical shift in perspective. It is a dream about the agonies of fatherhood, about the unalterable pain of watching the death of a beloved child. And this dream, and not another, follows in the train of oedipal and preoedipal dreams, which center on the child's experience. Although some of Freud's dreams provoke association pointing toward his adult role, most of them have to do with overcoming the censor, altering his relationship with his father, or wishing for or believing in achievement.

We are suggesting that this beautiful and powerful dream is a container for an image of Freud's mature reality. There is no unanalyzed child left in this man. As a creator, as a scientist, as a human being, he has in the course of the self-analysis altered his relation with his (dead) father, understood and therefore conquered Oedipus, and succeeded in the interpretation of dreams. The child is burning. And this child is the father of the mature man. The child is the book, now completed, and Freud's fears for its acceptance in society as a container for his new identity.

Chapter 11

CHANGING LIFE
Maturity—40 to 65

More quickly in women, more slowly in men, an alteration in the balance of the drives occurs during the years from 40 to 65. An increased libidinal tempo accompanies hormonal changes which for several years signal the menopause and the climacterium. These initial years of new libidinal thrust animate the generative surge that accompanies maturity. Much as orality peaks in the primal scene, childhood masturbation intensifies in the oedipal period, and adolescent genitality flourishes in the efflorescence of somatic and hormonal changes, maturity arrives with a libidinal necessity of its own.

As the libidinal tempo slows—a little earlier in women, a little later in men—the aggressive forces come into ascendancy again. Changes in the relative strength of the drive in response to hormonal pressures require changes in the formal identity structure to accommodate to the change-of-life.

The change in identity structure which must accommodate the changing biological balance of the drives is reflected most profoundly in the individual's relationship to society. During adult life the individual identified himself as an integral part of society, as an individual contained within the structure of society. With the coming of maturity, the individual, particularly the creative individual, feels the necessity of making a change in society.

The aim is not the adolescent one of revolutionizing the authority structure; rather it is toward fashioning a new perspective of the social order itself. The mature individual realizes as he remakes his identity that social order is maintained through similar coextensive perceptions in many individual minds. Thus the institutional character of social order (which is more or less taken for granted in "adult life") is questioned in maturity. Recognition of the relativity of social forms and of their accessibility to alteration by the individual changes the relation between the individual and society in maturity.

THE MATURE CREATOR

We have seen that the adult creator finds his alternative identity in the work. He remakes, or changes, his identity as a creator in the course of his adult works. He endows his work with a structure or with characters which, in their entirety, comprise a whole provisional being. This provisional alternative identity meets the major criterion of the creator's syndrome: that there be an alternative to the normal resolution of the traumatic challenge to identity which occurs in each stage of life.

There is a shift in the focus of the alternative identity presented in the works of the mature creator. He wants to make a statement of social significance through the impact of his collected works. The mature creator comes to believe that his works—collected, or retrospected—contain a unique social significance which distinguishes him as a creator. The reputation of the creator is identified with the social significance of his work, and contributes to the creator's sense of social identity.

Reputation mediates between the creative and his normal identity.

In this era, being refused a social reputation on the basis of his works is the professional creator's major trauma. He resolves this trauma syndromatically through his pursuit of the fantasy of greatness. The creator denies his lack of distinction by identifying himself with great past creators whose distinction and reputation have become legendary. Our thesis in this chapter is that the identification with historically mighty predecessors is an aspect of a fantasy of immortality. The creator is looking with denial toward a future where individual identity must perish. Thus the creator's search for an identity extended into the historical past is a wishful attempt to establish a present identity secured from the aging process.

The creator's fantasy of achieving immortality through the effect of his work on social communication externalizes for him a provisional social identity mediated by his mature works. This illusion has much to do with the mature creator's changing view of his audience. The audience is equated with a society which, if it recognizes the creator's greatness, can confer awards or distinctions which bestow the social illusion of immortality on the creator. In maturity, the work-inspiring power of the muse is increasingly assigned to a specialized province of culture.

This is to say that in the mature stage the creator perceives the inspiring muse figure as having taken up residence outside himself and society. Thus certain historical figures take on the significance previously granted to a more personal muse. As the creator strives to enter the social mythology, he looks to historical predecessors to embody the inspirational themes that give rise to the generation of new works.

We would like to bring the reader up to date on the progress of the creator's syndrome in maturity. By this time of life the creator has come to know very much about his creative states and about his own creative process. He understands that there is a contrast between his professional identity as creator and his ordinary day-to-day identity. He understands that there is a sequence which he must follow to bring his works from conception to the light of day. The sense of inspiration has shifted away from the love affair with the muse, or away from the later apportionment of that kind of love to a mate. The mature creator develops, still syndromatically, an alternative to ordinary identity comprised of an alternative self.

This development in the creator's syndrome is prefigured by a change in consciousness which attends middle age. The middle-aged person is aware almost continuously of his own mortality. Thus the chief anxiety of the age is fear of death. The alternative identity as creator takes on a detached imperviousness, as if the creative state were truly removed from the consciousness of mortality. We would like to exemplify this development by citing clinical material from the analysis of a 58-year-old writer.

PSYCHOANALYSIS OF A MATURE WRITER

The patient is a writer who had been in analysis for three years at the time of the session we are considering here. He entered analysis at the point of divorce from his wife of 30 years. He had maintained a satisfying affair with another woman for 10 years, but had finally become frightened of being found out, and of the other woman's wishes for more of him. He expressed similar feelings about a new woman he began seeing. He is genuinely fond of her, but he fears that she will infringe on his life and on his time for writing.

In the sessions preceding the present one he had begun to become aware that his mother's first marriage, ending with her husband's death, had had a more profound effect on the patient's life than he knew. His mother had overprotected him and had sought to revive the love she had for her first husband in him, her only son. This shed some light on the mother's wish to live through her son's creative accomplishments. The writer had begun his affair at the point of his mother's death. He had begun to write when he was only seven years old. From the beginning he felt that the activity afforded him relief from the feeling that his mother was always hovering over him.

The patient's claustrophobic feelings, which are connected with a sense of being smothered by his mother or some other woman, play a prominent part in his analysis. He has always found it a relief to have some other man share the responsibility for a woman he is involved with. He maintained a close, unconsciously homosexual, friendship with the husband of the woman with whom he had the affair. His wife's therapist was an integral part of his sense of relationship with his wife. At the time of the session the analyst was similarly experienced as part of his relationship with the new woman. She also has an aged father for whom she cares. The patient expresses strong wishes that she will care for him in his old age as his mother cared for him in his young age. But he fears that she will take over his life, just as he feels that she takes over his genitals through her avid interest in them.

During the three years in analysis the patient has set out consciously to make a name for himself. He wants his works to have the same lasting significance which he feels is ascribed to works of his contemporaries. He believes their works are no better, and perhaps not as good as his own. He has felt that some basic change is necessary if he is to be satisfied with his life and to accomplish more with his work.

The session begins with a dream which heralds psychic change and which contains in its structure the elements of change. The dream structure is formal and simple, though with internal complications—like his writings, which are abstract and broad in their scope.

> It's as though I were watching a play. [He laughs, and says that although he felt detached, it was after all his dream.] There is a man in bed, fully dressed. He gets up and leaves the room. He goes to the other side of a partition, and there is an identical

appearing man. They talk. The other man says, "We are preparing you, and you will find it isn't such a difficult experience." He has a red jacket, and he says, "Put this on." I knew he represented death. The one with the jacket is the spirit, and the other one is the body. I thought, "I didn't realize it was time." The first man puts on the jacket and his body stays where it is, while his spirit goes with the other man who must be death's assistant. The first man who is spirit now says, "It wasn't as difficult as I thought it would be."

There is a sense of traumatic disengagement in the dream. We are reminded of Freud's formulation that the presence of the self objectified in a memory is evidence for screening. The writer is a neutral observer of the action of the dream, but in the same way that he joked in the beginning of its telling, he is a part of the action. His identity is split. The red jacket is vivid, overdetermined. It bears the trademark of screening.

The first association is to an airplane ride the day before, when the patient was literally above the action of the world. He felt anxiously shut in and afraid of a crash. He thought of what he would leave behind—his works. He said that he guesses that is a wish for immortality. The analyst reminds him of the theme of the previous session, the fact that his mother had overprotected him as if she were afraid he might die. He then recalls, for the first time, the actual episode (when he was 12) of his mother first mentioning her dead first husband. The patient's father hushed her. It was the first the boy knew of his mother's first marriage. He wonders aloud why his father hushed his mother. "What did my father think: I should have a virgin mother?"

Then he mentions that he is due for a physical examination. In the past his lover would urge him to get his physical; now he wants the analyst to protect him. The analyst points out that the fully clothed man on the bed is the patient on the analytic couch. The analyst is represented by the spiritual, less corporeal figure. The analyst is working with the patient toward a successful relationship with the new woman, but unconsciously the patient fears that he will leave the analytic couch for the embrace of the angel of death.

The patient says, "You and I are preparing me not for dying, but for living." Then he associates to his former lover's father, who is dying while his wife remains devoted and by his side every moment. He thinks of his son, with whom he has recently re-established a relationship after it had been dormant for several years. "Hey, I did it. I'm communicating with him." He adds that he had done this on his own without the help of his former lover, who used to watch over his emotional life with the same devotion with which her mother is now watching over her father—the same devotion with which the patient's mother used to watch over him. The analyst points out that if the patient feels that he can accept the fact of his own future death, then he need no longer feel that a woman must watch over him in this enveloping way.

He thinks of "the father, the son and the holy ghost" and of his son, the new generation, embodying immortality. Then he says, "Yeh, you're right. I get up from the analytic couch and leave something of the past, its gone, yeh, leaving a shell behind. That feels more comforting than death." His final association is to giving a red jacket which had formerly belonged to his daughter to the new woman. He identifies the red jacket with her vagina. He says that his relationship with her feels more real, less like a play.

As a structural dream of identity, the dream heralds a change in this artist's conscious reflection. He identifies his reflection with the neutral identity of the analyst, and in this new identification of his reflective identity he is able to accept the existential fact of his death. The new reflection splits the objective identity of this mature adult into the physical being that is subject to aging and the socially immortal spiritual man of the world who works as a writer making objects of lasting significance.

We would now like to go on to examine a contemporary work by a mature author. This work is another prime example of the autobiography of the creator during a period of transformation in creative identity. Saul Bellow gives evidence of knowing much about his own creator's syndrome. This knowledge allows him to send his creative self on fantastic journeys of self-discovery.

HUMBOLDT'S GIFT BY SAUL BELLOW

Bellow's work, *Humboldt's Gift,* brought this author the highest prize of social distinction which society can confer on its creative individuals, the Nobel Prize. It has been noted that the work which stimulated this acclaim is itself concerned with evaluating the meaning of such distinction, for the major character of the book, Charlie Citrine, has been awarded the Légion d'Honneur and the Pulitzer Prize. The book itself, though it makes light of such honor, is concerned on one level with the relationship between social distinction and the life of the creative person, and on a transcendent level with the emotional import of a belief in immortality, on the creative imagination.

"Humboldt's gift" is the gift of the imagination. The final gift portrayed in this work is a movie scenario which aptly sums up the creative condition in the life of an author. Thus Charlie Citrine, the hero of the novel, is able to portray the life of the author as creator and the main character in the novel simultaneously.

Humboldt, who is also a character in the novel, stands for Charlie's emotional, literary, and socially influencing predecessor. This search for public figures from the past whose images have taken up residence in the mythology of the culture is a common theme in the works of maturity. The reason for this, we think, is that in the era of late maturity the recognition of mortality is ascribed to the real objective self-representation, while the wish to continue the life of the creative imagination is ascribed to some other inspirational figure which has already been granted a sense of social immortality.

We contend that an inspirational figure in maturity, such as Humboldt, carries with it the whole ontology of the muse. Being a book about the author's creativity, all of the main figures may be seen in light of the ontology of the muse. Thus Charlie's inspirational figure is represented not only by Humboldt, but by Humboldt's wife Kathleen as well. The character Cantabile functions in this novel as the boy who will not take no for an answer. He is another necessary mediator of Charlie's experience in this novel. It is the essential function of these muse characters to mediate the relationship between reality and the creative imagination. The muse characterizations function as ongoing mediators of the relationship between reality and the creative condition. The kindred nature of the characters gives energetic thrust to the action of the whole novel.

The symbol of the characters' energetic interaction is money. Charlie, like the real author, is enmeshed in a continuing monetary strangle which, each time it erupts, gives rise to new action and consequent new reflection by Charlie on the relevance of immortality themes to his life. Money represents the generating energy which must be present to overcome the limitations imposed by reality. These limitations include the loss of sexual gratification when one's object is the beautiful and phallic Renata, the loss of creative thrust, and the loss of physical vigor. Charlie's brother Ulick is a kind of negative double who is dedicated to the proposition that the acquisition of money can hold all forms of death more or less permanently at bay. This more worldly side of Charlie is counterposed against his own whimsical innocence about money.

Now we would like to make these points in a convincing way by looking at what appears to be breaches in the course of the action of the novel. *Humboldt's Gift* is interlarded with reflective meditations on the role of immortality in the life of the artist. Rudolph Steiner's transcendental speculations are made the centerpiece of this aspect of the work. On the face of it these meditations seem to intrude on the fast, often comic action of the novel; but upon consideration, these transcendental speculations become the intrapsychic glue which binds together the serious social purpose and the creative aspects of the book. At precisely those moments when the action takes Charlie into the greatest threat of social trauma, he stops the action to make another point about his relation to life as a creative person. We will bring into consecutive focus those portions of the novel told in the breaches.

Bellow begins the novel with a retrospective account of his first meeting with Humboldt. The account contains a reference to Charlie's most primitive sense of the creative gift. It is written as loose irony from the vantage of the late mature Charlie looking back to the young writer Charlie looking back to his own origins as a writer.

> And money wasn't what I had in mind. Oh God, no, what I wanted was to do good. I was dying to do something good. And this feeling for good went back to my early and peculiar sense of existence—sunk in the glassy depths of life and groping, thrillingly and desperately, for sense, a person keenly aware of painted veils, of Maya, of domes of many-colored glass staining the white radiance of eternity, quivering in the intense inane. (p. 2)

This statement, made fully ironic by "inane," contains reference to the earliest sense of infantile existence—visual and not quite real—emerging into a real sense, with the most primitive of language calling the visual imagery into account. There is a sense of creating the world here, and being created by it, and the inanity refers to the general amorphous blankness which precedes specific consciousness and which is forever a backdrop to the specificity of experience.

Charlie goes on to tell all about Humboldt—his extreme thirst for knowledge, his passion to envelop all of the real world, sometimes assuming clear manic proportions. This is, we think, a description of the wish to attain all gratification—everything —from the muse. Charlie presents the book's first dream, a vivification of the dead, but still ubiquitous Humboldt.

He was sitting beside me at the soda fountain with a Coke. I
burst into tears. I said, "Where have you been? I thought you
were dead."

He was very mild, quiet, and he seemed extremely well
pleased, and he said, "Now I understand everything."

"Everything? What's everything?"

But he only said, "Everything." I couldn't get more out of
him, and I wept with happiness. Of course it was only a dream
such as you dream if your soul is not well. . . . I have a hunch
that in life you look outward from the ego, your center. In death
you are at the periphery looking inward. (p. 9)

This last statement foreshadows the long dream of immortality which animates this book as its conceptual context. It is
a statement about taking on the sphere of immortality as the
proper sphere for the residence of the muse in late maturity.
The human danger of aging is countered by the identification
of the creative imagination with what endures in society and
nature. Something like God's perspective (outside of the ego)
provides a reflective cohesion which can include both the immortal and the mortal in its scope.

The imagery shifts away from Humboldt to Cantabile,
who comes marauding into Charlie Citrine's life on the wings
of fantastic, invidious, thoroughly American brutality. Cantabile careens into Citrine's life by smashing the hell out of Citrine's silver Mercedes. Then Cantabile orchestrates a series of
incidents meant to scare Citrine out of his wits. In the midst of
great comic, but still more real than surreal, danger, Citrine
launches into a meditation and a memory.

I was taken aback to see eyes move in faces, noses breathe, skins
sweat, hairs grow, and the like, finding it comical. This was
sometimes offensive to people born with full oblivion to their
immortality.

This leads me to recall and reveal a day of marvelous spring
and a noontime full of the most heavy silent white clouds like
bulls, behemoths and dragons. The place is Appleton, Wiscon-
sin, and I am a grown man standing on a crate trying to see into

the bedroom where I was born in the year 1918. I was probably
conceived there, too, and directed by a divine wisdom to appear
in life as so-and-so and such-and-such (C. Citrine, Pulitzer Prize,
Legion of Honor, Father of Lish and Mary, husband of A., lover
of B., a serious person, and a card). (p. 86)

He goes on to tell that this incident of his trying to peek
into the genesis of his immortality was no different from the
ongoing incident in which Cantabile is trying to find his own
immortality by peering into the life of Citrine. In other words
Cantabile was in his own way trying to fathom the basis of his
own position in life by attaching himself like a parasite to
Citrine. Charlie need no longer fear for his life. In his state of
traumatic detached reflection, his mundane life and experience
is merely a kind of record keeping imprinted on a piece of a line
which has no beginning or end.

The connection between Humboldt and Cantabile is established when Cantabile reveals that one reason for his "abduc-
tion" of Citrine is that Cantabile's wife is doing her PhD thesis
on Humboldt. Citrine talks about the link between Humboldt
and Citrine in the life of his mind when he says this to himself
on the day after the big adventures with Cantabile:

I myself, a nicely composed person, had had Humboldt expressing himself wildly on my behalf, satisfying some of my longings.
This explained my liking for certain individuals—Humboldt . . .
or even someone like Cantabile. (p. 103)

Humboldt and Cantabile, and of course their wives as fused
parts of the muse figure, stand for the wakening influence of the
imagination, for Citrine goes on to divulge that he was at work
on a significant work exploring the "chronic war between sleep
and consciousness that goes on in human nature" (p. 104).

He goes on to espouse Rudolph Steiner's assertion that
between the act and its execution by the will there lies a gap of
sleep. If we understand Citrine—or Bellow—the imagination
takes a person out of the state of sleep preceding the act. If we

understand him, the imagination integrates the most primitive, undifferentiated portions of the mind and makes of them a force which instigates a generalized readiness to action, much like acetylcholine acts within the reticular system to produce a background for wakefulness, although it is not in itself responsible for the transmission of particular contents of consciousness. Citrine undertakes meditations meant to strengthen that part of the will which can evoke the wakefulness of the imagination. On the morning after the Canbile experience he meditated on Humboldt:

> Such meditation supposedly strengthens the will. Then gradually strengthened by such exercises, the will might become an organ of perception. (p. 107)

Now we contend that the will used in this way refers to reflection as an organ of perception, insofar as it perceives the nature of experience. The identity change which a creative person undergoes in the course of a work changes the perspective of reflection. In this case Citrine (Bellow) identifies Humboldt with his reflection. It is in this way that the muse figure comes to organize the reflective imagination. Citrine goes on to quote a poem of Humboldt's which had eluded him until the present moment of meditation.

> Mice hide when hawks are high;
> Hawks shy from airplanes;
> Planes dread the ack-ack-ack;
> Each one fears somebody.
> Only the heedless lions
> Under the booloo tree
> Snooze in each other's arms
> After that lunch of blood—
> I call their living good!

> . . . The imagination must not pine away— that was Humboldt's message. It must assert again that art manifests the inner

> powers of nature. To the savior-faculty of the imagination
> sleep was sleep, and waking was true waking. (p. 107)

Citrine's meditation lasted for a long time since he was preparing himself to go to court to face the last judgement in his divorce settlement trial. He uses the theme of the imagination to protect himself from the very real social attack on his means of survival. It is proof again that art intervenes between the traumatic perception and the act which, undertaken, must be clearly conceived. Charlie Citrine comes out of his long meditation with a sense of re-enforcement of the identification of his reflection with Humboldt. Notice the legal argument inhering in his words:

> At this moment I must say, almost in the form of deposition, without argument, that I do not believe my birth began my first existence. Nor Humboldt's. Nor anyone's. On aesthetic grounds, if on no others, I can not accept the view of death taken by most of us, and taken by me during most of my life—on aesthetic grounds therefore I am obliged to deny that so extraordinary a thing as a human soul can be wiped out forever. (p. 136)

Citrine goes on to say—and we ask the reader to hear his argument as a purely subjective proposition—that the dead inhabit the areas of the brain which store the memory of those we have loved once, and continue to love in the unconscious. In other words, Humboldt, the loved image of a man, has taken up permanent residence in the area of memory which remains in contact with the raw undifferentiated drive for wakefulness and new experience. It is no different from Freud's proposition that the repressed comes into contact with the same unconscious that arises in contact with the neuropsychological origins of the mind. If Citrine is allying himself with the dead but ever glowing coals of old love, then his present experience takes on meaning only when it can fan the embers of old love. He goes on:

No, the dead are about us, shut out by our metaphysical denial
of them. As we lie nightly in our hemispheres, [Isn't Citrine
referring to the hemispheres of the brain as much as the earth?]
asleep by the billions, [Isn't Citrine referring to the neurons?] our
dead approach us. Our ideas should be their nourishment. We
are their grainfields. (p. 136)

Cantabile comes to Charlie with propositions to save Charlie's financial skin. Perhaps they should arrange a kidnapping
of Charlie's children, or put out a contract on Charlie's wife.
He has another, a homosexual proposition, to share his lover
with Charlie in a sexual act for three. But Charlie is in the midst
of working out his new identity, learning that the all-out fight
to preserve his own creative life denies the necessary acceptance
of mortality. Charlie (Bellow) is developing the perspective that
his necessary identity must ally itself with the dead who still live
on in his memorial imagination.

I want it to be clear, however, that I speak as a person who had
lately received or experienced light. I don't mean "The light."
I mean a kind of light-in-the-being, a thing difficult to be precise
about, especially in an account like this, where so many cantank-
erous erroneous silly and delusive objects actions and phenomena are in the foreground. . . . Only I seem to have forgotten that
in the first decade of life I knew the light and even knew how
to breathe it in. But this early talent of gift or inspiration, given
up for the sake of maturity or realism (practicality, self-preservation, the fight for survival), was now edging back. Perhaps the
vain nature of self-preservation had finally become too plain for
denial. (p. 171)

Before he goes on to tell us about the most luscious woman
he has known, the most desireable sexual prize of his life,
Renata, Charlie sets out his new beliefs as a thesis. The lesson
we are to learn is that the most compelling object of our passions and our interest is not strong enough to sustain a lack of
boredom. His thesis is that our ethical and our social political
self, our mundane self, is in conflict with our aesthetic, immor-

tal self. Without the participation and perspective of the immortal, creative, imaginative self, boredom and denial of talent
are our lot. He seeks to be stimulated beyond the border of
ordinary self-preservation. He seeks the trauma that can take
him into a recognition of the essential imaginative side of life.

In the court the judge takes away all of Charlie's money.
Charlie is moved to remember Humboldt's central conclusions
about money:

> . . . in the unconscious, in the irrational core of things money was
> a vital substance like the blood or fluids which bathed the brain
> tissues. (p. 233)

Then Charlie goes on to think of a different kind of man
than the "ethical" judge—he goes on to think of the father of
one woman he took in lieu of Renata when Renata had left him
for a time to go with her mortician who could offer more money
than Charlie. The father had explained to Charlie that in sleep
the soul enters into a discourse of direct communication with
the essential consciousness of the inanimate universe—the essence of nature whose representative in the mind is the imagination. Once again in the theme of Charlie's sexual life a man and
a woman are together. The woman stimulates his desire while
the man elicits his imagination. Taken together with the man
who stands for the imagination, the woman is not boring; taken
separately, the woman is only a sex object in the world.

As Renata is in the process of leaving Charlie because he
has no money to keep her, Charlie comes upon the legacy which
Humboldt has left him. It is a legacy which Humboldt owes
him because they had been blood brothers, had signed a check
together in blood, which Humboldt had cashed in the midst of
a manic storm of resentment at Charlie's success, feeling that
Charlie had made a great commercial success of a play Charlie
had written based on Humboldt's character.

They are brothers of the imagination, and Humboldt's
legacy is a gift which outlines the very process of literary cre-

ation, and which dramatizes as a movie scenario the interaction between ordinary life and the life of the creative imagination. As the corner piece of this book it is the story of how the book was written, and it shows in this play within a play, this movie within a book, the essential transformation of identity which Bellow undergoes in facing the transition in his identity to one who has become a more aged creator. The reconciliation of identity as creator and identity as a normal social person is the task of the work.

The plot of the movie scenario is very simple. A creative author who is unable to feel the necessary stimulation of love and involvement in his work has an affair full of beauty and love. He experiences an opening to sensation and perspective. He creates a beautiful work placed in a setting outside of society and faithful to this imaginative experience. But he cannot publish it because he would lose the marriage which constitutes his ordinary social life. Therefore his agent suggests that he restage the entire affair, this time with his wife. He does that but it turns into parody, and then loss, since his wife knows it is not she who formed the essence of his published experience. He then loses the woman with whom he had the affair because he was not faithful to her. At the end he is a success, but he has lost both his wife and the other woman. Bellow's story is told as an aside in this movie scenario, for Humboldt is made to say,

> When the artist antagonist has learned to be sunk and ship-wrecked, to embrace defeat and assert nothing, to subdue his will and accept his assignment to the hell of modern truth perhaps his Orphic powers will be restored, the stones will dance again when he plays. Then heaven (creativity) and earth (real life) will be reunited. After long divorce. With what joy on both sides, Charlie! What joy.
> But this has no place in our picture. (p. 334)

It turns out that Humboldt had left the same legacy, the same story to his wife, Kathleen. In one sense, then, Humboldt is saying that Charlie is his mistress, that he is undergoing the same trip with Charlie that he had undergone with Kathleen. This makes Charlie his mistress bonded in the imaginary world they shared. From Citrine's or Bellow's point of view, the double legacy makes the creative imagination be composed of two muse figures, the wedded Humboldt and Kathleen, the composite ordinary and extraordinary social figures.

When Kathleen comes to visit him, Charlie is in the hotel dining room without one of his shoes. Renata had taken the shoe with her in an act of pique with Charlie for renewing his connection with Humboldt and Kathleen. She had taken the shoe after removing it and using Charlie's foot secretly under the table to satisfy her lust, while Charlie was conducting a conversation about literary money matters. The ritual act connected Renata with the erotic world of complete satisfaction as the description of her complete orgasm attests. This is not the same satisfaction that can be provided by the literary imagination, and so she and Charlie must soon be parted.

> As for Renata smiling—her dark eyes, red mouth, white teeth, smooth throat— . . . I knew her theory well. Whatever was said, whatever was done, either increased or decreased erotic satisfaction, and this was her practical test for any idea. Did it produce a bigger bang? "We could have been at the Scala tonight," she said, "and part of a brilliant audience hearing Rossini. Instead, do you know what we were doing today, Thaxter? We went out to Coney Island so Charlie could collect his inheritance from his dear dead old pal Humboldt Fleisher. It's been Humboldt, Humboldt, Humboldt, like Figaro, Figaro." (p. 352)

Next in the progress of the book is an interlude with Ulick, Charlie's brother. Ulick must undergo open heart surgery to save his life. But his imaginative, money-food-hungering spirit is fastened with particular intensity to the capitalist dream of creating yet another paradise on earth worked by cheap labor, another playground fantasy formation for the rich of America, a fantasy playground that will return huge monetary rewards. Bellow declaims on the beautiful and awful American social fascination with the capitalism of technology, the refuge of the imagination corrupted at the social level. It is the imagination of the irrepressible American bad boy. Ulick and Cantabile form a social double for Charlie.

> The reason why the Ulicks of this world (and also the Canta- biles) had such sway over me was that they knew their desires clearly. These desires might be low, but they were pursued in full wakefulness ... Ulick was awake to money; I, with a craving to do right swelling in my heart, was aware that the good liberal sleep of American boyhood had lasted half a century. And even now I had come to get something from Ulick—I was revisiting the conditions of childhood under which my heart had been inspired. (p. 383)

Finally, Renata deserts Charlie in Spain, leaving him wait- ing for her in a hotel room, sending her mother and her son in her stead, to take advantage of Charlie's last few pennies. Charlie consoles himself:

> The job, once and for all, was to burst from the fatal self-suffi- ciency of consciousness and put my remaining strength over into the Imaginative Soul. As Humboldt too should have done. (p. 403)

The rest is a fantastic compensation. Cantabile comes to Spain to "help" in Charlie's negotiations over the movie rights to Humboldt's legacy. But essentially Charlie is done with Can- tabile, finished with Renata, the need for Humboldt is spent, and Citrine-Bellow is comfortable in his acceptance of the muse condition preceding old age, and entering into a period of rest and restoration in the confidence that the present work is completed.

Chapter 12

THE CREATOR'S DEATH

65 and Over

A biologically predetermined assault on identity structure occurs as the neuropsychological foundations of mental life are
undermined by organic causes. Although the onset and causes
are variable, sooner or later the prefrontal foundations of reflective identity are compromised, producing a tendency toward a
retrograde desynthesis in the levels of structured identity. As
anxiety signals the desynthesizing forces in the structure of his
mature identity, the aged person is forced to become aware of
the imminence of the end of his life. In the face of arterioscle-
rotic and senile changes in the organic basis for mental integration, the old person is forced to seek a more serviceable identity
in old age.

This chapter argues that the aged creator first tries to find
refuge in the alternative identity as creator—possibly producing some of his profoundest works—and then comes to terms
with the decline of his identity as creator. The fantasy of immortality which can inspire the aged creator is then subordi-

nated to the knowledge that only the process of life may be deemed immortal.

An ancillary notion is that the creator's alternative identity is more impervious to physical decay than is everyday identity. Perhaps the foundations of the creative alternative are more than usually generalized in the brain, and less dependent on the neurological systems that support the ordinary manifestations of identity. This is in line with Bellow's assertion that the part of his mind that is aligned with the creative imagination reaches back more easily to the most primitive foundations of mental life, those areas of mental life that do not necessarily particularize as specific conscious content, but which align instead with the general neurological forces that activate consciousness in the substructure of the human mind.

"BORGES AND I" BY JORGE LUIS BORGES

Exploring works of the aged creator which reveal necessary reconciliation with life's end, we will see that changes in identity structure must accompany this process. The muse is reincarnated to animate the creative works of old age. We find the aged creator putting forward an alternative double to his ordinary self. This double is endowed with all his creative abilities, maintaining the sense of past physical and mental vigor. In other words the creative alternative in old age may come to organize the whole of personality and to include the normal identity in one last synthetic movement which holds the line against a dissolution of reflective consciousness. The final amalgam of creative and normal identity produces a new perspective of wisdom in old age. It is an era when the aged Borges may declare in "Borges and I" that, whether imaginary or real, remembered or current, all experience has an equal place in the perspective of his reflection:

The other one, the one called Borges, is the one things happen to. I walk through the streets of Buenos Aires and stop for a moment, perhaps mechanically now, to look at the arch of an entrance hall and the grillwork on the gate; I know of Borges from the mail and see his name on a list of professors or in a biographical dictionary. I like hourglasses, maps, eighteenth century typography, the taste of coffee and the prose of Stevenson; he shares these preferences, but in a vain way, that turns them into the attributes of an actor. It would be an exaggeration to say that ours is a hostile relationship; I live, let myself go on living so that Borges may contrive his literature, and this literature justifies me. It is no effort for me to confess that he has achieved some valid pages, but those pages can not save me, perhaps because what is good belongs to no one, not even to him, but rather to the language and to tradition. Besides, I am destined to perish, definitively, and only some instant of myself can survive in him. Little by little, I am giving over everything to him, though I am quite aware of this perverse custom of falsifying and magnifying things. Spinoza knew that all things long to persist in their being; the stone eternally wants to be a stone and the tiger a tiger. I shall remain in Borges, not in myself (if it is true that I am someone), but I recognize myself less in his books than in many others or in the laborious strumming of a guitar. Years ago I tried to free myself from him and went from the mythologies of the suburbs to the games with time and infinity, but those games belong to Borges now and I shall have to imagine other things. Thus my life is a flight and I lose everything and everything belongs to oblivion, or to him.

I do not know which of us has written this page. (Borges, 1964, pp. 246–247)

Borges expresses the wisdom of old age. He understands that the inherent biological reality of his mind and body is a part of the structure of overall reality. His inner nature is part of eternal nature. Through accepting that his creative alternative has the same relation to the overall reality of life as his normal self, he is able to achieve the wisdom reflected in the quoted passage.

As the aged creator becomes aware of the difficulty in

exerting the mental functions he had taken for granted all along, he comes first to want to deny these changes. He attempts to take refuge in some creative state mediated by the false belief in immortality. This belief is first vested in the muse, which itself is felt to be immortal as some angel might be. But the animating spirit of the work in old age must be transformed into the ultimately accepting principle of mortality. After his identity change has been completed, the aged creator must reflect in his works an acceptance of an identity based on a reality which will include neither the aged person nor his creative alternative. This forms the dynamic conflict that pervades the creative work of old age.

YEATS: A POET LOOKING TO OLD AGE

What in the development of Yeats's creator's syndrome lent itself to such a productive creative identity in old age? Creativity is a process which repairs identity, and provides psychic cement when trauma threatens to rend mental continuity beyond repair. The older artist identifies with his own creativity to circumvent the destruction of aging. For this reason the muse of aging seems to mediate the creator's entire personality.

Yeats's life is a prime example of this function of creativity. Throughout his life Yeats was beset by disintegrative forces which threatened to throw him into psychosis. But he met every challenge with a creative response of unusual vigor, and the result was that he was much healthier and better in his creative identity than he was in his normal identity. Throughout his life Yeats tried to live as the pure creator. This effort lent him an air of madness or extreme eccentricity. Nevertheless, this effort averted madness, and Yeats's identity really cohered, held, for the first time as he entered old age.

Yeats's creative states were characterized by an effort to

release the concrete antecedents of abstractions and representations. The search is evident in his interest in automatic writing and in his courting of the hypnagogic state in which certain kinds of phraseologies came to him starkly, and at times quite audibly. Yeats was also engaged in a conscious search for the Irish language of concrete rhythmic expression. As a poet he caught the fugitive phraseology of his hypnagogue much as the boy Yeats had captured the butterfly by day, the moth by night, learning when each species would come, in what size and variety, hour by hour.

Years was fixated on a particular aspect of his oedipal development. He was devoted to capturing the language of the conscience in the process of its development. In other words, Yeats took in moral injunctions—with their rhythmic force—and made formulations of them, and then made symbols of the formulations. Yeats fixated on the formation of conscience. Yeats's oedipal period was characterized by an attempt to circumvent the moral authority ordinarily represented by the father.

Yeats begins his *Autobiography* (1965) with lonely images of living with his maternal grandparents in Ireland. In the first two pages he refers to four scars: the cracked Irish wall, the long scratched stern of a toy boat, the broken wing of a duck he wounded with a stone, and a scar on his grandfather's hand made by a whaling hook. The imagery points to an oedipal child who feels alone and unprotected, liable to castration, and seeks to identify himself with the strongest possible masculine representation. To the boy Yeats, his grandfather is almost a legend, close to God in the child's mind. According to the information in Ellman's (1948) biography Yeats' father went off to London to become an artist when his son was not yet two years old. The family moved between Sligo, where the mother's family lived, Dublin, and London where the father was being schooled in Pre-Raphaelite art.

In the second part of his reveries, Yeats tells us of the process of his conscience forming.

One day some one spoke to me of the voice of the conscience, and as I brooded over the phrase I came to think that my soul, because I did not hear an articulate voice, was lost. I had some wretched days until being alone with one of my aunts I heard a whisper in my ear, "What a tease you are." At first I thought my aunt must have spoken, but when I found she had not, I concluded it was the voice of my conscience and was happy again. From that day the voice has come to me at moments of crisis, but now it is a voice in my head that is sudden and startling. (1965, pp. 5–6)

We can surmise that his conscience spoke to him at a time when he was in Sligo, away from his father, for Yeats goes on to describe his grandfather's shipwreck, occurring on a night when the boy allegedly dreamt of a shipwreck. Yeats adds to his own legend, then, saying that he must have seen a supernatural white sea bird, symbolizing death in the corner of his room.

Apparently the effort Yeats put into making his grandfather a grand figure screened him from feelings of awe about his father. The original feelings of awe about the father return in full force later in Yeats's life. His father was away over the Irish Sea when Yeats was a boy in Sligo. Ideas about his "death" must have taken hold of the oedipal boy's fancy. Yeats's wishes for his father's death were so strong and so well screened by his belief in his own magical powers that Yeats's conscience could not gel. The legend Yeats promulgates of his own gift at prophesy both screens and reveals the oedipal fantasies striving for realization in the child's mind.

We have seen before, with Sartre, how the grandfather image can substitute for a more distant, less threatening version of the authority of reality over the young child whose conscience is in the process of formation. Yeats continued to believe in the extreme mutability of reality. He believed that he could affect future events through a manipulation of symbols. The symbols Yeats chose were muse symbols, and symbols of bisexuality. Yeats tried to get control of the formation of conscience in order to manipulate reality to yield him the child-hood masturbatory-illusory pleasures he wished. He elevated the representation of his father to the bisexual "pregnant father." Images of masculine fertility appealed to Yeats all his life, and these images were intimately connected with the identity screens which he used to cloak his own identity.

Given the young magician's strong fixation to the formation of conscience, and to its mastery through his creative illusions—it is not surprising that in latency Yeats's fantasy of family romance hypertrophied. At the age of 50, writing his autobiography, Yeats still mythologized his early years, trying to make himself sole child of his legendary grandfather.

Yeats recounts that after he had moved to London to join his father when he was eight, the family would return to Sligo for weeks at a time. "Perhaps my mother and the other children had been there [in Sligo] all the time, for I remember my father now and again going to London." (p. 18) Yeats prefers to image himself as young follower of his heroic grandfather. If the rest of the family, including his mother, enters the picture, it is as distant, unimportant siblings. He tells about the death of a younger brother as if he were the only child at Sligo: "My realization of death came when my father and mother and my two sisters were on a visit. . . . My brother Robert had died" (p. 16). Thus much of Yeats's early life, including the first years of his latency, is shrouded in family romance, lending mythification to his early Ireland, identified with the legendary grandfather hero.

In London Yeats was a timid, obsessive, solitary, yet daring child. He compulsively collected wood to make the great ship of his dreams, and he would force himself to fight English boys although he did not really feel connected to or involved in the fight. This quality of effortful performance remained characteristic of Yeats all his life and entered thematically into the composition of his poetry and plays. What he lacked in natural ability as a fighter he made up for in perseverance. He could not be beaten, but he could not win either. If he ran a race

he would be careful to show no signs of fatigue. He was interested in maintaining an image of himself as extraordinary to
compensate for feelings that he might easily be destroyed.

Yeats could make the artificial fight because he believed in
the power of his legendary Irish heritage. His father's creator's
syndrome also became increasingly available to Yeats's identification. In this way his normal identity also participated in the
wish to be a creator, because that was the profession of his
father. Yeats wanted to surpass his father as a creator at the
same time that he wished to identify with his father's bisexual-
ized image of creativity.

Yeats tells of four works which affected his preadoles-
cence: "The Lay of the Last Minstrel gave me a wish to turn
magician that competed for years with the dream of being killed
on the seashore" (p. 38). Then he tells of his father disapproving
of his reading "boy's papers" without realizing that it was just
a retelling of *The Iliad* he was interested in. Yeats mentions
sentimentally in one of his rare references to his mother, that
she would read him "The Ugly Duckling." When he was 11 his
father took him to see *Hamlet,* which remained fixed in his
mind. There is one element of significant similarity in these four
recollections. Yeats's first identification with the swan is seen in
his affinity for the family romance of the ugly duckling. The
Hamlet image refers to his wish to kill his father.

Yeats collected butterflies throughout his latency, and well
into his adolescence. His fascination with butterflies and birds
places him in the company of every single one of the creators
we have examined. His expeditions to find butterflies would find
him finally by the sea at Sligo. In his adolescence Yeats made
a romance out of his adolescent masturbation. He would go
with green nets to a cave overlooking the sea, spend half the
night dreaming of poet-magicians, masturbating (he tells of
these expeditions after a quick reference to his young adolescent
sexuality), identifying himself with Shelley's "Prometheus." He
made fires in the cave and roasted eggs under the ground, and
as we know from his later *A Vision,* this was an activity which

symbolized giving birth. He mentions more than once that his father read to him from Shelley's "Prometheus." Yeats was searching for a muse to love and he seems to have found only his father. At the end of adolescence he went to art school, where he toiled to become an artist, to share his father's vision.

Finally a legitimate muse personage came to him. Maud Gonne came to his father's house to talk politics. She was a revolutionary who believed killing was necessary to redeem Ireland. In the presence of this handsome, six-foot woman, Yeats' took courage to oppose his father. Maud Gonne was a bisexual representation whom he could love as he loved the heroines of the great poets, and so he could defuse the identification with his father. It was liberating to be free of the wish either to kill his father, or to be penetrated by his father on the rocks by the sea where Yeats gave birth to his vision of becoming an adult poet.

Yeats's adult life was characterized by his search for some unifying mythology of social life which could give him courage. His love for life, for Maud Gonne, for his father seemed unrequited, but he persisted. Lady Gregory, understanding his timidity and his talent, regularly lent him her summer place, to rest and write and gather courage.

Two events forced Yeats into maturity. Maud Gonne married, blocking Yeats's illusion that he could find the reality of love with her, and his father went to America. It gradually dawned on Yeats that his father's move was permanent. Yeats continued to correspond with his father on aesthetic matters, but as long as he did so Yeats could not feel that he himself was the aesthetic authority in his own life. Ezra Pound sensed this when he brought himself into Yeats's life the same year that Yeats's father went to America, when Yeats was 43.

In his early 50s Yeats still felt incomplete. Neither his work as a dramatist nor as a politician provided him with a feeling of closure and satisfaction in his identity. Lady Gregory was getting older, and she no longer felt that she could continue to protect Yeats, so she and Pound, who had become Yeats's personal secretary, proposed that Yeats should marry Georgie Hyde-Lee. And so Yeats married when he was 52, in 1917.

On their honeymoon Georgie engaged in automatic writing, probably to release some of the tension she felt with her panicky husband. Yeats seized upon this new activity of his fellow spiritualist wife with a perverse fervor. Soon Georgie was spending up to several hours a day transmitting embodied voices to Yeats. The voices were masculine. Yeats referred to them as "he" and "them."

He was entranced with Georgie. She contained masculine power in a female body. Yeats possessed her in this guise. She put herself into a trancelike half-waking, half-sleeping state for Yeats. He loved it. It was the time of hypnagogue, the state of mind in which abstraction gives way to concrete antecedents, and in which identity gives way to the fragmentary voices that have gone into the composition of the object world.

His wife phallicized, or fatherized, made into the male muse, Yeats was free to love her, to be inspired by her, to have children with her. Yeats was finally in a position to forge a complete artistic identity for himself. He collected the communications he received from Georgie in her trancelike states and used them as a basis for a symbolic mythology which he constructed. He constructed a loosely woven fabric for his own identity as a creator, embroidering it with the generality which he felt applied to all of mankind. This identity structure of his middle age served him reasonably well until his father died in 1922.

During the period of political unrest which preceded this event, Georgie and Yeats had gone to live in Yeats's symbolic tower. The tower, complete with spiral staircase, reassured Yeats of his phallic completeness. After his father's death however, Georgie and the tower were no longer sufficient to help Yeats keep his identity centered. And so Yeats set off in earnest on a restoration and elaboration of *A Vision,* meaning to heighten the symbolic truth to a point where it could no longer be doubted. In this activity, and in the poems that became part of that activity, Yeats made a new creative identity for himself. This time it was an identity that would serve his entrance into old age. It was, finally, a stable identity.

We would like to present some excerpts from *A Vision* and the attendant poetry, to show Yeats's identity formation as he entered or prepared to enter the old age of a creator. This work of Yeats shows the same fixation which spiralled through all the stages of his life. It is the muse, Yeats's creative double building a mask to screen the boy-man from threats to his body and phallic integrity.

The theory of *A Vision* centers on a gyring interpenetration of subjective and objective consciousness determined by the phases of the moon. This is an apt framework to represent Yeats's relationship with the still menstrual Georgie. She represents an outward identity for Yeats in this theory of identity which Yeats constructed. In Yeats's theory a person has a subjective will and an objective mask which must be synthesized. In addition, a person has a subjective creative mind which must be correlated with "the body of fate." He exalts the creative man to an identity which participates in historical mythological forces.

In *A Vision* the creative man Yeats creates a mythic artifice to account for the creation of his own symbolic work. It is a story containing Yeats's quintessential fantasy life. Robartes, the Greatfather brings Aherne, sonlike, the sacred written truth. The beneficiaries of this truth are Huddon, Duddon, and Denise. In this ménage Huddon doesn't mind sharing the sexual rights to Denise with Duddon. (Thus Duddon must represent the boy Yeats.) Duddon is supported because Huddon buys his paintings. (Yeats sent his father in America money to supplement the father's sale of paintings. Father and son reverse roles in the story and in Yeats's life.)

Robartes's bisexual gift is none other than Leda's egg. The egg carries the myth of perfect bisexually synthesized personality. It must be placed on the desert floor by two special carriers, Mary and John (characters so ordinary they must be Yeats and

Georgie). The egg will hatch a new life, the new birth of the poet in old age.

The latter part of *A Vision* is entitled "Dove or Swan." It purports to tell the future. It is launched with the poem "Leda." This poem, then, is central to Yeats's new identity in old age. Yeats is Leda, the mythical bisexual consecration whose nativity and issue is the poem. It is—is it not—his most beautiful poem. The imagery of the poem condenses all the epochs of Yeats' development as a creator: Imagine that Yeats the creator is Leda, the swan god his father. Then the imagery condenses the primal scene, the bisexual oedipal identity, the coupling with the muse in adolescent epiphany, the permanent juncture of muse and poet—man and wife—and finally the knowledge which comes from the intrapsychic supplanting of the dead father. This is the imagery of Leda, a congerie of Yeats's identity themes.

Inspired by Leda, Yeats's vigorous language and rigorous, passionate honesty propel "Byzantium" and "The Tower" forward into an *agone* of relation. There are, implicitly, two sorts of reflection—personal and historical. Reflecting, objectifying, the generically "romantic" soul studies "monuments of its own magnificence" and is so gathered "into the artifice of eternity." The final ideal is immortality in immortal work—the muse finally released from its bondage to flesh.

> Once out of nature I shall never take
> My bodily form from any natural thing,
> But such a form as Grecian goldsmiths make
> Of hammered gold and gold enamelling
> To keep a drowsy Emperor awake;
> Or set upon a golden bough to sing
> To lords and ladies of Byzantium
> Of what is past, or passing, or to come.

Revolving the compass of experience like a monk searching for the *primum mobile,* Yeats opts for the artifice of eternity in a movement of illogic or faith that presupposes some essential self enduring beyond all that sensual music of dying generation and the sensuous dress of imagery.

"THE TOWER" BY WILLIAM BUTLER YEATS

"The Tower" is a poem in which Yeats decries the plight of a body no longer adequate to express the poet's own identification of himself as a creator. In it Yeats is foreshadowing a time when his muse, his poetical imagination, must go packing whether or not he wishes it.

> What shall I do with this absurdity—
> O heart, O troubled heart—this caricature,
> Decrepit age that has been tied to me
> As to a dog's tail?

It is a rhetorical question, one addressed to the subjective self, a question which is posed reflectively out of the ego ideal sense which requires perfection of bodily form from him. Reflectively, he caricatures his body, derogates it, and mocks it by comparing it to a dog's body. He achieves affective relief through this device.

> Never had I more
> Excited, passionate, fantastical
> Imagination, nor an ear and eye
> That more expected the impossible—

The poet reflects that after all his *sensory appreciation* is as great as it ever was, and he refers to this objective function as well as the function of imaginative synthesis by the metonymous use of ear and eye to stand for these functions. In the past the ear and eye reached their objective status as vehicles for the subjective expression which he could bring to them. Thus his expectation of the impossible is the poetry which he can construct through the auspices of his senses. The speaker cannot believe that his body is no longer a tower of strength, housing his organs of perception in an objective, affirmatory way.

> No, not in boyhood when with rod and fly,
> Or the humbler worm, I climbed Ben Bulben's back
> And had the livelong summer day to spend.
> It seems that I must bid the Muse go pack,
> Choose Plato and Plotinus for a friend

As a solace he recalls that his youthful sensuous urge was no greater than his urge is in the present time. He personifies the mountain of his locale, and its broad back is foil for his bent frame. With this strengthening image formed as a wish, Yeats enters into the realm of memory, but this memory is short-lived, unlike the livelong day of his earlier summer, and he is brought up short to the present. And so he must ask again rhetorically whether it is his muse, his creative identification, which must go pack.

The images of time which accord with the reference to memory stand in the development of the mind as building blocks for subjective identity. It becomes clear that the poem is unravelling the strands which had been woven once into the composition of identity. The poet takes a distance and stands apart in his rationality, in his reflection, wondering whether all that is left for him is monuments of unaging intellect.

> Shall he be content
> In abstract things; or be derided by
> A sort of battered kettle at the heel?

This last is ambiguous, a metaphor for his own mocking shadow. This self-image is tied to the aging body like a dog's tail. The ambiguities blend and bring us back to an earlier section of the poem, as Yeats has already returned to an earlier image of himself. He uses the device of self-mockery, dragging this cacaphonous image, this destroyer of music, behind him. To be mocked by one's own shadow is self-directed irony, and its purpose must be to begin to destroy the value in the objective image of the body so that its loss will be tolerable. We see the reversal of direction in old age, in which the body is to be derided, where as once it was the source of pride. The phallic wane is imaged in the humble worm which the boy hung before him full of hope. We notice also that the rhetoric has begun to be overcome by regular rhyming and Yeats's indominatable rhythm. In this way he asserts his claim to the muse. Then he begins:

> I pace upon the battlements and stare
> On the foundations of a house, or where
> Tree like a sooty finger, starts from the earth;
> And send imagination forth
> Under the day's declining beam, and call
> Images and memories
> From ruin or from ancient trees,
> For I would ask a question of them all.

He takes a distance from the battle like some old general who is going to resurrect each battle before going forth again, possibly to final defeat. The ancient foundations are the foundations of his body, and his mind objectified. Now we can begin to see the tower acquire some personal symbolism, not only as the site of his life in reality, but embodying as well the sense of his personal past. Yeats self-consciously sets out to question the survival of his poetic identity. Can he any longer marshall his images and his memory and make them come forth like a tree from the ruins?

He will tell tales. He makes legend and allegory, and uses humor, and immerses himself in his Irish heritage and recalls feelings of fun and humor, fellowship, the blind poet, and the indescribably beautiful peasant girl who drives men's wits astray until tragedy intervenes for one who drowns in the great bog. He is pacing in his mind, brooding now and recalling the feeling of the strength of his poetry and finally breaks through for a moment to say:

O may the moon and sunlight seem
One inextricable beam,
For if I triumph I must make men mad.

His solution is to be mad himself, to condense all his years, to make time succumb to his creative power, but to do so he must reduce the blind poet and the peasant girl to one, "Homer that was a blind man" and Helen to one; himself who is aging objective presence and himself the muse to one. He must undertake the madness which he realizes is apart from reality and substitute that for reality in order to be in the state in which he can create. It is himself as poet that Yeats is creating, just as one's self-identification is first created and then recreated. He must combine, into Ireland, the symbolically castrated blind poet and the beautiful peasant girl who is Yeats's legendary muse. He must compound himself, the blind poet, together with Maude Gonne, his tragic muse. He must create the poet out of this stuff.

And I myself created Hanrahan . . .
I thought it all out twenty years ago;

And he continues then bitterly that Hanrahan's tricks turned a pack of cards into a pack of hounds. He sees his imagery running too fast, too easily, and he begins to parody his own style. What's the use of style, he asks, when one can no longer believe in the trick of creating it. Yeats is now in a mood very near depression. His poetic frenzy can't save him from it, although he tries to save himself through self-parody. It is a way of lowering his self-esteem gently, but a self-destructive element emerges in the process. The aggressive signals of the parody go beyond the overhanging detachment of the superego's humor. Once Yeats could create an alternative self out of Hanrahan, and Hanrahan was accepted as a good fellow.

Hanrahan rose in a frenzy there
And followed up those baying creatures towards—

O towards I have forgotten what—enough.
I must recall a man . . .
An ancient bankrupt master of this house.

Yeats himself, the narrator, breaks through into the present because his mood cannot be contained by poetry used defensively. As the bankrupt master of the house he feels emptied of his passion, but he turns to the tower he lives in, and the word *house* acts as a transition, a way of changing the focus from his reflection on his intrapsychic state to reflection on his ancient house. Now he will proceed on a different level, less personal, and more real in the sense of having existed in the world. The metaphor of objectification will proceed farther from his own body and mind and on a more general level where less immediate pain is present, where more can be absorbed by poetic devices.

Before that ruin came, for centuries
Rough men-at-arms, cross-gartered to the knees
Or shod in iron, climbed the narrow stair,
And certain men-at-arms there were
Whose images, in the Great Memory stored,
Come with loud cry and panting breast
To break upon a sleeper's rest
While their great wooden dice beat on the board.

Yeats thinks of those men who had come before him to the tower, at first admiring them, comparing his present state with theirs, beginning a mockery of them because he has made them so godlike. But again the feelings become too strong; there is a kind of resentment in the implied metaphor of his Great Memory partaking perhaps of the Divine Memory, and feeling that his own representation cannot take on these greats. They become for him a nightmare image, like the return of the repressed. Now he must weaken them—which he does by saying that they are no more gods or giants than Hanrahan and the boys at their dice. He concludes that he cannot dispense with Hanrahan. Because he is still asking what to do with his aging body and because these mighty predecessors can give no answer, he decides ruefully that he must ask Hanrahan who will be allowed to continue to exist. He tells these poor giants of his dreams, these figures from an early childhood of presences,

> Go therefore; but leave Hanrahan,
> For I need all his mighty memories.

Yeats has become Hanrahan, his own creation, which can no longer be an imposter. Hanrahan is privy to all the memories of potency.

Thus Yeats attempts a temporary regression. As once he progressed from the omnipotent three-year-old to the phallic boasting four-year-old, so must he again. Yeats the narrator talks to Hanrahan, with slight ironic humor, but fondly, for his intrapsychic friend is muse among the Irish people.

> Old lecher with a love on every wind,
> Bring up out of that deep considering mind
> All that you have discovered in the grave,
> For it is certain that you have
> Reckoned up every unforeknown, unseeing
> Plunge, lured by a softening eye,
> Or by a touch or a sigh,
> Into the labyrinth of another's being;

Yeats speaks to Hanrahan, his scribe with a strong poetic voice, with strong and sexual poetic rhythm, re-enforcing the sexual metaphor. He tells Hanrahan ironically that since he has taken him on many a sexual plunge, perhaps he can also bring back information from the grave. Sexuality was dangerous, after all, because the sexual plunge may be metaphorized into the plunge into the labyrinth of another's being. It is like the legendary plunge to the death into the great bog of Cloone. There is danger in that lure, which might bring Yeats out of his own identity, and so cause psychological death. Requited love may separate the artist from the essence of his muse, that creature who is compounded at least in part of unrequited feeling. But at this point the imagery is a kind of reassurance, because it is the ravage of old age, rather than love of a woman, that threatens extinction or decomposition of the poet. Yeats steps back to consider this safer question:

> Does the imagination dwell the most
> Upon a woman won or lost:
> If on the lost, admit you turned aside
> From a great labyrinth out of pride,
> Cowardice, some silly over-subtle thought
> Or anything called conscience once;
> And if that memory recurs, the sun's
> Under eclipse and the day blotted out.

Yeats calls forth the familiar pain of his idealizing impotence, which can be set almost right by the poet. He substitutes that pain to make the image of the day decline blot out. He lets memories of lost love overshadow age. As the poet he makes an image of eclipse to almost prove the reality of the substitution which he is making. He can accept the trauma of aging by comparing it with lost loves of the past, already realized. The regular consequence of trauma is a detachment from its source and a development of greater reflective insight built over the foundations of past traumas. In the added pride of having faced his earlier trauma, Yeats is ready now to stand in the dignity of his age.

> It is time that I wrote my will;
> I choose upstanding men
> That climb the streams until
> The fountain leap, and at dawn
> Drop their cast at the side
> Of dripping stone; I declare
> They shall inherit my pride.

He returns to the phallic, sexualized imagery of his youth and to the imagery of subjective assertion in overcoming obstacles, to the people of Ireland who have joined that pride. He asserts that with that pride, with which he has built his personality and with which the people have built a country against obstacles, he can now face his present dilemma. So he summons up his central muse:

> Or that of the hour
> When the swan must fix his eye
> Upon a fading gleam
> Float out upon a long
> Last reach of glittering stream
> And there sing his last song.

Now Yeats has summoned up his swan, his bird, the symbol of life and death, of the power of poetry, his poetry to encompass life and death. It is with the voice of this illusion that he can sing most brilliantly. It is in the guise of this symbolic omnisexual allusion that he can condense the sensuous imagery of light into beams or gleams which contain a wealth of images, a horn of plenty. The light, or the sound of the fabulous horn, the essential senses which compose reality, are enough to stimulate all of his imagination when he is in this mood of triumphant assertion over his whole internal world. It is as if he could summon up reality. This suggests that the experience of knowing that one can summon fantasy to collate the impressions of the senses gives the power to the activity of condensing images to make illusions, new objective forms. Yeats is determined to face the frustration of aging with his poetry standing up ready to communicate to those who would also be poets.

> And I declare my faith:
> I mock Plotinus' thought
> And cry in Plato's teeth,
> Death and life were not
> Till man made up the whole,
> Made lock, stock and barrel
> Out of his bitter soul,

Aye, sun and moon and star, all
And further add to that
That being dead, we rise,
Dream and so create
Translunar paradise.

Rhapsodically, with his song ringing beyond the absolute
notions of God's province, Yeats sets his creativity in this place
of all creativity, asserting that it is his power over life and death.
He has risen before on wings of his song to overcome the
abstract necessity of conscience. He will not settle for the well-
ordered thoughts of the reasonable man. Rather he will force
his poetry on reason once again. Yeats is creating new forms to
cope with his old age.

I have prepared my peace
With learned Italian things
And the proud stones of Greece,
Poet's imaginings
And memories of love,
Memories of the words of women,
All those things whereof
Man makes a superhuman
Mirror-resembling dream.

He asserts that the mirror-resembling dream, which is his
poem, is also mankind's ongoing poem of itself, alive because
it is filled with faith and belief. He is speaking now of the
inclusive forms of identity which man makes toward the ending
of the poem of his life. In the formation of experience we are
interested in those surfaces where experience is transformed
into some sense of a lasting essence, where it becomes part of
the reflective activity itself. This is certainly an aspect of the
experience of identity building. Yeats describes this process:

As at the loophole there
The daws chatter and scream,
And drop twigs layer upon layer.

When they have mounted up,
The mother bird will rest
On their hollow top,
And so warm her wild nest.

But of course the sentence beginning "As at the loophole there . . ." is no sentence at all. It is a dependent clause and referable only to the preceding sentence, which happens to be another stanza and belongs to another unit of thought. This suggests that the space between the stanzas functions as a place holder for a missing clause or unit of thought. It also suggests that, for Yeats, a connection and a discontinuity existed between the specific matter of personal inspiration and the notion of some force for creation beyond the self. Surely, the loophole is a window directed in, objectified—it is an entrance to the creative identification. The building daws, bird-symbols of nature creating, fill in the superhuman mirror-resembling dream, creating an object of fragments as Yeats has created a pillar of descriptive fragments. So Yeats identifies with a mother bird at rest atop creation, atop a phallic creation, a tower. But, chiefly it is as if Yeats were turning backward to the female, mothering muse as we turn back to mother earth as phallic power and identification wane in reality.

This is an image of beauty, and in the beauty is a subjective composition of identity. All the while the mother bird is waiting to give her own form to complete the nest—another home. And home, tower, body have taken on the function of imposing poetic form. The beauty is in the indigenous sense of composing, of making the form of the poem, twig by twig. And in development the sense of making the ego ideal is that of yielding the subjective libidinal possibilities to some internal guiding principle. The loophole is the way into the experiencing mind from the reflective vantage point—if the idealized mother imago is present, the poet can write with her voice—a perfected form. With this evidential beauty of assertion, Yeats is free to make his statement of the acceptance of his aging body in a calm way; he has proved that his muse has not foresaken him.

> I leave both faith and pride
> To young upstanding men
> Climbing the mountain-side,
> That under bursting dawn
> They may drop a fly;
> Being of that metal made
> Till it was broken by
> This sedentary trade.

He issues one last reproachful denial, blaming his poetic necessity for the ruin of his body. He must do this because he is willing his trade to those who come after him, and they must finally suffer, as he did, the dissolution of the poetic dream of their youth—without solace—with only the necessity to continue their trade.

> Now shall I make my soul,
> Compelling it to study
> In a learned school
> Till the wreck of body,
> Slow decay of blood,
> Testy delerium
> Or dull decrepitude,
> Or what worse evil come—
> The death of friends, or death
> Of every brilliant eye
> That made a catch in the breath—
> Seem but the clouds of the sky
> When the horizon fades,
> Or a bird's sleepy cry
> Among the deepening shades.

There is a great beauty of sadness here as Yeats finally turns his bird to creating the tones of death itself. It is not the dull decreptitude as much as the dying which the poem evokes in the end. He brings all of his imagery to a combined resolution; time, light, the body, his past, the friends, the stuff of imagery, all fade in a saddening demonstration of the sense of dying. Yeats uses the poetry to create the mood which he anticipates. This is the use of fantasy to prepare oneself for the trauma of events. But he is right; he is experiencing his death, because all of that experience is in the anticipation. Nothing gives more form to the poet's or the individual's reflection than the realization that reflection stands between being and extinction.

KING LEAR—SHAKESPEARE'S GREAT WORK ABOUT OLD AGE

One of the great advantages accruing to those who do (or can) maintain their creativity into old age is an increased access to the channels of identity synthesis. The terrible poignancy that can pervade the literature of aging often has to do with the recognition of death and, with it, the approaching end of a process as habitual as thought or breath. Although, heaven knows, there are enough other reasons for the poignancy. Still, this is the time when the spent but still fertile poet, anticipating the end of creativity, writes:

> That time of year thou may'st in me behold
> When yellow leaves, or none, or few, do hang
> Upon the boughs which shake against the cold,
> Bare ruined choirs, where late the sweet birds sang.

This theme animates *King Lear.* We will take the play as an example of a single mind in the process of entering and accepting old age. The Fool, who is the play's muse, must facilitate the resolution of this identity problem. He disappears half way through the action when the infirm notions of Lear's wishes for immortality have been clearly demonstrated to the king. Lear's passage through the storm is his entrance into old age. He accepts it, and is simultaneously reconciled with Cordelia, who embodies both his capacity to love and his acceptance of death.

The essence of reflection is to maintain a perspective on all motives whether they are sexually or aggressively colored. Neutralization is a function that holds these motives up against the considerations imposed by reality, personal limitation, social values and so on. Identity structures this capacity for neutralization. In old age there is a tendency for aggressive forces to break loose, because the self-representation on which the objective portion of identity depends is disrupted with the infirmities of old age.

When aggressive motives are increased, the process of synthesis which is inherent in neutralization looses scope. By this we mean that the capacity to sublimate with love is used by reflection to hold potentially destructive motives in check. When the aggressive motives are increased, the capacity for sublimation may become insufficient to maintain neutrality in perspective. In our consideration of the mind of Lear, we shall see that the failure in neutralization sets the regressive portion of the creative process into motion. The new capacity for neutralization based on a synthesis of subjective identity with a more extended sense of nature is the reparative identity change that comes only at the end of a long creative process.

In *King Lear,* a play about identity change, the dramatic structure is controlled by the phases of the creative process. In this context we take both Lear's mind, and the process of a change in his mental representation of himself, as the subject of the play. The characters represent aspects of Lear's character and of the world as conceived by that personality.

But how does the play's organizing consciousness speak simultaneously to Lear's identity problem, Shakespeare's problem as a mature creator, and the play's dramatic problem of making a compact with the audience? We contend that the generic structure of tragedy speaks to all these concerns. For

Shakespeare, tragedy renders the possibility that he might lose his creative abilities. Suppose Shakespeare's need to prove his ability through the making of the play is equated with Lear's ability to pass through the identity crisis of old age. Writing the play would prove Shakespeare's capacity for remaking his identity as creator.

But in maturity one cannot remain for long in one's capacity as creator. One must enter into the state of creating and resolve the creative state during the course of the production of the work. Then one returns to the normal state of being one single contributor to society, as opposed to one speaking through the work to all of society. If the problem of returning to the normal (museless) state is introduced into the work itself, then the work must dispose of its own artifices in the course of its resolution. Now this statement approaches certain of the generic requirements of tragedy, for in a tragedy the characters must partake of the destiny that the tragic form and the course of the work have set for them.

Even though Lear successfully accepts his old age and reciprocally acknowledges love with Cordelia, and even though Edgar and Gloucester acknowledge their love as father and son, still the tragic course of the play requires that Lear's forces cannot win the civil war that has taken over the kingdom. This is so because Lear's time of maturity and leadership have passed. Though he accepts old age, still, he is not immortal. He must accede to nature, which in this case is equated with the inevitable movement of the form of the tragedy. Ripeness is all. The old must fall from the tree when they are ready, regardless of the quality of the fruit. The supraordinate neutrality of nature must be preserved at all levels.

The play must come to grips with requirements along multiple levels. First, the sovereign cannot transcend God's authority, because that authority inheres in nature. Second, the play, while providing a social lesson, must not transcend the institution of sovereignty which permits it to be produced. Third, Shakespeare must produce a work that proves his mature identity as a creator by dramatically resolving the whole structure of the play. Fourth, Lear's identity change must be authentic despite the use of those dramatic artifices that carry the creative process forward. Fifth, all these problems must resolve in a way that is consistent with the formal structure of tragedy.

King Lear exemplifies one more aspect of identity change in old age. In maturity, social-political life is internalized, becoming a part of individual reflective identity structure. At the same time the individual grants this side of life a continuity beyond the individual. This mature accommodation is no longer sufficient in the final stage of life. The aged creator identifies reality with a "nature" that transcends social institution, seeing social institutions as transient as personal mortality.

In the tragedy of Lear, Shakespeare explores the relationship between personal mortality and the social institution of sovereign rule. The only reality force that endures during the course of the play is that of human nature, which is identified with nature on a grand or universal scale. This is the extra-psychic reality which the aged person must come to accept as the objective foundation of reflective identity. The muse is finally absorbed into this identity structure of old age. The social institution of sovereignty is maintained only through the supraordinate neutrality of nature.

Lear's identity change bears witness to this truth about identity in old age. It is only through allying himself with the universal forces of continuity that the aged person makes a new identity serviceable in the extremity of all loss. Pervasive "nature" maintains the sense of continuing reality outside of the scope of the action and determines the outcome of the play.

Works of literature that deal specifically with identity change take on a formal structure synonymous with the creative process. The five movements of *Lear* recapitulate the creative process. The creative process is used for identity change when, given the prevailing reflective order, an age-appropriate life problem is incapable of resolution. Tragedy is a generic form of identity change structuring the inexorable progress of dissolution in the prevailing reflective order. Because he is king, Lear's identity extends beyond his own reflective cohesion; it symbolizes and controls his kingdom as well. Disintegration and reintegration of social cohesion in Lear's kingdom follow the process that accounts for Lear's identity change. This is implicit in the moral lesson offered by *Lear,* as it is staged by Shakespeare for his public. The moral equivalent of violent rage loosed within the personality on aspects of personal identity—which is what we usually call Lear's madness —is the social/moral equivalent of civil war.

Since it is a play about the change in identity in old age, we expect the creative process to abet the movement of the action, and to be itself a subject of investigation in the play. The Fool, who represents the indwelling muse of the play, takes on the function of preserving perspective and the ability to love during the course of the action. The Fool picks up where Cordelia disappears in the beginning of the play, and disappears when Cordelia re-emerges as the embodiment of the capacity to love later in the play. The Fool is concerned with Lear's abdication of responsibility for his own mortality in the beginning of the play, and later with the preservation of Lear's identity, when Lear's identity has so regressed that it is insufficient to maintain the reflective cohesion of the play. Lear's identity must function throughout the play in order for the thread of action to maintain its artistic coherence.

Here is a summary of the course of action in the play as it accords with the phases of the creative process: The first movement deals with an insoluble problem to identity cohesion; the second movement portrays a metaphoric transformation of this problem; the third movement reveals a full regression to contact with the unconscious sources of the problem, and reveals the seeds of future identity; the fourth movement shows a progressive movement toward restoration of new identity; and the fifth movement concludes with a full resolution of the identity problem, and returns to reality.

Phase 1—Frustration

Briefly, the first movement of the play concerns an insoluble problem for Lear's mature identity. He cannot accept his mortality because he cannot accept the anticipated decrease both in his ability to love and in his ability to govern. In reaction he trys to substitute the wish to be loved and taken care of in exchange for an abdication of his power. These false resolutions of his identity dilemma set a regressive process into motion in his mind. By renouncing Cordelia and Kent, he renounces respectively his capacity to love and his capacity to govern effectively. For the mind this is tantamount to the loss of the capacity for mental synthesis. The subjective portion of Lears' reflection is left without the capacity to produce reliable judgments.

By choosing Goneril and Regan, Lear places himself in the laps of the characters who represent the aggressive, destructive forces in the kingdom. The objective spatial kingdom is divided into two parts. If the kingdom represents the objective realm of Lear's reflection, then Lear has given up his capacity to govern this realm in the hope of becoming absorbed into the structure of that realm. This is to say he subordinates the objective side of his reflective identity to a false representation of objective strength. The inability to maintain an effective identity under these circumstances mobilizes a kind of regressive searching in the mind of Lear.

Phase 2—Regression

As the process develops in the second movement, Lear uses his Fool as the muse, or instrument for searching back into the past for solutions to his current dilemma. Kent returns in new form, disguised. Such disguises, by reducing identity to symbolic or metaphoric equivalents, carry regression to a point where structural alteration of the identity in the mind of Lear may occur. In the scenes of the second movement, Lear's phallic, initiatory potency, as represented by his entourage of knights, is reduced by Goneril and Regan, first to 50 knights, then to 25, and finally to none. Kent, his executive arm, is put into the stocks. Thus the source of his subjective initiative is reduced to a state of helplessness.

Phase 3—Primary Process

In the third movement the process of identity transformation reaches the stage of primary process. The storm clearly expresses Lear's identity stripped of all previous manifestations. Lear's mind is reduced to the level of primitive experience. Finally, in a kind of play within a play, with the aid of Edgar and the Fool, Lear manages to accomplish a change in his structure of identity. We stress that it is a play within a play, occurring in Gloucester's farmhouse when Goneril and Regan are on mock trial, because a play within a play connotes a change in the level of identity structure. In this play, death, or its immediate alternative, madness, must be weighed and accepted. The play within a play is a kind of extended personification demonstrating Lear's traumatic reality finally coming into reflective terms. It is necessary to regress to the foundations of the most infantile sense of identity to produce any structural alteration in identity, because it is only in primary process that the mind comes into sufficient contact with the drives for new experience to produce a profound transformation. Using his muse, and the pretense of madness which is conveyed by Edgar, Lear realizes that Goneril and Regan are purveyors of aggression who operate predominantly from outside of his sense of internal reality. Lear realizes that his newly rediscovered love for humanity is incompatible with the false values of Goneril and Regan.

Phase 4—Revision

In the fourth movement, Lear's identity resolution becomes apparent. First he re-experiences his whole sense of personal development in terms that are altered from this previous experience. He re-represents his life's experiences to himself. This resolution is accompanied by an intense shame about his renunciation of Cordelia's real love. The fact that Lear can experience this shame means that he is able to love again, and what's more, to realize that he and all other creatures should love. In his recovery, and in the resolution of the process of identity change, Lear realizes that he is "a foolish, fond old man." However, his wisdom and his identity change have come too late to avert the final enactment of tragic action.

Phase 5—Resolution

The final movement of the play brings harmony between the intrapsychic realm which had been the kingdom of Lear's mind, and the extrapsychic realm where action occurs. The new accord is fashioned out of a full circle, so that the kingdom becomes the dominion of the matured Albany. Albany comes to understand, through the course of the play, that human society and the will to govern that society cannot usurp the powers inherent in nature. Human passions must not lead to actions that are incompatible with the ultimate authority and continuity of life in nature. Understanding this, Albany and Edgar are in a position to take up rule of the realm where Lear and Gloucester had dropped it in the beginning of the play, when they began their intense search for false values.

The creative process of the play took the identity change full circle. Lear began by giving up his grasp on his mature identity prematurely. His mind was launched into a crisis which was finally resolved by his emergence into a new identity as an old man. With the passage successfully completed, a new mature identity can emerge in the social realm of the kingdom, namely Albany's passage from adulthood to maturity. In this overall shift in the ages and stages of men, the play presents the very neutral reflection that men as part of the natural order must age and change and pass away. It is this reflection that neutralizes the destruction inhering in the tragic action. Albany's ability to take this perspective indicates that the tragedy is at a close. Conceivably, Albany's development parallels Shakespeare's own development as a creator.

A TEXTUAL ANALYSIS OF THE MIND OF LEAR

Act I

The play begins:

> I thought the King had more affected the Duke
> of Albany than Cornwall.

Since Albany is the ultimate arbiter of neutrality and reality and emerges as the new king, this statement makes it clear that before the time of the play the king had loved neutrality, the impetus to sublimate with love, more than he had wished to loose his aggression in a destructive way. The notion of a desynthesizing split in the King's reflective consideration of his kingdom is introduced. The king is unwilling to accept the challenge of identity change in old age:

> Lear: ... and 'tis our fast intent
> To shake all cares and business from our
> age, conferring them on younger strengths
> while we unburden'd crawl toward death.

Goneril, with her deceitfully false and destructive identity representation, appeals to his fantasy of immortality, implicit in his disavowal of the challenge of old age.

> Goneril: Sir, I love you more than word can wield
> the matter;
> Dearer than eyesight, space, and liberty;

Goneril states that she loves him beyond her own subjective life, as if he were all of her reality. The idealizing "love" is actually narcissistic, with unconscious aggression structuring the omnipotent wish to usurp the whole field of intrapsychic and extrapsychic reality. Regan continues just as deceptively:

> Regan: ... I profess
> Myself an enemy to all other joys
> Which the most precious square of sense possesses,
> And find I am alone felicitate
> In your dear Highness' love.

Regan insists that she renounces all of her own subjective experience, even her sexual pleasure, in favor of basking in her father's adoration. The roots of deception are to be found in the abrogation of personal experience, particularly in the renunciation of sexual pleasure.

Cordelia loves her father "According to my bond; no more nor less." She loves him sincerely, according to the subjective experience of her capacity to love. Lear concludes that it is "nothing." Thus Lear gives up the synthesizing capacity of love to show him what he truly wants in exchange for the illusion of meaning which is carried by mere words without their connection to the experience of love. He trys to believe that his words, unconnected to his own experience, can carry the full weight of nature's reality and authority.

> Lear: ... Only we still retain
> The name, ...
> Kent: ... Answer my life my judgment,
> Thy youngest daughter does not love thee least,
> Nor are these empty-hearted whose low sound
> reverbs no hollowness ...
> Lear: ... On thine allegiance hear me!
> Since thou hast sought to make us break our vow —
> Which we durst never yet—and with strained
> Pride to come between our sentence and our power—
> Which nor our nature nor our place can bear.

Lear gives up his internal reality as king in exchange for the omnipotent fantasy that his words convey the authority of nature. He tries to maintain dominion in the mind of his kingdom through the sway of evocation of his words, his vow—but his words are hollow because they are not re-enforced by an acceptance of his own capacity to love.

When words lose their capacity to bind experience, the stage is set for a tragic loss of judgment. Cordelia says she lacks:

> ... that glib and oily art
> To speak and purpose not,
> Since what I well intend,
> I'll do't before I speak—

For Lear, renouncing Cordelia has the effect of depleting his capacity for new experience, while banishing Kent cordons off his capacity for neutral reflection on experience. Cordelia goes off with France, who becomes the repository for the redeeming wish for social and judgmental neutrality and continuity.

In the second scene Edmund takes up the theme of verbal deceit with his false letter, compromising Edgar's love for his father. Gloucester serves to externalize Lear's intrapsychic conflict by taking part in a subplot which is more overt, that is, where the action occurs in the common realm of external reality. Gloucester expresses a sense of strangeness:

> Gloucester: These late eclipses in the sun and moon
> Portend no good to us. ... And the noble and true-
> hearted Kent banished! His offense, honesty!
> Tis strange.

Gloucester can't believe in love or honesty anymore. Reflective structure, perspective, begins to break down. Thus Lear has encountered an insoluble dilemma for his identity to encompass. Kent and Cordelia, his truth and his love, cannot pull him through. Therefore he must resort to the realm of the imagination. The creative process begins to take hold as Kent returns disguised, and as the center of rational perspective comes to rest in the Fool. Now Lear, and his story, must be carried along in guises, devices, ironies, allusions, and the like, while the aggressive forces take hold in the realm of reality. This is an apt description of the necessity that drives the creative person toward a creative solution of seemingly insoluble identity problems.

In Scene IV Lear receives some new help in his attempt to maintain his dignity and his integrity. Kent returns in disguise. He opposes Goneril's attempt to destroy totally Lear's social integrity. The Fool appears, ironic. His irony helps Lear reestablish a sense of connection with his experience. The Fool can speak the truth as long as it is in the guise of false identity. This is irony. For instance, when the Fool interprets that Lear gave away his (phallic) power he concludes his speech with:

> Fool: ... If I speak like myself in this,
> Let him be whipped that first finds it so.

The Fool goes in and out of Lear's identity, relentlessly interpreting that Lear has given up his wits and his true self.

> Fool: That Lord that counsell'd thee
> To give away thy land,
> Come place him here by me—
> Do thou for him stand.

The Fool counsels Lear to give up the false identity which he assumed and to take back his own identity as king. The Fool counsels him to let the Fool be the fool. Lear has placed his true identity into the realm of the imaginary. He thus enters into alliance with all those devices of mind that can make the traumatic become bearable. Overwhelmingly painful experience can be represented to reflection through the assumption of false identity.

Lear has abrogated his mature identity. He cannot identify

with himself as the real King. When Goneril finally comes to the king, frowning, the Fool says:

> Fool: Thou wast a pretty fellow when thou hadst
> no need to care for her frowning. Now thou art
> an O without a figure. I am better than thou
> art now: I am a fool, thou art nothing . . .

Indeed, Goneril treats him as if he no longer exists as a real person. She is in charge of the aggression which can determine what is real, while the king has neither control of aggression nor love, having renounced Cordelia's love as nothing. The Fool gives all of his interpretations in front of the disguised Kent, who in this way is treated as intrinsic to the King's real identity.

> Lear: Doth any here know me? This is not Lear.
> Doth Lear walk thus? Speak thus? Where are
> his eyes? Either his notion weakens, his
> discernings are lethargied—Ha! Waking? 'Tis
> not so! Who is it that can tell me who I am?

Lear feels depersonalized, strange. His reflection, the coordination of his thoughts, loses accord with his experience. It is as if his reflection were asleep. But he can still test the reality of sleeping and waking, and therefore he has not succumbed to psychosis. Rhetorically he questions his source of personal identity, but his experience cannot answer. The Fool tells him that only his shadow, the negative of his identity, can tell him who he is, for Lear has sided with that portion of the mind which should only evaluate traumatic experience, not provide him with his sense of reflective identity.

Goneril's destruction of his sources of identity continues. She tells him he should not have passion, prowess, potency—that his phallic knights are in excess. The sense of the castrating mother returns to Lear. That sense is one of the foundations of the literary personality. The unacceptable traumatic appreciation of castration leads to the assumption of fantasy as a protector of real identity during childhood development.

> Lear: —O most small fault,
> How ugly didst thou in Cordelia show!
> Which, like an engine, wrench'd my frame
> of nature,
> From the fix'd place; drew from my heart all love
> And added to this gall. O Lear, Lear, Lear!
> Beat at this gate that let thy folly in
> [strikes his head]
> And thy dear judgment out. Go, go, my people.

Act II

In Act II the consequences of a breakdown in identity structure are dramatized. Since Lear's identity is no longer available to structure his reflection, and since his identity structures the play, the action turns to the consequences of the loss of identity. These consequences include a lack of judgment on the part of those in authority, unleashed aggression, primitive unmodulated affective expressions, social disturbances leading toward war, in short, all of the earmarks of tragedy on every important level.

Lear's affect shifts from intemperate rage and self-pity to anxiety and deep sorrow. These are more painful affects and reveal to Lear the full extent of his trauma. When he realizes that Regan too is but a carrier of aggression, and that Cornwall contrives to paralyze him by putting Kent in the stocks with full disregard for the former authority of the King, he wails:

> Lear: O, how this mother swells up toward my heart!
> Hysteria passio! Down, thou climbing sorrow!
> Thy element's below!

The anxiety and the grief over loss of identity, over the loss of impact of his words, signal a shift in Lear's hold on his

reflective structure of false identity. He feels that he is no more
a man as these woman's tears swell up in him. Severe physiological discharges indicate a breakdown, or a breaking through of
drives beyond the capacity of reflection to bind them. His tears,
which he calls women's tears, the natural appeal to the return
of some missing mother, presage the storm.

> Lear: ... I have full cause of weeping, but this heart
> Shall break into a hundred thousand flaws
> Or ere I'll weep. O feel, I shall go mad!

Act III

In Act III Lear comes into full contact with the experience
of his losses. It is a question of whether the nature in him, the
very neurological framework which supports his reflection, will
hold. The "thought executing fires" of the intrapsychic storm
threaten to defuse the very mold which makes thoughts come
from words and from experience and from the drives. Kent
echoes the danger with the thunder:

> Kent: Man's nature cannot carry
> Th' affliction nor the fear.

But the Fool's humor and Kent's steadfastness do not fail
Lear. The Fool wants to make a codpiece a covering for Lear's
head. This action functions to preserve Lear's sense of humor.
Humor is the natural device which maintains denial against
overwhelming trauma, at the same time that it allows sufficient
perception of the traumatic experience to allow reflection to
continue its function of judgment, guiding experience. And
Lear begins the work of preserving his moral judgment. Moral
judgment is the repository of humor.

> Lear: ... Close pent-up guilts,
> Rive your concealing continents, and cry

These dreadful summoners grace. I am a man
More sinn'd against than sinning.

Lear turns kind to his Fool. The Fool, in an attitude of affectionate humor, shows the return of synthesis in reflection in the mind of the play.

Fool: [sings] He that has and a little tiny wit—
With hey, ho, the wind and the rain—
Must make content with his fortunes fit,
Though the rain it raineth every day.

Showing the readmission of love to experience, the Fool's words take on ever greater rhythm. The mind of the play begins to resonate a deeper beat that seems to search out the foundations of language. The generative phonemics of speech seek out the words which must be found to make meaning become real again. The mind of Lear is approaching the neuropsychological margin where the drive attaches to morphemes and is bound.

Fool: When priests are more in word than matter;
When brewers mar their malt with water;
When nobles are their tailors' tutors,
No heretics burn'd, but wenches' suitors;
When every case in law is right,
No squire in debt nor no poor knight;
When slanders do not live in tongues,
Nor cutpurses come not to throngs;
When userers tell their gold i' th' field,
And bawds and whores do churches build:
Then shall the realm of Albion
Come to great confusion.
Then comes the time, who lives to see't
That going shall be us'd with feet.
This prophecy Merlin shall make,
For I live before his time.

With this curious and oracular speech, the Fool brings himself into coincidence with the muse of long ago. The false identity inhering in Lear's immortality fantasy is exposed in this irony, played on time. The coextension of past and future also reflects the movement of the play into the realm of primary process. Time and space and person are condensed in this portion of the play. We see that the muse function is also altered: The fool mediates the regression of the mind of the play to the realm of the primary process. In this speech the fool communicates the loss of rationality in the whole kingdom of the mind of the play. It is an irony employed in the service of regression to the very foundations of new, and potentially authentic experience.

Lear re-experiences the origins of identity in the hovel in the storm. His way is the way to the sea, to the primitive sources of his suffering. Even if his reflective consciousness is swallowed up in the "bear's mouth" which opens to the sea, even if he must re-experience himself being swallowed up, he must re-establish contact with his own body and his own representation.

> Lear:　Poor naked wretches, wheresee'er you are,
> That bide the pelting of this pitiless storm,
> How shall your houseless heads and unfed sides,
> Your loop'd and window'd raggedness, defend you
> From seasons such as these?

Lear becomes concerned with the subjective states of those who have existed in his external realm without his taking notice before. Now he feels a sense of kinship with them, and it must be through a realization of the nature of what is external, but also alive, that he will restore the objective continuity of his reflection.

It is at this point that Edgar, as Lear's objective representation, intersects Lear's consciousness. In a movement of primary identification, Lear experiences himself becoming Edgar. This is like a rebirth of objective being. Edgar acts as an agent provocateur to Lear's most primitive and infantile organizations of objective experience. Edgar impersonates one who has been driven mad from a surfeit of sensual pleasures. He pretends that a particular devil has had each of his "five wits" to excess. Shakespeare has a theory of mind which he draws upon. There is an implication that the devil is a father figure who, acting from external reality and internal reality simultaneously, makes a slave of the person's senses and desires. For Edgar this idea is structured like a delusion with a kernal of truth, since his father, Gloucester, has taken on the aspect of some tormenting devil which keeps him running from his true identity.

Lear's sanity goes on trial in Gloucester's farmhouse, with Edgar as the presiding judge, and the Fool and Kent as jury. Goneril and Regan are condemned as wantons who pretend like bitches to be loyal to a master whereas they are in reality aggressively serving only their own ends. The play within a play, or trial within a play, is a device which focuses the attention of reflective consciousness on pretense. It is a curative procedure. The muse is therapeutic agent in these circumstances. Edgar's utterances are chants, rhythmed in nursery rhymes. This brings reflection back into coincidence with the foundations of its origins in primary versions of speech. The trial is convened:

> Edgar: Let us deal justly.
>
> Sleepest or wakest thou, jolly shepherd?
> They sheep be in the corn;
> And for one blast of thy minikin mouth
> Thy sheep shall take no harm.
>
> Purr! The cat is gray.

Lear is drawn in fully to the device of Edgar's "counterfeiting." He sees his daughters all as dogs. Edgar chants an almost magical intonation condemning Goneril:

> Edgar: Be thy mouth or black or white,
> Tooth that poisons if it bite;
> Mastiff, greyhound, mongrel grim,

Hound or spaniel, brach or lym,
Bobtail tyke or trundle tail—
Tom will make him weep and wail;
For, with throwing thus my head,
Dogs leap the hatch, and all are fled.

With his incantation, he is exorcizing the devil for Lear.

The devil represents all false identities. Edgar, Kent, and the Fool help Lear rid his reflection of all the false representations which have led the action to this juncture. The Fool's work is done at this point in the play—he has led Lear back to the earliest sentience, in the process ridding him of all false structures and putting him in touch with the foundations of his experience again. Lear is mad now, only insofar as he has regressed to the foundations of his speech and experience. At this point Lear falls into a curative and timeless sleep, and he will be born back to Cordelia when he awakes.

But the false representations of Lear, which structure his wish that Regan and Goneril would love him, have also served the function of preventing the outbreak of violence in the realm. Throughout the play Lear's intrapsychic world is closely mirrored by the sociopolitical world played out in the subplot of Gloucester and his sons. At this point in the play, the violence inherent in the external world controlled by Goneril and Regan, and their ilk, is loosed. Cornwall enucleates the eyes of Gloucester, who declared his allegiance to the king. The theme of vengeance takes hold of the action and moves it along. The unleashed aggression must progress—after the first enucleation, Regan runs through the servant who trys to save Gloucester's other eye—to a state of warfare.

The act of putting out the eyes draws the violence of the intrapsychic and the extrapsychic world into harmony. The eyes are the organ of perception of external reality, and they serve to represent the attachment to reality. Enucleating Gloucester's eyes moves the aggression in the sociopolitical side of the play toward its inevitable destruction of life. Vengeance requires that all of the false characters be killed. The activation of free aggression at the end of Act III must surely lead the intrapsychic drama toward a reawakening.

Act IV

Act IV is a movement dramatizing the reconstruction of the psychological world. First Gloucester re-emerges to new intrapsychic life after his external reality has been destroyed. Then Lear comes slowly back to his senses, emerging through a series of condensed images which recapitulate the stages of development leading back to his final emergence as an old man. First he reconstructs his inner bodily reality, and then he goes on to reconstruct the facets of object relations. Much in this portion of the play sheds light on the construction of reality. Lear's entrance into Act IV is literally a movement from the primary process of sleep to the hypnopompic imagery of waking. At the social level of the play, Albany emerges for the first time as the purveyor of neutrality. It becomes his task more and more to maintain the thread of social order as the false artifices of social aggression are destroyed.

As Act IV opens, Gloucester, seeking to find the very edge of England and to plunge into the nonbeing outside of the reality of the play, encounters his son Edgar, still in the guise of a madman. Edgar is musing that the worst is upon him when he finds still worse in his father's bleeding eye sockets. "This is the worst" is a response to trauma. It is a statement that one's capacity for new reflective neutralization has been exhausted. Thus reality testing is called into question and used as a device as Gloucester tells Edgar that he, Edgar, came into his mind as his son the day before when he saw the poor naked fellow, the "madman" who is in reality Edgar in disguise.

> Gloucester: As flies to wanton boys are we to the gods.
> They kill us for their sport.

> Edgar: [Aside] How should this be?
> Bad is the trade that must play fool to sorrow,
> Angering itself and others.

In this aside Edgar is suddenly talking with the voice of the author Shakespeare. Shakespeare is commenting rather directly, through Edgar to the audience, that the playwright must not play overly much on pity. Otherwise the audience must finally turn away because a surplus of emotion will ultimately liberate anger. Shakespeare is announcing through this aside which interrupts the artifice that it is time to begin to dispose of the artifices that have born the tragedy along. Edgar, in his guise as madman, has all along carried the potential to give up this artifice and to begin to return the play to normal. Edgar has represented the part of Lear's mind that has suspended rationality to produce a change in identity structure. Now that the change is at hand, Edgar can stop playing madman. (Lear has never been insane.)

There is the artifice of the play itself which is never completely suspended until the play is over. There are also levels of artifice within the play consistently carried by each character. In the regressive portions of the play, Lear's real identity is suspended and carried in an irony which conveys reality as if that were artifice, by the Fool and by Edgar. At this moment in the play, as Edgar gives up his artifice, there is no longer a defense against Lear recovering his true identity. This recovery of true identity constitutes the waking, or progressive portion of the play.

The other main level of artifice is one that mirrors the artifice of the Fool and Edgar in a negative way. The artifice of Goneril and Regan, and of Edmund, is an artifice of deceit and false pretense for the purpose of conveying reality which is false. Gloucester would not bear witness to the false reality, so his eyes were put out. In the present section of the play, breaking the levels of artifice means that the deceivers must be disposed of.

Gloucester makes Edgar, a wanton son, an instrument of the gods, of cruel amoral nature. This irony highlighting unreality protects Gloucester from the impact of loving a son who has been banished from his intrapsychic reality. Since sorrow is an entirely real affect discharging overwhelming pain in the sphere of intrapsychic reality, the devices of unreality must yield. In the same way the audience is moved to real feelings when the provisional sense that it is only a play breaks down. Identity as real reflective synthesis cannot be worked out in its entirety in artifice. A play cannot suddenly become entirely real. Therefore, in preparation for the play's end, the tragedy must dispose of its artifice in some consistent way. The play must be a real lesson in order to maintain the neutrality of the compact of communication between the playwright and the audience.

In Scene II Albany becomes the reflective perceiver of the internal reality of the play, much as Kent had been during the regressive phases of the drama. Goneril loves him no more than she loved her father. Albany brings tragic necessity into focus. The unneutralized aggression of the play, emanating from Goneril as she pursues a total affiliation with Edmund, must be brought to justice.

> Albany: If that the heavens do not their visible
> spirits send quickly down to tame these vile
> offenses,
> It will come.
> Humanity must perforce prey on itself,
> Like monsters of the deep.

In Shakespeare's compact with the social authority of his day, it was necessary to resolve his tragedies. Order must be restored and England must be preserved as a harmonious state existing within the neutrality of natural order. In this act of reconstruction and resolution, the drives must be reunited if reflective order is to prevail in the end. Cordelia, re-emerging from France, brings back into the play a more overt and direct expression of love. At this progressive stage in his identity cycle Lear must re-emerge from the deep of his contact with the source of his drives. Love must re-enter from below, as it were, from instinctual sources.

> Cordelia: All blest secrets,
> All you unpublished virtues of the earth,
> Spring with my tears! Be aidant and remediate
> In the good man's distress! Seek, seek for him!
> Lest his ungoverned rage dissolve the life
> That wants the means to lead it.

In Scene IV Edgar practices an immense conceit on Gloucester, who is intent on suicide. It is a conceit heavily laced with irony. Gloucester is willing to sacrifice his internal reality to spend all of his aggression in an act of contrition, as he spends his remaining fortune on his disguised son. Edgar leads him to the verge of nothing, where Gloucester hurls himself into the void, only to wake up as from a dream of nonidentity restored to total affiliation with his son, in contact with his love and in almost total contact with the internal reality of the play. Edgar's "possession" by the devil becomes an explanation of Gloucester's behavior. The devil is an incarnation, a false identity built of aggression. The conceit, another "play within a play," is reparative, exaggerating the representational qualities of human life. It gives reflection an extended metaphor on which to construct new identity in the same ruins where deceit had taken it away. Lear undergoes a similar repair with the conceit of a doctor in attendance upon the rebirth of his new identity in old age.

In Lear's speeches of renaissance he recalls the whole subjective experience of the play, but more, he re-experiences his whole childhood libidinal development. Lear comes first to a recognition of himself, and then he recognizes Gloucester, the inner reality of his reflective mind. Gloucester hears and feels the king's real identity.

> Gloucester: The trick of that voice I do well remember.
> Is't not the King?
> Lear: Ay, every inch a King!
> When I do stare see how the subject quakes.
> I pardon that man's life. What was thy cause?
> Adultery?
> Thou shalt not die. Die for adultery? No.
> The wren goes to it, and the small gilded fly
> Does lecher in my sight.
> Let copulation thrive;

We think that Lear is describing his affective response and his reflective defense to the primal scene. It is the idea of copulation taking place before him, and a feeling that he could not abide that in the past, but that now he can. His own oedipal wishes toward his daughters are brought into that scene, and as he continues associating, the other great trauma of childhood becomes apparent.

> Lear: Down from the waist they are Centaurs,
> Though women all above.

It is the representation of the phallic woman which defends against castration anxiety. The phallic woman becomes the available representation for the muse and thus structures the realm of the imagination. The oedipal identification with the phallic woman provides an artifice for identity, a means of organizing traumatic perceptions so that they are available to the reflective imagination.

At the end of his speech of recovery and resolution, Lear describes the terrors of the primary process, equating it with a great pit that lies within the phallic woman.

> Lear: There's hell, there's darkness, there is the
>   sulphorous pit;
>   burning, scalding, stench, consumption. . . .
> Gloucester: O, let me kiss that hand!
> Lear: Let me wipe it first; it smells of mortality.

Death in the smell of the woman's genitals—the love of Cordelia as the entrance to death.

Lear produces more sexual imagery from his memory of images of internal reality.

> Lear: Thou rascal beadle, hold thy bloody hand!
>   Why dost thou lash that whore? Strip thine
>   own Back.
>   Thou hotly lusts to use her in that kind
>   For which thou whippest her. . . .
>   Get thee glass eyes
>   And, like a scurvy politician, seem
>   To see the things thou dost not.

There is revenge in experiencing internal reality in this way. Lear identifies with the image of some father figure who beats the sexual woman, whom Lear has just accused of unleashing the power of the demons on his manhood. Lear can identify a representation of himself with the representation from his internal reality of the man who beats the sexual mother. And with this self-identification with the aggressor of his internal reality, he emerges to recognize Gloucester, the father figure of external reality. Finally Lear emerges from what had become a deep dream of near castration, wherein he was ready, like the oedipal son, to kill or be killed. It was necessary for Lear to encounter all of the traumatic imagery of his childhood to be reborn into his natural identity as an old man. At the end of Act IV Lear has found his new objective identity. He says to Cordelia:

> Lear: Pray, do not mock me.
>   I am a very foolish fond old man,

Fourscore and upward, not an hour more nor less;
And, to deal plainly,
I fear I am not in my perfect mind.
Me thinks I should know you, and know this man;
Yet I am doubtful; for I am mainly ignorant
What place this is; and all the skill I have
Remembers not these garments; nor I know not
Where I did lodge last night. Do not laugh at me;
For (as I am a man) I think this lady
To be my child Cordelia.

He is deeply ashamed as he returns to his identity, an affect like guilt which cannot maintain its signal function of reflection unless the structure of identity is intact. The shame signals a return of complete love for Cordelia. This restores the King to full reality, and as Freud understood in his "Three Caskets," Cordelia represents the reality of death to the King. As the subjective source of love for the mind of Lear, she also represents the missing mother of the play. As Freud pointed out, the mother of old age conveys an acceptance of death just as the mother of youth conveys an acceptance of life.

Act V

In the last act mortality has been accepted by the mind of the play, but it remains to restore the natural order, the harmony between the inner and the outer reality. Consider the fate of the main characters. The Fool, having no real being, being muse, disappears. Cordelia, Lear's love and subjective vehicle of death, is choked off. Goneril, Lear's aggression, kills Regan and then puts an end to her own inner reality. Oswald and Edmund, purveyors of aggression from the external reality, are killed by Edgar, restoring natural order. As he dies, Edmund, taken up by the synthesis of new identity, goes against his deceiving nature to try to save Cordelia whom he has sentenced. Thus all the aggression is becoming neutralized once again, as the false artifices of tragedy are removed. Gloucester died in his internal reality with an excess of love, bursting his heart in reconciliation with Edgar. Kent will die when the cords that bind him to the subjective Lear are broken off with Lear's death. Lear dies, in one last denial of the death of his own love of Cordelia, in the recognition that she is really dead. France returns to his own country maintaining the continuity of that external social order which does not impinge on the presented one.

For Lear, for the mind of the play, Cordelia's death does crack "the vault of heaven." Only the death of love can crack the ultimate biological, neurological neutrality which supports the most profound reflection, the sense of ongoing existence in reality. At the end Albany reflects neutrally on the identity of age, and he understands his own matured reflective identity, which has now come to constitute the kingly social order which leaves the play behind.

> Albany: The weight of this sad time we must obey,
> Speak what we feel, not what we ought to say.
> The oldest hath borne most; we that are young
> Shall never see so much, nor live so long.

BIBLIOGRAPHY

Bate, W. Jackson. *John Keats.* Cambridge: Harvard University Press, 1978.

Bellow, Saul. *Humboldt's Gift.* New York: Viking Press, Avon Paperback Edition, 1976.

Bonnerat, Louis. *Matthew Arnold, Poète: Essai de Biographie Psychologique.* Paris: Impramerie F. Paillart, 1947.

Borges, Jorge Luis. *Labyrinths: Selected Stories and Other Writings.* New York: New Directions, 1964.

Carroll, Lewis. *The Complete Works.* New York: Random House, 1979.

Corbett, Edward P. J. *Classical Rhetoric.* New York: Oxford University Press, 1974.

Craig, Hardin and David Bevington, (Eds.) *The Complete Works of Shakespeare.* Glenview Illinois: Scott, Foresman and Company, 1973.

Deutsch, Babette. *Poetry Handbook.* New York: Funk and Wagnalls, 1962.

Eissler, K. Creativity and Adolescence. *The Psychoanalytic Study of the Child,* 33: pp 461–517, 1978.

Eliot, T. S. *The Complete Poems and Plays.* New York: Harcourt, Brace and Company, 1952.

Ellman, Richard. *James Joyce.* New York: Oxford University Press, 1959.

Ellman, Richard. *Yeats, The Man and the Masks.* New York: Macmillan, 1948.

Erikson, E. H. Identity and the Life Cycle. *Psychological Issues.* New York: International Universities Press, 1959.

Freud, Sigmund. *Project For a Scientific Psychology.* Standard Edition Vol I, London: Hogarth Press, (1895), pp 287–397.

Freud, Sigmund. *Screen Memories.* S.E. Vol III: 301–322, (1899).

Freud, Sigmund. *The Interpretation of Dreams.* S.E. Vols. IV and V, (1900).

Freud, Sigmund. *On Narcissism.* S.E. Vol XIV:67–102, (1914).

Freud, Sigmund. *From the History of an Infantile Neurosis.* S.E. Vol XVII: 3–122 (1918).

Freud, Sigmund. *On Humor.* S.E. Vol XXI:160–166, (1927).

Freud, Sigmund. *Fetishism.* S.E. Vol XXI:149–157, (1927).

Freud, Sigmund. *Civilization and its Discontents.* S.E. Vol XXI: 57–145, (1929).

Frye, Northrop. *Anatomy of Criticism: Four Essays.* Princeton: Princeton University Press, Paperback Edition, 1973.

Greenacre, P. Regression and Fixation. *Journal of the American Psychoanalytic Association,* 8:703–723, 1960.

Greenacre, P. *Emotional Growth.* New York: International Universities Press, 1971.

Harold, Frederick Charles and William D. Templeman (Eds.). *English Prose of the Victorian Era.* New York: Oxford University Press, 1966.

Hawthorne, Nathaniel. *Selected Tales and Sketches.* New York: Holt, Rinehart and Winston, 1970.

Hawthorne, Nathaniel. *The Scarlet Letter.* New York: Macmillan Co., 1927.

Hemingway, Ernest. *A Farewell to Arms.* New York: Charles Scribner and Sons, 1929.

Holland, Norman N. *The Dynamics of Literary Response.* New York: Oxford University Press, 1968.

Isakower, O. On the Exceptional Position of the Auditory Sphere. *International Journal of Psycho-Analysis,* 20:340–348, 1939.

Joyce, James. *Ulysses.* New York: Random House, 1942.

Joyce, James. *A Portrait of the Artist as a Young Man.* New York: Viking-Compass, 1968.

Keats, John. *Selected Poems and Letters.* Edited by Bush. Cambridge, Mass.: Houghton Mifflin—Riverside Edition, 1959.

Kris, Ernst. *Psychoanalytic Explorations in Art.* New York: International Universities Press, 1952.

Lowry, Howard, Foster and Willard Thorp (Eds.). *An Oxford Anthology of English Poetry.* New York: Oxford University Press, 1956.

Luria, Alexander R. *Higher Cortical Functions in Man.* New York: Basic Books, 1966.

Normand, Jean. *Nathaniel Hawthorne—An Approach to an Analysis of Artistic Creation.* Translated by Derek Coltman. Cleveland: The Press of Case Western Reserve University, 1970.

Patrick, J. Max (Ed.). *The Complete Poetry of Robert Herrick.* Garden City, New York: Doubleday-Anchor Books, 1963.

Sartre, Jean Paul. *The Words.* Translated by Bernard Frechtman. Greenwich, Conn.: Fawcett Publications, 1964.

Schur, Max. *Freud: Living and Dying.* New York: International Universities Press, 1972.

Sidney, Sir Phillip. *Selected Poetry and Prose.* Edited by David Kalstone. New York: Signet Classics, 1970.

Thomas, Dylan. *The Collected Poems of Dylan Thomas.* New York: New Directions Publishing Co. (paperback), 1971.

Tillotson, Geoffrey, Paul Fussel, Jr. and Marshall Waingrow (Eds.). *Eighteenth Century English Literature.* New York: Harcourt, Brace and World, 1969.

Trilling, Lionel. *The Selected Letters of John Keats.* New York: Doubleday-Anchor Books, 1956.

Untermeyer, Louis (Ed.). *Modern American Poetry—Modern British Poetry.* New York: Harcourt, Brace and Company, 1950.

Vygotsky, L. *Thought and Language.* Cambridge: M. I. T. Press, 1965.

Winnicott, D. W. Transitional Objects and Transitional Phenomena: A Study of the First Not-Me Possession. *International Journal of Psycho-Analysis,* Vol 34:Part 2, 1953.

Yeats, W. B. *The Collected Poems of W. B. Yeats.* New York: Macmillan, 1957.

INDEX